Structural Transformation and Agrarian Change in India

The landlord and his emaciated labourer are symbolic of Indian agriculture. However, this relationship is less assured as large landowners have fallen from their superior position. This volume explores how this emblematic pair is becoming a thing of the past.

Structural Transformation and Agrarian Change in India investigates whether family labour farms are gaining prominence as a consequence of the structural transformation of the economy. The authors work alongside Weberian methodology of ideal types and develop different types of family farms; among them family labour farms that rely mainly on family workers, contrasted with capitalist farms that depend on hired labour. Agriculture is shrinking as a part of the total GDP at the same time as agricultural labour is shrinking as part of the total labour force. The changing agrarian structure is explored with the use of unique long-term survey data and statistical models. Results show that India is approaching farm structures that are typical of East and South East Asia, with pluriactive smallholders as the norm.

This book successfully criticizes popular narratives about Indian agricultural development as well as simplistic evolutionist, Marxist or neoclassical prognoses. It is of great importance to those who study development economics, development studies and South Asian economics.

Göran Djurfeldt is Senior Professor at the Department of Sociology, Lund University, Sweden.

Srilata Sircar is currently a Doctoral student at the Department of Human Geography, Lund University, Sweden.

Routledge Studies in Development Economics

For a complete list of titles in this series, please visit
www.routledge.com/series/SE0266

119 **Peripheral Visions of Economic Development**
New frontiers in development economics and the history of economic thought
Edited by Mario Garcia-Molina and Hans-Michael Trautwein

120 **The Political Economy of Natural Resources and Development**
From Neoliberalism to resource nationalism
Edited by Paul A. Haslam and Pablo Heidrich

121 **Institutional Innovation and Change in Value Chain Development**
Negotiating tradition, power and fragility in Afghanistan
Holly A. Ritchie

122 **China's War against the Many Faces of Poverty**
Towards a New Long March
Jing Yang and Pundarik Mukhopadhaya

123 **Exploring Civic Innovation for Social and Economic Transformation**
Edited by Kees Biekart, Wendy Harcourt and Peter Knorringa

124 **Trade, Investment and Economic Development in Asia**
Empirical and policy issues
Edited by Debashis Chakraborty and Jaydeep Mukherjee

125 **The Financialisation of Power**
How financiers rule Africa
Sarah Bracking

126 **Primary Commodities and Economic Development**
Stephan Pfaffenzeller

127 **Structural Transformation and Agrarian Change in India**
Göran Djurfeldt with Srilata Sircar

Structural Transformation and Agrarian Change in India

Göran Djurfeldt with Srilata Sircar

LONDON AND NEW YORK

First published 2017 by Routledge

2 Park Square, Milton Park, Abingdon, Oxfordshire OX14 4RN
52 Vanderbilt Avenue, New York, NY 10017

Routledge is an imprint of the Taylor & Francis Group, an informa business

First issued in paperback 2019

British Library Cataloguing in Publication Data
A catalogue record for this book is available from the British Library

Library of Congress Cataloging in Publication Data
Names: Djurfeldt, Gèoran, 1945- author. | Sircar, Srilata, author.
Title: Structural transformation and agrarian change in India / Gèoran Djurfeldt with Srilata Sircar.
Description: Abingdon, Oxon ; New York, NY : Routledge, 2017. | Includes bibliographical references and index.
Identifiers: LCCN 2016020492| ISBN 9781138913677 (hardback) | ISBN 9781315691312 (ebook)
Subjects: LCSH: Agriculture--Economic aspects--India. | Land tenure--India. | Farm tenancy--India. | Rural development--India.
Classification: LCC HD2072 .D6135 2017 | DDC 338.10954--dc23
LC record available at https://lccn.loc.gov/2016020492

ISBN: 978-1-138-91367-7 (hbk)
ISBN: 978-0-367-87199-4 (pbk)

Typeset in Times New Roman
by Fish Books Ltd.

Contents

Illustrations

Figures

Map

Tables

Acknowledgements

Throughout the years Björn Holmquist has been a guide for the lead author in the statistical jungle and in learning statistical modelling. Sultana Nasrin has very capably assisted in setting up the datasets and running some of the models used in this book. William English and Jean Francois Trin Tanh did the initial slogging in extracting data from ARIS REDS. Venkatesh Athreya and Staffan Lindberg have been quarrelsome constants in my life-course, agreeing only on one point: *empirical reality is the final arbiter*. My wife, Agnes Andersson Djurfeldt is my partner not only in life, but also in our professions as social scientists, always questioning my language and logic, and their theoretical and methodological rigour.

Others have contributed in innumerable ways to making this book finally appear from the press: Peter Timmer, Andrew Foster, Hans Binswanger-Mkhize, Anirudh Tagat, Masud Chaudhary, Himanshu, Gopal Karanth, Surinder S. Jodkha, Rahul Mukherji, Lisa Eklund, John Harriss, Pierre-Marie Bosc, Karin Arvidsson, María Archila, Erik Green, Christer Gunnarsson, Magnus Jirström, Montserrat Lopez Jerez and other participants in several seminars at Lund University (Afrint and RUDE groups, Sustainable Society group at the Department of Sociology, and at the Department of Statistics). Thanks also to the Faculty of Social Sciences, Lund University who founded the Rural Development Group (RUDE), of which this study is one output.

The case study presented in Chapter 3 (by Srilata Sircar) has been carved out of field notes, participant observation, and key informant interviews conducted for her doctoral project at the Department of Human Geography, Lund University. The field work was supported by grants from the Swedish Society for Anthropology and Geography (SSAG) and the Margit Althin Fund of the Royal Swedish Academy of Sciences.

Srilata Sircar is grateful to her supervisor Agnes Andersson Djurfeldt for extensive comments on an early draft of the chapter, and to Staffan Lindberg for feedback on a later draft. She would also like to express her thanks to lead author Göran Djurfeldt for the opportunity to contribute to this book and the faith he has shown in her.

Introduction

Unlike family farms, which are more or less universal, family *labour* farms are far from so and usually regarded as rare in India. Instead the old-fashioned landlord together with emaciated labourers are often seen as emblematic of the country and its agriculture. This books tests the contrary hypothesis that family labour farms are more common than usually made out and, perhaps more controversial, they are increasing in prevalence, as a consequence of the agrarian transformation.

The Year of Family Farming by the United Nations Food and Agriculture Organization (FAO) was celebrated in 2014 and Chapter 1, dealing with the concept and universal history of family farms was written in response to that, although it appears in print somewhat belatedly. In the ensuing Chapter 2 we confront theories of structural transformation (ST) and their application to India, and more specifically to its agrarian ST. As a conclusion to that chapter, we formulate the overall hypothesis of the book on the increasing prevalence of family labour farms and the mechanisms of that increase, which are connected to wage competition with the service and industrial sectors.

Chapter 3, written by Srilata Sircar deals with the phenomenon of and theories about third tier urbanization. These are crucial to an understanding of agrarian ST that is occurring under the radar, as it were.

Since the empirical analysis uses statistical modelling and since a large part of the intended audience may feel insufficiently grounded in statistics, Chapter 4 contains a short introduction to the subject of causal inference through statistical modelling.

The detailed hypotheses discussed in Chapters 5 to 7 are derived from the overall hypotheses mentioned and deal with the drivers of (1) mobility out of and into the farm sector, (2) mobility in size-class of cultivated area, and (3) changes in relative income. The analysis draws mainly on unique Indian panel data collected since the late 1960s and until 2012 in connection with the ARIS REDS and HDPI-IHDS surveys.

In the concluding Chapter we argue that standard narratives about Indian agriculture are flawed and that our results should help in undermining them. Volatility is high and more is to come!

Lund, March 2016
Göran Djurfeldt and Srilata Sircar

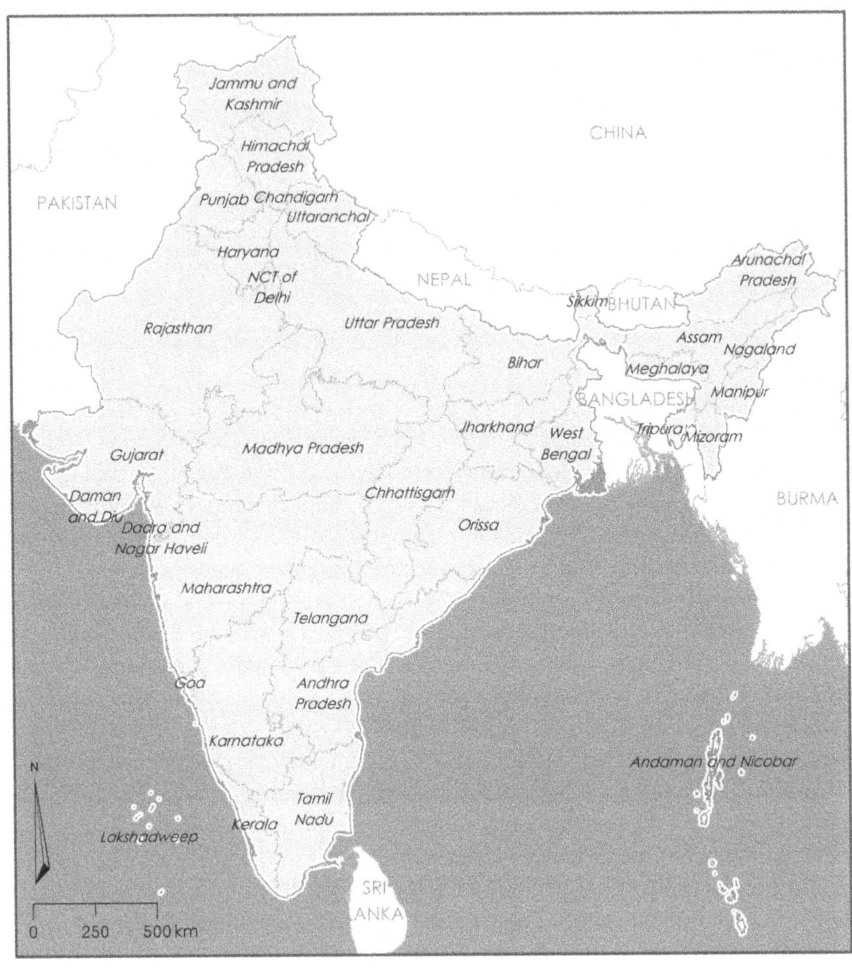

Map I.1 State map of India

Source: These data were extracted from the GADM database (www.gadm.org), version 2.8, November 2015. They can be used for non-commercial purposes only. It is not allowed to redistribute these data, or use them for commercial purposes, without prior consent. See the website for more information.

1 Capitalism and family farming

This book aims to test a general proposition about family farming as gaining strength from structural transformation in India.[1] We obviously need to start by defining our terms. We will expand on the definition of structural transformation (ST) and agrarian transformation in Chapter 2. Briefly put we refer to a social and economic process during which the industrial and service sectors are growing in proportions of GDP and of the total labour force. A main question in this book is therefore: What happens to the agrarian sector, when the economy as a whole is transforming?

Referring not specifically to India, but more generally to historical experiences of ST, mainly in the west, there are two classical attempts at answers to what happens to the agrarian sector during the transformation. The first one is associated with neoclassical economics, with Marxism and with modernization theories in sociology and political science. For reasons that are interesting as such, but which we will avoid here, the second type of answer was never part of any major intellectual or academic tradition. This alternative answer has to do with family farming.

The first classical answer to the above question is that 'traditional' agriculture, however defined and termed, transforms into capitalist agriculture with large farms dependent on hired labour. Such farms are expected to be more efficient and to outcompete smaller farms dependent on family labour. The alternative classical answer is associated with names such as the Russian agricultural economist A.V. Chayanov (1888–1937), and the German Social Democrat Karl Kautsky (1854–1938) who were critical of the belief in the superiority of factory-like organization of farming.

While the concept of structural transformation (ST) will be introduced in the next chapter, we will here devote ourselves to family versus capitalist farming: What are their respective characteristics? Why these contrary expectations where one camp is convinced of the technical superiority of capitalist organizations in agriculture, while the other is sceptical and points to the resilience of family farm organization? What follows is an outline of a perspective from economic sociology on agrarian structures[2] and their transformation.

Neither of the authors is an economist. Our perspectives come from sociology and geography and our methodology is mainly Weberian (after Max Weber, 1864–1920). A key concept in Weberian sociology is that of an ideal type.

Max Weber coined his term of ideal type as a key concept in his methodology, following his conclusions from the great methodological debate among German historians in the late nineteenth century. It is mainly a critique of Hegelianism, which at the time had a deep influence among historians and philosophers, including Karl Marx and the Marxists. The Hegelians were conceptual realists, working from a master concept, like Hegel's 'Spirit', from which an understanding of empirical reality in all its complexities was to be deduced. Previous to Weber, the alternative to conceptual realism among historians had always been an empiricist or *atheoretical* approach. Using an ideal-type approach places the Weberian in a mid-position between conceptual realism and empiricism.

Using this approach we will sketch two ideal types of production units, *family* and *capitalist* farms. We will also discuss the ideal type agricultural labourer. With these definitions in hand, we briefly discuss Lenin's theory of capitalist development, which as a figure of thought has more in common with classical notions in economics (for example with Arthur Lewis) than one would think.

In continuing, we take account of a fact which is often neglected in theories of agricultural development that tend to regard rural economies as purely agricultural. We use a term from rural sociology, i.e. pluriactivity. The term highlights the fact that members of farm households often combine several income earning activities. Economists refer to the same phenomenon with an acronym: RNFE, rural non-farm enterprise (or employment, one could add), while geographers use the terms, 'multi-local' or 'multi-spatial' livelihoods. Along with many others we argue that in order to understand agricultural development, currently and globally, we have to abandon the tendency to view the farm sector as purely agricultural.

Drawing on the discussion of pluriactivity and the three ideal types of capitalist farms, family farms and agricultural labourers, we formulate a typology of *really existing* farms.

As we will see, family farms persist and even increase their predominance globally, despite many prognoses of pending demise. One of the reasons for this is exactly pluriactivity and another one is technology and the fact that farm technologies have proven to be more scale-neutral than what has been and is still often presumed. This is why ideal, or near the ideal typical capitalist farms are rare historically, as well as currently. We continue with a discussion of agrarian policies, in the west, in India and elsewhere, which in turn lays the ground for the question to be researched in later chapters: the position of family farming in India and the hypothesis about its increasing prevalence.

Ideal types of farms

We use 'ideal type' as defined by Max Weber:

> An ideal type is formed by the one-sided accentuation of one or more points of view and by the synthesis of a great many diffuse, discrete, more or less

> present and occasionally absent concrete individual phenomena, which are arranged according to those onesidedly emphasized viewpoints into a unified analytical construct.
>
> (Weber 1997, 1949: 90)

Ideal types feature prominently in a Weberian toolbox. Contrasting ideal types of farms, in our case, with really existing ones is an important methodology aimed to better understand the complexity of the real world. It helps in making sense of an empirical material, as well as in understanding how preconceived notions form our understanding of reality. Systematically collected empirical material, i.e. not only anecdotal or piecemeal evidence, but hard evidence, in the form of macro- and micro-level statistics, and reviews of existing research, historically as well as currently, helps in exposing the ideal type to a kind of test of its empirical adequacy. This is turn aids the researcher in working out theoretically grounded typologies and empirically adequate accounts of social reality.

Working with such a methodology we will discuss three ideal types, viz. that of the family farm, counterpoised with the capitalist farm and the agricultural labourer, on whom the latter depends conceptually as well as really.

The main hypothesis in this work is that processes of structural transformation, historically, currently (and hypothetically in the case of India) will bring with them an increasing importance and eventual predominance of family farms. This obviously calls for an explanation but first of all a definition of 'family farm'.

Defining ideal types of farms

The International Steering Committee for the International Year of Family Farming, celebrated in 2014, developed the following conceptual definition of family farming:

> Family Farming (which includes all family-based agricultural activities) is a means of organizing agricultural, forestry, fisheries, pastoral and aquaculture production which is managed and operated by a family and predominantly reliant on family labour, including both women's and men's. The family and the farm are linked, co-evolve and combine economic, environmental, social and cultural functions.
>
> (FAO 2014)

Obviously political, the above definition was formulated by the Steering Committee, presumably after a lot of strategic and tactical deliberations and compromises. To function methodologically the definition is too broad and diverse. In order to work out an ideal type definition we need something sharper than the one cited. One of the background papers to the FAO report written by Lowder, Skoet *et al.* (2014) is of good help. The authors scrutinized 36 definitions of family farming and found that nearly all of them included an element of family management, and specify that part of the definition of a family farm is that a member of the household "owns, operates and/or manages the farm either in part or fully." Often a specification is added that concerns "a minimum share of labour that must come from the owner and his or her relatives."

A number of other criteria are often used to complement the definition, for example, that a family farm should not exceed a certain size in terms of area, or that the share of household labour should not exceed a certain level. The definitions examined by the authors apparently did not include either of the ones argued for by Djurfeldt (1996) and Errington (1996). In the stalemated debate both these authors insisted on one overriding element as essential in a definition of family farming: Djurfeldt insisted on a family labour criterion, while Errington as insistently clung to a family management criterion. With increasing age and experience they both should have grown less stubborn. Instead of clinging to an essentialist definition, we prefer an approach that distinguishes between three dimensions, along which different types of farms may differ from one another:

1 The proportion of family labour is high, as opposed to other types of labour, casual or otherwise.[3]
2 Management of the farm is predominantly taken care of by members of the family rather than by employed managers or agents.
3 The farm is to a large extent owned by members of the family or by kinship networks, as with customary lands, owned by communities rather than by their individual members.[4]

Various combinations of these three dimensions would give us three variants of ideal types: (a) *family labour farms* where most of the labour is put in by family or network members; (b) *family managed farms* where the management function is performed by family members, relatives or possibly by network labour. Finally, we get (c) *family owned farms*, where ownership is in the hands of a family or possibly a non-market network of some sort. A tenant farm would obviously not fulfil the last criterion, but may still be a family farm by the first two.[5]

Combining the three dimensions above yield the most inclusive definition possible: Family farms are either *worked, managed or owned* by families or through non-market networks. This definition implies that an overwhelming majority of all farms globally are family farms. The FAO report quoted above estimates the number of family farms worldwide to 570 million out of a total of 600 million (FAO 2014: 8). It adds that for most countries, family farms inclusively defined account for more than 90 and in many cases 100 per cent of all farms.

We are not content however with the inclusive definition above; a more exclusive definition of family farms is preferable for analytical purposes. Here we choose to define an ideal type family farm as dependent on family labour in production and primarily managed by members of the family. This definition would still include a huge majority of the 570 million family farms worldwide. What would it exclude?

The ideal type of capitalist farm

Of the 30 million farms that are not classified as family farms by the FAO definition the most important one, for analytical purposes at least, is the capitalist farm. We define the *ideal type capitalist farm* as an agricultural production unit in which all factors of production (land, labour, capital and management) are procured on the market: This is another way of saying that the factors of production are commodities and have market value. In terms of the three criteria discussed above, the ideal typical capitalist farm (or firm) is: (1) worked by labourers hired for wages (rather than recruited by non-market means, (2) managed by professional managers (rather than by family members), and (3) owned by corporations having invested their capital into the farm. The capital includes land that, as for family farmers, may be owned or leased.

To be financially sustainable the capitalist farm must, like all capitalist enterprises, in the long run yield a return of the capital invested, at rates that are comparable with other types of investment. More precisely, the investment in the farm needs to yield high enough returns on the capital invested in all factors of production, including the land.[6] Thus the capitalist farm must be competitive with other farms or firms operating on the same markets (here we are mainly concerned with output markets). Normally the competitors would include a large number of family farms. The extent to which they are competitive among other things is a question of economies of scale.

If there were economies of scale in agricultural production, as pointed out by Binswanger *et al.* (1995: 2664), capitalist farming would have upended family farms long ago. As we will see later, economies of scale are rare in agriculture and often obtain only in some of its branches.

As would be expected of an ideal type, few really existing landed properties live up to the ideal type definition of a capitalist farm, especially not the requirement to yield a return on the imputed value of the land or, if mortgaged, interest on the loan taken. Land not acquired as an investment, perhaps inherited, or land not mortgaged, may obviously be profitable in an account that does not include the value of the land. This makes it easier for such farms to compete with family farms that, by the way often enjoy the same advantage of mortgage-free land. However, capitalist farms suffer another handicap, which is their reliance on hired labour. Really existing, as opposed to ideal typical capitalist farms often save on labour costs by hiring what we call 'unfree' labour.

With these definitions of the ideal types of family and capitalist farms at hand we will proceed by discussing real types, as opposed to the ideal type of capitalist farming. It deserves to be stressed that ideal and real types are endpoints on a continuum from more to less abstract, from ideal type family farm or capitalist ones, to really existing farms. Contrasting the ideal type with what we know or have learnt about a real system is an important tool in deepening our understanding of the latter. When contrasting ideal type capitalist farms with really existing large estates, the aim is to deepen our understanding of the latter.

Large estates are seldom capitalist farms

Definitions of capitalist farming found in the literature are variable, but often reflect what we would argue are non-rigorous definitions of capitalism itself. It is commonplace to see authors, academic or popular, explicitly or implicitly using definitions of farms as capitalist because they are (1) market-oriented, (2) employ much labour, (3) are heavily mechanized or because (4) they are large in terms of area. A fifth point is that (v) capitalist farms seldom were established because they were technically superior but more often because powerful elites thought that they were. As we will explain neither of these five criteria would qualify a farm as capitalist in the ideal sense of the term and thus cannot be used in an ideal type definition.

Market orientation versus subsistence production

Why is not market orientation an indicator of ideal type capitalist farming? Such a farm is market orientated by definition, but so are most of the estimated 600 million farms found globally. Purely subsistence oriented farms, producing nothing for the market hardly exist, except as aberrations and in very remote areas.

The FAO report quoted exemplifies varying degrees of commercialization using statistics for eight countries. Out of these the least market orientated one is Nepal, where farmers in the lowest farm size quartile sell less than ten per cent of production, while those in the top quartile sell slightly more than 20 per cent. Tanzania unexpectedly is at the other end, with farmers in the lowest quartile marketing more than 60 per cent while farmers in the top quartile sell 66 per cent of their production (FAO 2014: 22). With a too schematic conception of subsistence production one could have expected poorer Tanzania to have a higher degree of production for own use than somewhat better off Nepal. We do not know why it is the other way round, but one may suspect that the reason is that family farms in Nepal are subsidized, not by governments as in Europe and the US, but by remittances from migrants to the Gulf and elsewhere. Thus, commercial production is not an exclusive criterion of capitalist farming and neither is subsistence production an indicator of non-capitalist agriculture.

The majority of farmers worldwide produce partly for subsistence, especially in poor and middle-income countries. They are usually referred to as smallholders in the development debate. By the criteria proposed here they are family labour as well as family managed farms, with the specific characteristic of being partly subsistence oriented. They make up a majority of the world's poor.

Acreage criteria

Smallholders are usually defined by an acreage criterion, for example farms below two hectares (Dixon, Tanyeri-Abur *et al.* 2004). Area is not a homogeneous variable however: two hectares in a near-desert area cannot feed a family, while two intensively cultivated hectares under a valuable crop can be quite a large unit in economic terms. In practical terms, the smallholder category lumps together farm types, which for analytical purposes one may wish to keep distinct. In this chapter we will avoid the term, although it will recur in the empirical analysis from Chapter 5 onwards.

Dependence on hired labour

Somewhat surprisingly perhaps we reject "dependence on hired labour" as a defining characteristic for the ideal type capitalist farm. Many landed properties in India or in other parts of the world, due to their size in terms of area or in turnover certainly depend on labour recruited either from outside the family or from community and kin networks. But being dependent on hired labour of various types does not make the employer capitalist in the ideal type meaning. More specifically, dependence on hired labour does not imply, as the ideal type requires, that such farms be constrained to make a profit on capital invested in land. We leave the issue of hired labour for now but will return to it later.

Mechanization

As everyone knows famers of all kinds use machines. Family farms of the kind found in Europe or the US are heavily mechanized. They still fulfil the criteria of family farms according to the definition above. In other words, reliance on machines does not make the farmer a capitalist, as we define these terms.

Size of farm

Similarly the size of a farm does not automatically reflect its organization of production. A large estate does not become capitalist just because of its size. The history of large, landed properties around the world suggests that unlike industries, large-scale estates have not emerged through economies of scale. They often have a completely different history. For instance, *latifundios* in Southern Spain (Djurfeldt 1993) as well as in South America have a common history as feudal fiefs. Take another example: The plantation sector in sub-Saharan Africa never proved its economic superiority, but was established by colonial and military might and often continues to be protected by the rulers of post-colonial societies, or taken over by them or their cronies. Malawi is a good example here (Prowse 2011, 2013). A recent World Bank study showed that such plantations cannot, except for certain crops, compete price-wise with the family farm sector (World Bank 2009).

Large landed properties are often created and protected by the State

Political considerations are evident in the establishment of large-scale farms. Take the now defunct Chinese communes: They would never have been set up were it not for the policy makers of the Chinese Communist Party having been taken in by the myth of "big is beautiful," inspired by scale economies in industry. Neither would they have been dismantled from 1978 and onwards if scale economies had been there. The reforms initiated by Deng Xiaoping established by administrative fiat a huge family farm sector in China. Thus the reforms added many millions of family farms to those already existing around the world. In terms of its addition to the country's food security, it was a uniquely successful reform (see for example Lin 1992, Riskin 1995).

Returning to the main argument: large landed properties seldom proved their superiority in terms of productivity, but were established by administrative or political interventions. Thus land tenure and other agrarian institutions have a political history that must be borne in mind when trying to understand their role in current or future food production. Historically political interventions often created large landed properties, as in Andalusia or in the former Spanish or Portuguese colonies in South America.

Corporate ownership

As argued initially, the ideal type capitalist farm requires that land ownership is corporate rather than family based. This criterion is more discerning than might be expected. When Deininger and Byerlee recently tried to estimate the number of capitalist farms worldwide they found only one good example: the Swedish Black Soil AB which bought up large tracts of land in the black soil areas of Ukraine cultivating them by means of so-called precision agriculture where tractors and combine harvesters are steered by Global Positioning Systems (GPS) and where fertilization regimes are worked out by means of satellite imagery (Deininger and Byerlee 2012). Since Black Soil AB is a public limited firm, listed on the Stockholm Stock Exchange, it fulfils the rigorous definition of an ideal type capitalist farm (and firm), dependent for its long-term survival on generating profit on the capital invested in the firm, including the land.

A recent article in *The New York Times* was titled "Cash Crops with Dividends: Financiers transforming strawberries into securities."[7] The article points out that the rush for land investments (land grabs) that got into a high spin following the global food price crisis in 2008 had already begun to lose speed six years later. A new financial product is however exemplified in the article and pioneered by a private (not public) company, American Farmland. The new product is an example of what the journalist calls the latest twist, in which investors and bankers are "combining crops and the soil they grow in into an asset class that ordinary investors can buy a piece of" (Stevenson 2014). This is an example of the *financialization* of land, which fulfils one criterion of the ideal type of capitalist farming. So far it has been rarely fulfilled however.

In addition to American Farmland, only two other farm companies are listed on the NASDAQ stock exchange, Farmland Partners and Gladstone Land Corporation, and indeed, investors interviewed by the journalist are still unsure if in the long run land it is a worthwhile investment. This is in the heartland of world capitalism and given that we have been fed with prognoses of the imminent takeover of world agriculture by capitalism, at least since Lenin's "The Development of Capitalism in Russia" (1960, 1899),[8] this is not overly impressive.

In the US and other western countries it is not uncommon to find farms which legally are corporations but more often than not are entirely or majority family-owned and thus do not qualify as ideal type capitalist farms. They are not constrained to generating profit on the value of the land and not subjected to the discipline of the financial markets. Unlike a capitalist firm there is nothing that forces the owners to close shop if the farm is not profitable.

With this discussion of ideal types we move over to the development theory associated with those envisioning a future in which agriculture is dominated by capitalist farms.

Classical Leninist theory

The process of capitalist development in agriculture as envisioned by Lenin (1960, 1899) is much akin to what a classical development economist like Arthur Lewis had in mind. Lewis referred to a "traditional sector," the main function of which was to deliver surplus labour to the modern sector as the structural transformation proceeded. When surplus labour was exhausted agriculture had to be modernized and develop into capitalist agriculture.

Lenin said much the same, as is schematically illustrated in Figure 1.1. For him, development of capitalist agriculture is one of differentiation. In the process middle peasants either, for the majority, become dispossessed after losing out in competition on the market and join the ranks of the agricultural proletariat or, for a minority, graduate to the class of capitalist farmers.

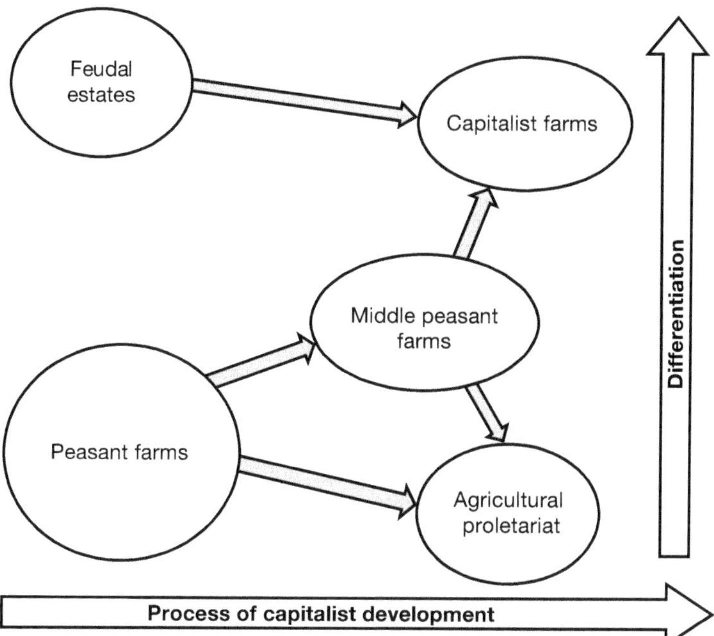

Figure 1.1 The development of capitalist agriculture according to Lenin

The emergence of capitalism in farming according to the varieties of the Leninist model, must be one of the most frequently failed prophecies in intellectual history. Given the estimate that out of about 600 million farms worldwide, as already pointed out, only a handful can be deemed capitalist in the ideal type sense of the word, the expectation that they would take over the entire global farm sector can only be explained by ideological and political factors.

Putting it starkly: waiting for the technological preconditions for capitalist farming to prevail is like waiting for Godot in Beckett's play. He never arrives. Therefore we remain sceptical when Deininger and Byerlee (2012) argue that technologies like precision agriculture have now developed so far that, finally and with a delay of a century, large landed properties have gained a productivity edge over (smaller scale) family farming. The latter allegedly lost their competitive advantage in terms of family labour and family management. We are not yet willing to accept this claim, for the simple reason that the new technologies will be getting cheaper as they spread and, although with a delay, become affordable also to family farmers; in the west they are.

With this we can move over to discuss the third ideal type we need, i.e. the one of agricultural labourers.

Agricultural labourers in segmented markets

If we were to define an ideal type agricultural labourer it is tempting to resort to the Marxist view, according to which the capitalist farm is unthinkable without the agricultural labourer, and the reverse. Whether originating from dispossessed peasants or from groups historically denied access to land, ideal typical agricultural labourers sell their labour power in ideal typical markets where the forces of demand and supply enact their inexorable laws. The glitch here is the virtual non-existence of such markets, since really existing labour markets tend to be segmented with different mechanisms of wage determination in different segments.

Taking the Indian case, agricultural labourers have long been recruits from socially discriminated groups, the Scheduled Castes (SC, so-called ex-Untouchables), Scheduled Tribes (ST) or from lower castes, in the Indian debate often referred to as Other Backward Castes (OBC). Discrimination implies a segmented market with the evident function of keeping wages low. In the absence of competition for labour from services or industries, discrimination thus means locking SC, ST and low caste labourers into low wage market segments, condemning them to lives in misery.

What is well known but less recognized is that agricultural labour markets also in the heartland of world capitalism tend to be similarly segmented. A classic study from the 1980s (Thomas 1985) of salad farms in California, showed that farm workers were recruited from highly segmented niches in the labour market, with illegal immigrants at the lower rungs doing the most tedious jobs at the lowest wages. Green card holders occupied a higher and somewhat better niche, like overseers, quality controllers etc. The only wages at competitive rates were paid to US citizens, typically as managers, security staff and others.

The European agricultural labour market has developed in a similar direction in recent years, when legal and illegal immigrants have swelled the labour supply and caused a downward trend in wages with the effect that nationals and citizens remain only in the best paid jobs (Kasimis and Papadopoulos 1997, Gatti 2007).

Thus the ideal type agricultural labourer is as rare a bird as the ideal type capitalist farm. Anecdotally, it can be remarked the majority of the members in the Swedish agricultural labourers union work, not in agriculture, but on golf courses, in parks and in gardens. The Leninist theory of capitalist development is off the mark also in this respect. To describe really existing agrarian societies, we need real types adapted among other things to segmented labour markets. This does not mean that the Weberian type is not a useful tool, merely that it is not a descriptive, but an analytical device.

From ideal types to real ones

In Figure 1.2 we summarize the typology to be used in this book. The figure emphasizes the point that real agrarian structures are far from the ideal types as defined above, whether we speak of really existing capitalist farms or family farms, or for that matter agricultural labourers. In the case of capitalist farms there is an especially glaring misfit between prognoses of their increasing dominance and the fact they are exceptionally rare, not only in numbers but also in terms of shares of production.[9]

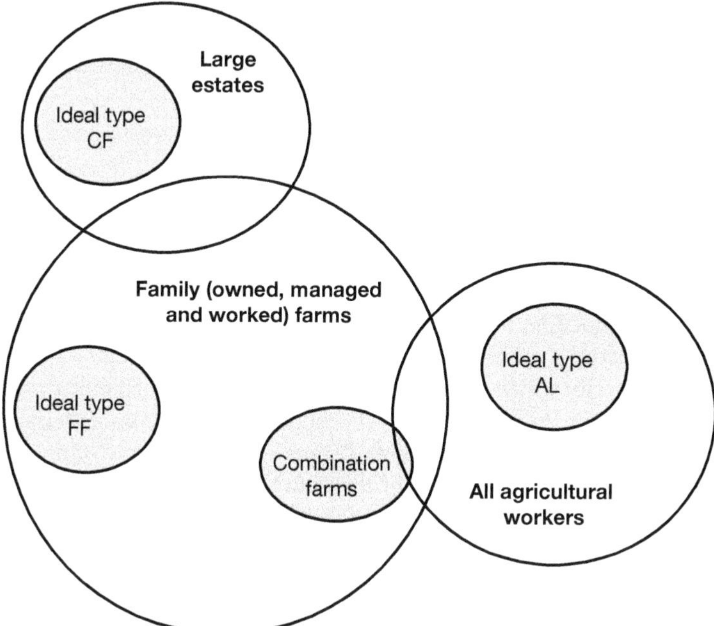

Figure 1.2 A typology of current agrarian societies

Note: CF refers to capitalist farms, FF to family farms and AL to agricultural labourers

In Figure 1.2 the ideal types are small shaded circles within bigger white ones. Firstly, all agricultural labourers make up a much bigger circle than the ideal type agricultural labourers and, although it is difficult to find data on this, we would contend that "free" or non-discriminated labour has shown no secular trend to increase its share of the larger circle. Moreover agricultural labourers are sometimes farmers as well, as denoted by the overlap between the two white circles of family farms and agricultural workers. Secondly, the ideal type capitalist farm circle is a small part of all large estates; moreover the corresponding shaded circle is not completely within the large-landed property circle, because some really existing farms dependent on hired labour are small in terms of acreage, but large in terms of economic turnover, for example in the horticultural sector. Thirdly the white family farm circle contains a new category, here called combination farms, which denotes farms where farming is not full-time, but is based a combination of farming with off-farm jobs. This type of "pluriactivity," as rural sociologists term it, is not new to agriculture. We will return to the issue in a while.

We argue that this typology is more accurate in describing contemporary agrarian societies and that analytically, together with the ideal types, the typology can be used in analysing the development of agrarian structures.[10] With this methodological tool in hand we can ask questions about the nature, prevalence and development of family farming in a given society: are there family labour and family managed farms and to what extent are they family owned? The typology further leads us to enquire about large estates dependent on hired labour, their history and their form of labour recruitment. Do they use "free" or "unfree" labour? Are their labourers free to negotiate their wages and organize, or are their wages kept low by their being discriminated against by citizenship, ethnicity, race or caste? To what extent are or were they historically protected by legislation, subsidies or privilege?

In the following section we first go deeper into the characteristics of family farms.

The competitive advantage of family farms

Within the Marxist tradition since Marx himself, family farms have been seen as a class facing extinction. For Lenin, the peasantry was doomed to disappear and split into two parts, a minority which would develop into an agrarian capitalist class, and a majority which would lose their land and be forced either to join the ranks of the agricultural proletariat, or its counterparts in the cities (Lenin 1960, 1899, Djurfeldt 1981). A presumption of superior productivity within capitalist agriculture underpinned this vision of the future. When compared to peasant or family farms capitalist agriculture, or factories in the field would be like industry compared to crafts and a thing of the past, a museum artefact.

That craft production has difficulties in competing with industrial organization is evidence to the superiority of what Marx called the capitalist mode of production (1977). Like Adam Smith before him (1904 (1776)), he argued that this superiority stemmed, not only from mechanization , but also from the advanced division of labour within the factory, with labourers specializing in different part of the production process rather than producing the whole product, as the artisan would.

This type of specialization of labour holds only to a limited extent on really existing capitalist farms, i.e. estates depending on hired labour. Strikingly such farms depend on masses of workers to perform tasks that are not easy to mechanize, like picking of strawberries, wine or tomatoes.

Large estates find difficulties in competing with family farms, precisely because they are not factories in the field, as the discussion above clearly illustrates. Historically, as well as currently, large estates generally have not had access to technologies, which are not also available to family farms. Both in Europe and the US, there are small differences in technology between the two sectors. The main difference between them lies in the armies of labour, often from segmented or unfree labour markets, absorbed by farms dependent on such labour. This is in contrast to a much greater dependence of family farms on own labour.[11]

While theoretically it is plausible that their mode of organization gives a competitive edge to estates dependent on hired labour, historically as well as currently, this is seldom the case. By contrast, given the access to the same technologies the 'staffing' of farms under family management provides their competitive advantage. Hired (non-family) labour is less motivated to work, and more prone to foot dragging than family labour (Chayanov, 1986; Scott, 1985; Eswaran, 1986). Family members on the other hand work for themselves or for their families, including for their kids and future generations. This is a potent motivating force. During crises family labour is often prepared to work for little or no remuneration, which is the fundamental reason for the resilience of family farms (Chayanov 1986). This is contrast to farms dependent on hired labour, for which the wage bill is largely inelastic.

There is an on-going debate within agricultural and development economics on economies of scale within farming (for overviews, see Eastwood, Lipton *et al.* 2010, Chand, Prasanna *et al.* 2011 and for India Dyer 1998). With few exceptions, scale in many studies is proxied by area, either of farm or of area under specific crops. There are evident problems with this operationalization, however. Area is not a homogeneous variable. Whether we speak of farm or plot size, the productivity differences between different farms or plots are vast and depend not only on soil fertility, but also on irrigation, drainage and other factors. Models regressing productivity on farm or plot size, as a result, get large residuals, not easy to minimize and not prone to be normally distributed. In our view, this is the fundamental reason why the many studies on economies of scale in farming have yielded little in terms of generalizable results. Thus we would argue that farm (or even plot) size is not the relevant operationalization, while farm type is. We know of only one study, which has used this insight, a World Bank study of the profitability of a selection of crops, comparing family farms and large estates in sub-Saharan Africa (World Bank 2009). It concluded that in most crops, family farmers are competitive with the estate sector.

Eastwood and Lipton argue that the competitive advantage of family farms over large estates will gradually disappear and Deininger and Byerlee would seem to agree (Lipton and John 1991, Eastwood, Lipton *et al.* 2010, Deininger and Byerlee 2012). All three teams of authors mention precision agriculture and geo-sensing, which in their present form require large farm areas to motivate the investment. As already pointed out and in in line with Moore's law,[12] currently large-scale technology is likely soon to be available to smaller-scale farmers. Be that as it may, this sketchy overview seems to indicate that we are far from the point of time when capitalist farms for technological reasons will replace family farms.

This argument for family farming and its competitive advantages can be put in economic terms by referring to Coase's theory of the firm (Coase 1937) and the concept of transaction costs (Williamson 1979). Coase's article became a classic because he pointed out that neo-classical economics could not explain the emergence or existence of the firm. This is where Williamson and his terminological innovation enter: the firm is a way of minimizing transaction costs by internalizing them into an organizational unit. One can argue along the same lines about family farming, and family business in general: by internalizing labour costs into the farm (or firm) one reduces transaction costs. Using family instead of hired labour, transactions costs are lowered because the need for supervision is nearly eliminated and shrinkage or foot dragging avoided. This is not necessarily a disadvantage to family workers and need not imply self-exploitation, as has sometimes been alleged. On the contrary, by increasing the quality of the labour input, the remuneration to family labourers may be higher than it would have been to the hired labour it replaced.

The remuneration of family labour is crucial. While the remuneration of hired labour is often simply a sum of money that of family labour is a bundle of utilities, food, shelter, affection and love, not easy to evaluate in economic terms. The economic parts of the remuneration can be regarded as the correspondence of a wage, or what Eastwood, Lipton and Newell call a reservation utility (Eastwood, Lipton *et al.* 2010). Thus one can say that as long as the reservation utility of family labour is higher than prevailing agricultural wages, one can expect a tendency for hired labour to be replaced by family labour (Schmitt 1991). An upward pressure on wages, for example due to competition with the industrial service sector, would have a similar effect.

Supermarketization and vertical integration

Many perceive the spread of supermarkets in middle- and low-income countries as the new threat to the world's family farms. The basic argument is that the giant supermarket chains, Wal-Mart, Carrefour and the others prefer to deal with a few big suppliers rather than a whole lot of small-scale producers. As supermarkets invest in erecting procurement chains for fresh fruit and vegetables, with the high quality demands of discerning middle class consumers in view, they tend to prefer large estates for production. In the process of supermarketization family farmers are deprived of some their markets. So goes the argument.

While this is undoubtedly becoming a huge part of all food retailing and procurement, we believe that its consequences for family farming worldwide may not be as apocalyptic as could be feared. Even in markets controlled by huge corporations, family farms enjoy advantages that serve them well.

In his mostly unspoken criticism of Lenin and the Bolsheviks, the Russian agricultural economist and pioneer of family farm studies, A. V. Chayanov proffered an alternative scenario to Lenin's horizontal concentration (see Figure 1.1 on page 9), which he styled vertical integration. Chayanov studied how urban-based merchants contracted with family farmers to produce cotton and other cash crops and offered credit to facilitate farmers' investments. He also studied the European cooperative movement during travels in Europe and wrote about his vision for the future of family farming (Chayanov 1977):

> If to this we add in the most developed capitalist countries, such as those in North America, widely developed mortgage credit, the financing of farm circulating capital, and the dominating part played by capital invested in transport, elevator, irrigation, and other undertakings, then we have before us the new ways in which capitalism penetrates agriculture. These ways convert the farmers into a labor force working with other people's means of production. They convert agriculture, despite the evident scattered and independent nature of the small commodity producers, into an economic system concentrated in a series of larger undertakings and, through them, entering the sphere controlled by the most advanced forms of finance capitalism.
>
> (Chayanov 1986, 1966: 262)

The leading current expert on supermarketization is Thomas Reardon with a long list of publications to his credit. He is careful to stress the enormous speed with which the process has enveloped the developing world including the poorest parts of sub-Saharan Africa. It is worth noting however that, with its restrictions on foreign direct investment in retailing, India is less drawn into the process than many other countries (see for example, Reardon, Timmer *et al.* 2003). Reardon *et al.* summarize studies on sub-contracting to farmers as follows:

> Companies in general tend to source from larger farmers and eschew smaller farmers in scale-dualistic contexts. However, there are various exceptions to this pattern, where companies source from small farmers even when large farmers operate in the same sector… Companies source from small farmers in contexts where small farmers dominate the agrarian structure… When companies source from small farmers, they tend to source from the subset with the requisite non-land assets (such as irrigation, farmers' associations, farm equipment, and access to paved roads). However, where companies need or want to source from small farmers but the farmers lack needed credit, inputs, or extension, companies sometimes use "resource-provision contracts" to address those constraints… [Studies] tend to show positive effects on small farmers of inclusion in modern channels, including on incomes and assets of farmers, and positive externalities to the local labor markets.
>
> (Reardon, Barrett *et al.* 2009)

Concluding from the above: alarm bells seem to prematurely signal the pending demise of the world's family farmers. As is the case for advanced technology, apocalyptic messages are too rash. In the longer run, neither supermarketization, nor precision farming need be as deleterious to family farming as some foresee.

A safety valve for farmers is pluriactivity, which we will presently discuss.

Pluriactivity and combination farms

The term 'combination farm' used in Figure 1.2 on page 11 is a direct translation from Norwegian 'kombinasjonsjordbruk'. Used in a classical work in Scandinavian sociology by the late Ottar Brox (Brox 1969), the term denotes the combination of activities and income sources in agrarian livelihoods. Brox' example related to the combination of small-scale agriculture with fishing along the North Sea coast and in the fjords, especially in Northern Norway where living exclusively on farming was well nigh impossible. Later rural sociologists have adopted a French term, 'pluriactivity' to describe such combinations, common all over but less visible because censuses and surveys long recorded 'primary' and at best 'secondary' occupations.

Pluriactivity is not a new phenomenon: Combination farms were common centuries ago, both in Europe and elsewhere (Holmes and Qataert 1986), for example with farmers from mountainous areas migrating in the off-season to the plains to gain extra there. The fisherman-farmer (Brox, op. cit.) and the logger-farmer combination is also age-old (Bjerén 1981). There is no doubt however that with the ST we can expect an increasing degree of pluriactivity, involving the whole cast, fishermen, loggers, herdsmen, agricultural labourers, family farmers and well as owners of large landed properties.

There was a spate of interest in pluriactivity in Europe in the 1990s that resulted in a number of publications, still worth reading. In a study from 1992, Fuller and Ray summarized the situation in Europe, the US and Canada. They noted an association between pluriactivity and farm size within countries. Operators of larger farms were associated with lower participation in off-farm work in Canada, the US and the ten member countries of what was then called the European Community. The authors further mentioned that the participation in off-farm work by spouses was not related to farm size. Off-farm incomes were important all over, especially in the US and Canada where on the mean they made up over 37 per cent of total income. Many farm households gained more than 50 per cent of their total income from such sources or from social transfers, remittances and return on investments (Fuller and Ray 1992: 206–9).

A study by MacKinnon and Bryden compared conditions within Europe in the early 1990s.[13] The authors concluded that, when comparing the remuneration of family labour in agriculture and other sectors of the economy, a large proportion of farms across Europe did not provide a full-time wage. For nearly a half of the sampled households, farm-based income provided less than a third of household income; for only around forty per cent did it provide more than 70 per cent of income. Only 28 per cent of the sample farms drew 90 per cent or more of their income from the farm. The authors concluded that 62 per cent of farm households in the sample were pluriactive on their definition (Mackinnon, Bryden *et al.* 1991: 61–2).

Since the 1990s interest in these issues seems to have waned both among researchers and policy makers and newer publications are difficult to find. It is unlikely however that pluriactivity would have decreased in the OECD countries.

Both neo-Leninists and neo-classical economists have had a tendency to interpret pluriactivity as a temporary phenomenon, when households due to the ST transfer out of the agrarian sector. Both camps have tended to underestimate the sustainability of combination farms and the livelihoods associated with them.

In conclusion, pluriactivity is more than a transitory phenomenon and is another way in which the prognoses about the development of capitalist agriculture, at the expense of family labour have come to shame.

The dice seems to be loaded against capitalist and for family farming. In the Indian case, scholars of various persuasions, Marxists and others have been looking for capitalist farming for 70 years without finding much of it. So we will turn the question upside down. In the empirical analysis we will be asking: has seventy years of agricultural development in India promoted family farming and, if so, what kind of family farming?

Working with a Weberian methodology requires working not only with ideal and real types, but also with the history of the societies you are studying. Aspects of the history of family farming and large estates elsewhere than in India are relevant in our case. In further preparation for the empirical analysis we continue by discussing historical processes of agrarian transformation. We will start with the classical case of Britain, since the time of Marx at the centre of discussion of agricultural development.

Historical transformation of rural economies

As will be evident from the following, British agrarian society did not at all develop according to theoretical expectations.[14] The roots of the British estate system are medieval and can be traced to the peasant uprisings in the fourteenth and fifteenth centuries, which the peasants lost. "Their consequential loss of land laid the foundation for Britain's extremely polarized distribution of land" (cf. Brenner 1976). The Black Death contributed further to the establishment of this highly unequal agrarian structure, as did the Reformation, the dissolution of the monasteries and the appropriation of their land by the crown under Henry VIII. These estates were later awarded to the nobility (Tracy 1989, Part I). Thus a small landed elite of mostly noble families monopolized landed property.

The majority of the rural population lacked property and were compelled to seek their subsistence in the commons, until the early seventeeth century when the Enclosure Acts privatized the commons and deprived the peasantry also of this source of sustenance. From the eighteenth century onwards the poverty of the rural population drove the poor and propertyless to seek work as agricultural labourers, industrial workers, servants or, alternatively to seek poverty relief (Polanyi 2001, 1944).

The monopolization of land by the nobility meant that the property-owning peasants, in England called yeoman farmers, became a small minority in the countryside. Besides the propertyless and the landlords the most important group, although small in terms of numbers, was the estate tenants.

The landowners usually did not cultivate their land themselves, but leased it out. Tenants of large landed properties were pioneers in the application of what has been called "high farming." This was a highly productive farming system, building on permanent cultivation, i.e. without fallows. Stall-feeding of cattle, systematic manuring and crop rotation with nitrogen fixing fodder crops were major innovations in the new farming system. Increasing demand for cereals spurred by a growing urban and industrial population stimulated the innovations. High farming reached its peak under the latter half of the nineteenth century and before the agrarian crisis of 1870 (Chambers and Mingay 1966).

At this time Great Britain had a distribution of land reminding of some Latin American countries before the land reforms of the 1960s. James Caird, a contemporary researcher described the system as follows:

> When we come more closely to analyse the purely landowning class, the aggregation of land among small numbers becomes very conspicuous. One fourth of the whole territory, excluding those under one acre, is held by 1,200 persons, at an average of 16,200 acres; another fourth by 6,200 persons at an average for each of 3,150 acres; another fourth by 50,770 persons at an average of each of 380 acres; whilst the remaining fourth is held by 261,830 persons at an average each of 70 acres. An interesting compilation by the Scotsman newspaper shows that the peerage of the United Kingdom, about 600 in number, possess among them rather more than a fifth of all the land, and between a tenth and an eleventh of its annual income.
>
> (Caird 1961, 1878 quoted in Newby, Bell *et al.* 1978)

The British agrarian structure before 1870 lay quite close to the ideal typical capitalist farming described earlier. It had a small group of aristocratic landowners, renting out their land to capitalist tenants and with a mass of agricultural labourers doing the drudgery in fields and stables. The system fulfilled one of the definitional requirements of capitalist agriculture, viz. capitalization of the land. The nobility lived from their rents, and their tenants had to run an enterprise, which could finance not only the wages and the inputs of capital, but also the capitalized value of the land, in the form of rent. It is a historical irony that this system, which as we have seen hardly exists today, was at its high 150 years ago and since then it decayed.

The agrarian crisis from the 1870s onwards and what we today describe as the first period of "hyperglobalization" (see further below) brought about the downfall of the British system of capitalist tenants. Falling food prices are a deadly threat to landlordism, since they decrease the rental value of land. Landlord incomes tumble; the nobility cannot maintain their castles, their extravagant style of living or pay their servants. This was the destiny that befell many British landowners.

In 1873 the first signs of the coming crisis appeared. World market prices on farm products fell drastically and remained low for a number of years. The estate tenants took the first blow, but since prices remained low, landlords were gradually affected. Paradoxically, agricultural labourers were quicker to recover. The competition between agriculture and industry for labour resulted in scarcity of labour and partly protected the rural proletariat from the worst effects of the crisis (Perry 1972: 22).

The agrarian crisis has been interpreted as a delayed effect of the famous Corn Laws, adopted in the 1840s by the British Parliament in opposition to the landlords (Perry 1972: 14). The Corn Laws opened Britain to imports of farm products, but their impact was delayed by about 30 years, due to high transport costs that curbed international trade in bulky products like cereals. During the second half of the nineteenth century, rapid advances in shipping led to falling freight costs. After 1870 they were low enough to allow American and Argentinian cereals to compete with European ones, which set the bells tolling for British landlordism:

> The dismantling of the landed estates – the aristocratic diaspora from the land – although usually dated from the period immediately following the First World War… began much earlier. Nevertheless a deluge of land sales began in 1919, on a scale unprecedented since the dissolution of monasteries in the sixteenth century. Within three years, it has been estimated, one-quarter of the land surface of the United Kingdom changed hands. However, as Hobsbawm has remarked, one of the most noteworthy aspects of this forced aristocratic abdication was that it took place almost unnoticed at the time, outside the restricted coterie of landowners, farmers, and estate agents who were directly involved in the transactions. This, Hobsbawm adduces, indicated just how far the agricultural interest and the landowning aristocracy had become removed from the centres of economic and political power by the early decades of the twentieth century.
>
> (Hobsbawm 1969, Newby, Bell *et al.* 1978: 36–7)

The agrarian crisis thus brought a land reform, not by the State, but via the market. British estates were divided and taken over by smaller landowners. They were often ex-tenants, but land was also sold in smaller portions to family farmers (Harrison 1975). Although Britain still has a higher concentration of landownership than Western Europe, its structure is similar to that found in the rest of Europe (Gasson 1987)

The British case is a good illustration of the role of agricultural labourers in the ST. As Eastwood, Lipton and Newell remark (2010), the relation of the wages of labourers compared to the shadow price of family labour is decisive. In Britain prices of output fell while wages increased. This forced landlords to divest themselves of their land and made it possible for family farms to invest in it. The development in the rest of Europe was parallel.

The case of Europe

With partial exceptions of Mediterranean and Southern Europe, agrarian development in the rest of Europe from 1870 onwards resembled that of the UK. The estate sector contracted in favour of family farming. A classic study of this process is the one by Folke Dovring (1965, 1955). His is a comparative study of agrarian change in the whole of Europe, especially the period 1900 to 1950. As can be seen today the periodization used is not optimal. Today one would have chosen the period from 1870 to 1914 (the first period of hyperglobalization) and 1920 to 1939 (the interwar years, including the Great Depression). In the latter period 1930 is a divider, marking the beginning of large-scale subsidies to agriculture. Roosevelt's New Deal was a forerunner but Europe soon got equivalent programmes.

Dovring documents the development of landownership in Europe. With great skill he avoids the many traps laying in comparative analyses of ownership structures and farm population in different countries. He starts with the decile distribution of land and owners, as one does when calculating Gini indices, but he takes into account the heterogeneity of land and the possibility that the value of output on a small farm, as defined by area can be higher than that of a larger farm. These complications make area statistics of limited use, especially if the aim is comparative and historical. Dovring avoids this problem by using other statistics, for example man–land ratios and standardized labour time data, which began to be collected in many European countries towards the end of the nineteenth century. By triangulating the different sources of data, he arrives at a very interesting conclusion, with a bearing on other regions and historical periods than Europe in the early twentieth century:

> The weighted material underlines the rigidity of the farm structure in Western Europe, and also the similarity between countries. England, with the most extreme large-farm structure in Western Europe, has only one-tenth of its developed resources in farms larger than 200 hectares, or employing more than 10 men. The median is only 60 hectares and rather less than 4 man-years. On the continent and in Scandinavia, family farms and under-sized farms are entirely dominant, with farms requiring large amounts of hired labor definitely in a small minority.
>
> (Dovring 1965, 1955: 135)

The same pattern to a large extent holds even today, although the median size in terms of area has grown manifold while average man years of labour input is considerably lower, with a strong majority of farms needing one man-year or less (as documented by Bailey 1973 for the period after 1945).

The US

When discussing North American agriculture, it is often pointed out that the US has no feudal past and that this has left an imprint on its agrarian history. In general terms that may be true, but in a more detailed account it does not hold. True, large parts of the Mid-West were colonized by settlers that were allotted land parcels, in principle of equal size. This created the typical US settlement patterns, with farmsteads spread out over the landscape and with a low degree of inequality in terms of landownership. But there are many exceptions to this. Firstly, many settlers bought larger land parcels from institutional landowners, often railway companies that owned about 10 per cent of all land in the US (Pfeffer 1983: 554 ff.). More importantly there are regional exceptions to the settler story.

In the Southern States, the history of agriculture is rooted in the slave plantations, dominant until the land reforms after the Civil War. Many have wondered why after the abolition of slavery, the large cotton plantations were not converted to capitalist farms, with black wage labourers. The fact that they did not, again points to the constraints to the development of capitalist farms, in the real world, as opposed to theory. Most Dixie landlords preferred to lease out land parcels to sharecroppers to running their plantations with hired labour. This may have something to do with Roumasset's observation:

> Share tenancy gives the tenant a share of benefits from maintenance and land improvements and thereby lowers asset abuse relative to that of the fixed lease arrangement, while simultaneously lowering optimal supervision costs of labor, relative to wage contracts.
>
> (Roumasset 1995)

Since the Civil War Southern landlordism has given way to a smallholder structure. In the 1980s the South had a greater share of smallholdings than the rest of the country (Wilkening and Gilbert 1987) and this is probably still the case. On the other hand, California, Arizona, Texas and Florida continue to be marked by a huge concentration of landownership. Mind you, this unequal structure is not a product of capitalist development, but of history. Californian landlordism is rooted in the Spanish/Mexican past. The large landed properties formed at that time, to a large extent have weathered the times and kept their dominance in the State. In 1870, 0.2 per cent of California's population controlled more than half the agricultural area:

> To some extent this pattern of landholding is an artefact of the area's colonial heritage. With the completion of the Mexican–American war of 1846–48, American rule was simply exchanged for Mexican rule without any basic change in land tenure. Spanish land grants remained essentially intact but were appropriated through force and fraud by public officials, the railroads, and various powerful persons.
>
> In order to understand the present day industrialized agriculture of California, with its heavy labor requirements, it is necessary to keep in mind the interacting effect of two factors: land monopolization and the availability of large units of cheap labor. If the large holdings had not been monopolized from the outset, it is quite likely that many small acreage units should have developed... Conversely, if the owners of the large estates had been unable to

> tap huge reserves of cheap labor after wheat production ceased to be profitable, it is quite likely that the development of large scale intensive agriculture would have been retarded, perhaps never undertaken.
>
> (Pfeffer 1983: 543)

In California, as in many other parts of the world, large landed estates were created before capitalism developed and thus are no product of such a development. The history of large landed properties so far is a corrective to the evolutionist paradigms. However, the different historical trajectories of the cotton belt and the sun belt, calls for an explanation. In the former the plantations have been largely dismantled, while in the latter *latifundios* continue to dominate. Pfeffer's explanation of this paradox still holds and tallies well with the thesis advanced in this book: the problem of large landed properties has always been labour power. The access to disciplined labour at low wages is a perennial problem for large-scale production. In Western Europe as we have seen, the large estates had great problems in surviving the competition with industry for labour, even if mechanization was a countervailing force.

East Asia: Japan, South Korea and China: The industrious revolution

Japanese scholars have coined the concept of an "industrious revolution" applicable not only to Japan but to several East Asian countries, emphasizing the role of family labour, not only in farming but also in the non-farm sector and in the proto-industrialization of the Japanese and Chinese weaving and textile industries. Later the industrious revolution led to the emergence of a labour intensive pattern of industrialization, which made it possible especially for Japanese industries to compete with American and European industry (see for example the works quoted in Sugihara 2003). The industrious revolution also left a resilient imprint on the agrarian structure of East, as well as South East Asia, as documented in a recent study by Rigg *et al.* (2016).

It is doubtful whether the concept of an industrious revolution can be applied to India, to its farm sector or its protoindustrialization. On the contrary, the division of labour in the agricultural sector and in spinning, weaving and textiles, typically occurred between households, rather than within them, unlike in the Japanese and Chinese cases. This also applied to farming where in the Indian case family-managed farms were the rule, but not family labour farms. Over large parts of the country even small and medium farmers depended on hired labour, especially during the peak seasons and in ploughing, harvesting and threshing (Kumar 1965, Hjejle 1967). The presence of a large landless proletariat, either working as tenants or as agricultural wage labourers made it possible for landowning farmers to "outsource" the most demanding tasks in cropping. We would argue that this structural feature, distinguishing the Indian case from the East Asian ones, is crucial in understanding the background conditions for India's ST. It continues to mark the development in the sub□continent.

Another common feature of the East and South East Asian "tiger economies" is that they all had thoroughgoing land reforms before World War II (in the case of Taiwan under Japanese occupation)[15] or immediately after the war in the other cases. Land reforms largely did away with landlordism and created farm sectors dominated by family farms (Jirström 2005). Again India is a contrast: its abolition of tax farming (*zamindari*) is usually considered successful but, although attempted, reforms of the East Asian type have only been implemented with some success in the Indian States of West Bengal and Kerala.

India in earnest launched the modernization of its agriculture with the Green Revolution from 1967 onwards (Frankel 1978, Djurfeldt and Jirström 2005), but it did so with a legacy of a segmented rural labour market, with minorities consisting of millions of landless labourers and poor peasants, segregated by caste, tribe and religion and mostly living in abject poverty, together with a class of large landlords, entrenched in agriculture despite the half-hearted land reforms and, with fewer family labour farms and more family managed ones.

Summary and conclusions

The emergence or strengthening of family farms has historically been associated with the structural transformation (ST) of economies, which now belong to the most industrialized and urbanized in the world. In the west family farms have grown, not only at the expense of smaller units, but also at the expense of large farms dependent on hired or other non-family labour. As a result of mechanization and the decreased importance of hired labour, big estates have often been subdivided and converted to family worked farms. This leads to a general question for following analysis. Is family farming strengthening its position in India in tandem with its ST? Or is India no place for family labour farms?

Before we can dig into that: in the next chapter, we discuss the concept and process of ST, especially its consequences for agrarian society.

Notes

1 As will be evident in Chapter 2 we prefer the term agrarian structural transformation to 'agrarian transition', which is used by many Indian authors.

2 According to the FAO definition (FAO 2014), 'agriculture' refers also to forestry, hunting and fishing. We use it mostly to denote agriculture as such. We use 'agrarian' in a more extensive meaning than agricultural, referring not only to agriculture *per se* but also to its institutional context.

3 There is an intermediate category besides these two forms, which we call "network labour," including labour recruited through kinship or community networks.

4 In many sub-Saharan countries, but also elsewhere, the State or the President is considered the supreme owner of the land. Historically this is a late add-on, developed along with the colonial and post-colonial State.

5 As suggested by Pierre-Marie Bosc (personal communication) major emphasis should be given to the first two criteria.

6 Pierre-Marie Bosc suggests an alternative definition, not unlike ours: "a farm relying exclusively on hired labour without any family/kinship link between the workers and

the owners of the means of production, including (or not it can be leased) the land. I would not put first (or limit to a single criteria) the need to get a "good" rate of return (RoR) on investment. You may find corporations investing in agriculture for various reasons and not exclusively guided by the RoR. It might be part of a portfolio of activities that compensate the lack of appropriate return. Another point that I would like to share is the issue of assets mobility vs the conventional view of agriculture as a pure localised and immobile activity, deeply rooted... If you consider the funds (what scholars call "financialization of agriculture") I think there is another step or degree, or a kind of break or profound change of nature in the activity. They shape "pure" capitalist farming because they (1) work with hired workers, (2) look for high RoR, but (3) they add the mobility of their assets since they rent all the operational assets and hence reduce at nearly zero their immobilization: land, labour, mechanized operation are rented... and if the situation changes they can migrate to more favourable settings like industry does, when looking to low wages/high skills/low social regulations conditions. This is the case in Argentina, Uruguay and parts of Brazil where you also find the strong consolidated "family business farms" category (in our defintion)" (personal communication, January 2016).

7 Circulated by Craig Harris through the RC40 network of the International Sociological Association who added a comment: "further to financialization."

8 Not to mention his study of US agriculture where he made a similar prognosis.

9 Excluding the plantation sector where colonially established estates tend to survive.

10 Economists might like to compare our real typology, i.e. the white circles in Figure 1.2 with the typology developed by Eswaran and Kotwal. Their model is a partial equilibrium one and shows that with unequal access to capital (mainly land) and high supervision costs for labour, a four class structure can be expected to develop with (1) labourer-cultivators, (2) self-cultivators (family labour farmers in our terminology), (3) small capitalists and (4) large capitalists. An obvious weakness of this model is that pluriactivity and combination farms are not at all part of it. Garner, E. and A. P. de la O Campos (2014). "Identifying the 'Family Farm': An informal discussion of the concepts and definitions." *ESA Working Paper 14–10*. Rome, Agricultural Development Economics Division, Food and Agriculture Organization of the United Nations. Eswaran, M. and A. Kotwal (1986). "Access to Capital and Agrarian Production Organisation." *Economic Journal* **96**(382): 482–98.

11 Thus we are critical of Brookfield's characterization of some large landed properties as industrial farms (banana and sugarcane plantations for example). They may be large-scale, but they are not industrial in terms of technology or organization: Brookfield, H. (2008). "Family Farms are Still Around: Time to invert the old agrarian question." *Geography Compass* **2**(1): 108–26.

12 Moore's law states that the number of transistors in an integrated circuit grows exponentially and tends to double once in two years. For other electronic applications this has meant, not only miniaturization, but also decreasing costs, making the technology available to new groups.

13 These were results from a survey from 1987 of 300 farming households in 24 regions of Western Europe. The survey was not statistically representative in a strict sense, but 20 of the research areas were chosen to match the European Community as whole. Four areas were from non-EC countries.

14 The following builds on Chapter 3 in: Djurfeldt, G. (1994). *Gods och Gårdar: Jordbruket i ett sociologiskt perspektiv.* Lund, Arkiv.

15 There is a large amount of literature on the consequence for the farm sector of structural transformation, especially in South East Asia. See for example the articles collected in Eicher and Staatz (1990) and Tomich *et al.* (1995): Eicher, C. K. and J. M. Staatz, eds. (1990). *Agricultural Development in the Third World*. Baltimore, MD: The Johns Hopkins University Press.

2 Structural transformation and farming

In this chapter we define the concept of structural transformation (ST) and proceed by looking at its history. Although the classical theories saw the process as automatic, closer inspection, we argue, reveals a fundamental role in it for policy and other institutional factors. This leads us to review western policy responses to agrarian distress before looking at the role of agriculture in development policy more generally. Against this background, agrarian development policies in the ex-colonies and especially the Indian experience are reviewed. Looking at the historical evidence in the Indian case one can ask: what is the role of policy for her specific patterns of transformation? But before being able to address this question, we need to look at the concept of agrarian ST and its history.

The agrarian transformation

Timmer defines the concept of ST as follows:

> The structural transformation is the defining characteristic of the development process, both cause and effect of economic growth. Four quite relentless and interrelated processes define the structural transformation: (1) a declining share of agriculture in GDP and employment … (2) a rural-to-urban migration that stimulates the process of urbanization; (3) the rise of a modern industrial and service economy; and (4) a demographic transition from high rates of births and deaths (common in backward rural areas) to low rates of births and deaths (associated with better health standards in urban areas).
>
> (Timmer 2009: 5, numbering added by GD)

Being non-economists and following for example Giddens (1984), we would add to the above perspective by underlining that all social (and economic) processes, although they may appear "relentless," are driven by actors, acting within the institutional conditions and structural constraints they are facing. In aggregate their actions are the ultimate drivers of the process of economic growth and thereby of the ST. At the individual level, we would say that the drivers are, not utility maximization as a neo-classical economist might put it, but dreams of a better and more dignified life for oneself, one's family and kids.[1]

To return to the economic theories of ST: in their classical formulation these theories assumed that the transformation was industry-led. Theories of agriculture-led growth and transformation are a later development, which we will come back to.

In the classical view, as industry grows, it stimulates demand for labour, which, to the extent that workers already within the sector cannot meet it, has to be met by recruitment of labour from the agricultural sector.[2]

Growth in industry and services is linked to the agrarian sector through growing demand for agricultural products and for labour. Beginning with the former, increasing incomes in the non-agrarian sector leads to a growing demand for agricultural and livestock products and high value crops like vegetables, fruits, etc. To the extent that in a given country this demand is not met by imports,[3] it would stimulate the domestic farm sector.

In the early stages of agrarian transformation increased demand for farm products does not automatically lead to intensified cultivation or increased agricultural labour productivity. It may equally well trigger area expansion without increasing the productivity of either land or labour. There is plenty of historical evidence of this, both in pre-Green Revolution Asia and in Latin America as well as in current sub-Saharan Africa (see for example Jirström, Andersson *et al.* 2011). In the case of India, most land reserves were emptied in the 1950s and '60s so that agricultural growth after that depended on intensification through irrigation, multiple cropping and diversification into high value crops.

Increasing demand for farm products is not the only, nor even the most important driver of the agrarian ST. Demand for labour from outside the sector has the effect of pulling farm labour, part-time or full-time, out of the agrarian sector. Primarily, it leads to scarcity of hired labour in agriculture, but it may also drain the family farm sector of labourers. Thus stimulating pluriactivity, it further increases the number of combination farms (see Figure 1.2 on page 11) and the number of agricultural labourers who straddle the agrarian and non-agrarian sectors.

Scarcity of labour thus is a crucial factor, which together with growing demand for food products stimulates agrarian transformation. Labour scarcity in its turn fuels mechanization enhancing labour productivity (water pumps, tractors, harvesters) and improved seed and fertilizer technology (Reddy, Reddy *et al.* 2014).

Thus growth patterns in agriculture change during the course of the transformation from land extensive to land intensive ones, driven by the two factors mentioned: labour scarcity and growing demand for farm products. By implication the thesis pioneered by Boserup (1965) saying that intensification in agriculture is primarily driven by population growth, although possibly valid in a macro-historical perspective, does not hold water. The primary drivers of intensification are political interventions and economic processes, in their turn possibly stimulated by demographic factors (e.g. so-called demographic windows of opportunity). An evident example of this, recounted below, is the Green Revolution.[4]

Comparative studies of structural transformation

In economics, early studies sought to establish typologies of ST (for example, Chenery and Syrquin 1975) but, as Timmer points out, those attempts have largely failed, due to "the uniqueness of country circumstances, especially in terms of political economy" (Timmer 2009: 14).

The economic historian, Alexander Gershenkron was the first scholar to explore the "general hypothesis that very significant interspatial variations in the degree of industrialization are functionally related to the degree of backwardness that prevailed in the countries concerned on the eve of their 'Great spurts' of industrial growth" (Gerschenkron 1962: 1). Gershenkron contrasted the classical case of Britain with later industrializers like Germany, France and Russia and documented the importance of different institutions in the different cases, for example the industrial banks in the case of France and Germany (ibid: 11 ff.), institutions which played a marginal role in the classical English case. In Russia, in contrast, the State had to take a leading role, which it continued to keep also after the Russian Revolution in 1917.

His analysis of different historical cases led Gershenkron to be critical of the concept of "primitive" or "original" accumulation, i.e. the theory that a preceding concentration and wealth is a prerequisite for industrialization. Although possibly valid in England, it has been taken as a general theory of capitalist development, and a favourite among neo-Marxists even today. But as Gerschenkron said: "the concept of original accumulation is not just a magnificent generalization; it is too magnificent a generalization, in the sense that in order to accept it one has to make abstraction from equally magnificent details…" (ibid: 39).

Gershenkron adds that: "there is no assurance at all that previously accumulated wealth will in fact be made available for industrial development finance" (ibid: 40). He underlines the importance of avoiding supra-historical generalizations and rather goes into the specificities of each case, before trying to generalize about it. In demonstrating the specific drivers of industrialization among the late industrializers, he laid the foundation of an institutional and political economy perspective on ST.

More recently, Timmer and Akkus carried Gershenkron's approach forward. By means of an econometric analysis, they demonstrated the political influence on patterns of ST. By means of a time series regression of data from 87 countries covering the period 1965 to 2000 they traced the drivers of agrarian ST by modelling (1) the share of agricultural labourers in the total labour force; (2) the share of agricultural GDP in total GDP; and (3) the difference between the share of agriculture in GDP and in the labour force.

Regarding share of agricultural workers in the total labour force Timmer and Akkus' first model shows that, during the period mentioned and seen globally, there was a secular trend for the share of the workforce engaged in agriculture to decrease by about one per cent per year on average. The pace of this process is gradually slowing down as more and more countries are reaching very low levels of employment in agriculture.

The slowing down of the pace can be attributed to Engels' law, which says that as household consumption expenditures increase, the proportion spent on food goes down. This implies that as incomes and expenditure increase, demand for agricultural products also grows, but at a slackening pace. However, Timmer and Akkus see technical change as an independent force impacting on the patterns and pace of ST in different countries. They show that labour productivity in agriculture tends to rise faster than in other sectors of the economy. This is an effect of mechanization and of improved crop technologies and is a prerequisite for the decreasing trend of the share of agricultural labour in the total labour force.

In their second model, with the share of agriculture in total GDP as the dependent variable, Timmer and Akkus find that similar to the decline of agricultural labourers in the total workforce, the share of agriculture in total GDP declines even faster than the share of labour. This implies increasing inequalities in incomes between the agricultural and non-agricultural sectors. They conclude that "[it] is no wonder that countries seek mechanisms other than economic growth to equilibrate the employment and GDP shares for agriculture" (ibid: 18).

Dealing with the difference between the share of agriculture in GDP and in the labour force, Timmer and Akkus' third model shows that a main driver is the agricultural terms of trade.[5] World market prices are a major determinant of domestic terms of trade between agriculture and non-agriculture, but they account only for about 20 per cent of the variance in them. The rest is due to domestic factors. With the operational definitions of the terms used by Timmer and Akkus, it is easy to calculate the inequality in incomes between the agricultural sector and other sectors. Their model indicates that income inequality between sectors tends to increase during the early stages of ST.[6]

Overall the relation of sectorial income inequality to the level of GDP per capita is negatively U-shaped. The top of the U-curve in year 2000 is estimated to lie at a GDP level around 9000USD per capita. Below this level were for example Mexico, Uruguay and Argentina, while above lay Greece and South Korea among others. These examples indicate that a majority of developing countries confront this dilemma. As economic and agricultural growth proceeds, levels of inequality of incomes between the agrarian and non-agrarian sectors tend to rise and are likely to cause rural dissatisfaction and political problems. Governments and politicians tend to respond to these challenges by manipulating sectorial terms of trade. There are many historical and current examples of this. Let us first look at some western ones.

Western policy responses

Early examples[7] of policy responses to agrarian distress include Roosevelt's New Deal and similar programmes in Europe (see for example Skocpol and Finegold 1982). Their common element was price support, or guarantee price schemes. They were not exactly market or free trade friendly; on the contrary, they intervened in domestic markets in order to protect domestic agriculture against imports. To take an example close at hand, in Sweden this led to regular negotiations between the dominant Farmers' Organization (RLF) and the government, in which both parties agreed to minimum price levels for a number of regulated products (cereals, potatoes, sugar beet, oilseeds, beef, pork and milk). Prices were meant to guarantee parity between wages of organized industrial labour and farmers and to contravene any tendency for farm incomes to lag behind those of industrial workers.

With modifications, the system was in place until shortly before Sweden joined the EU (Djurfeldt and Waldenström 1996). Evaluations of the system argue that it froze crop patterns, discouraging farmers from growing other crops than those covered by the scheme. However, it did not prevent the exit of landless labourers and smallholders from the sector; on the contrary, helped by policies promoting what at the time politicians and bureaucrats called "rationalization" of the agrarian structure, mean farm sizes grew, as did the level of mechanization. Although the system was meant to protect family farming, it led to increasing differences regionally and between small and big producers. The former tendency was dampened somewhat by selective interventions in marginal areas, while the latter was held somewhat at bay by the tendency for increasing revenues to be capitalized in land values (Djurfeldt 1994: 136 ff).

Both in Europe as a whole and in the US, price support schemes from the 1960s onwards led to overproduction, with bottomless lakes of milk and towering mountains of butter and grain as a result. This again triggered export subsidies, for example the Public Law 480 scheme, which subsidized US export of surplus grain to India, among other countries.

The current agricultural and rural policies of the EU involve a basic income support, meant to stimulate farmers to sustain their farming or conserve an agrarian or "cultural" landscape. The classic Common Agricultural Policy (CAP) has been reformed, partly as required by trade agreements under the General Agreement on Tariffs and Trade (GATT) and World Trade Organisation. Today the EU devotes lower shares of its budget to price supporting measures and export subsidies (although the latter are far from scrapped) and more to rural development and support to non-farm activities. Policies are politically legitimated by the need to avoid depopulation of the countryside and to reward farmers and others for what is called their "ecosystem services." Although the portal paragraphs of the CAP refer to the ideal of family farming, most of the income support goes to large landowners, with the British queen as the single biggest beneficiary (Eaton 2012).

Development policies

Thus protective tariffs and subsidies to production as well as to export were the predominant policy responses in the west, while the discourse was completely different in the ex-colonies. Socialist planning became a dominant discourse after decolonization. Here Indian economists and statisticians, most famously P. C. Mahalanobis made a mark. He modified Wassily Leontief's input–output model, which was a precursor to computable partial and general equilibrium models, converted by Mahalanobis into a tool for planning, implemented from the Indian 2nd Five-Year Plan onwards (Rudra 1996).

What Mahalanobis did for planning, W. Arthur Lewis with his classical article "Economic Development with Unlimited Supplies of Labor" (1954) did for development economics. His dual sector model emphasized surplus labour within the agricultural (or subsistence) sector and the possibility to absorb it into the capitalist sector and the industrialization project. It is incorrect, however, to infer as many have done, from the dual sector model that agriculture could or should be left to fend for itself. As pointed out by Timmer, quoting the following passage from Lewis' article:

> Now if the capitalist sector [in the two-sector model, our addition GD] produces no food, its expansion increases the demand for food, raises the price of food in terms of capitalist products, and so reduces profits. This is one of the senses in which industrialization is dependent upon agricultural improvement; it is not profitable to produce a growing volume of manufactures unless agricultural production is growing simultaneously. This is always why industrial and agrarian revolutions go together, and why economies in which agriculture is stagnant do not show industrial development.
>
> (Lewis 1954, quoted by Timmer 1998)

Unfortunately, economists and planners de-emphasized this aspect of Lewis' model. In India and China, as pointed out by Mellor (1984: 74), planners were more influenced by the Soviet model and by the Russian economist G. A. Fel'dman for whom increase in the capital stock was the source of development, from which followed that this resource should be directed to heavy industry. In Mellor's words: "The push was always on industry" (ibid.).

In the case of India this led to a decrease in the total outlay allocated to agriculture and irrigation, from 34.6 per cent in the First Plan (1951 to 1956) to 17.5 per cent in the Second Plan (1956–1961) (Frankel 1978: 131), when the Mahalanobis model was fully applied. The rationale for de-emphasizing the modernization of agriculture uncannily reminds of contemporary discourses:

> ...the planners informed the National Development Council that "domestic output of fertilizer was expected to reach only one-half the projected level, and on account of the foreign exchange shortage, supplies of chemical fertilizers were bound to fall short of the demand which was itself increasing." The gap had to be filled through "greater efforts in the direction of green manures and other manurial resources." In fact, given the stringent financial situation, it was more important than ever that "local participation and community effort... be enlisted on the largest scale possible in support of agricultural programs."
>
> (Government of India Planning Commission 1958: 40 and page ii cited in Frankel 1978: 152–3)

The consequences of the neglect of agriculture became evident with the Bihar famine of 1966–1967. Its scale was dwarfed by the Bengal famine of 1943, before Independence. While the latter caused an estimated two million deaths (Sen 1981), the official toll in Bihar was a 'mere' 2353. The Bihar calamity was widely publicized within India and the threat of future famines threw agricultural policies into disarray thus contributing to the policy shift leading to the Green Revolution from 1967 onwards (Djurfeldt and Jirström 2005).

As Djurfeldt and Jirström (ibid.) emphasize, the policy shift in the late 1960s and early 70s took place more or less simultaneously in a number of developing countries (see also Perkins 1997). It was a parallel to the hyped export-led industrialization pioneered by South Korea, Taiwan and other East and South East Asian countries (Jirström 2005). To paraphrase Mellor: *the push was no longer exclusively on industry*. In India this made the Bihar famine the last one to have officially caused any deaths from famine. In China it made the colossal famine caused by the policy failure during the Great Leap Forward both the largest and the last famine in Chinese history. The twin investments in new seed technology and institutional reforms that came with the household responsibility system from 1978 onwards turned the tables (see for example Riskin 1995).

The Green Revolution exemplified agriculture-led ST, where multiplier effects are reversed compared to the classical model discussed above. Massive investments in agricultural research, leading to new crop technologies, in infrastructure (irrigation, road construction), agricultural extension and credit led to increased demand for industrial products and services, stimulating growth of the latter.

Among the conclusions emerging from Djurfeldt's and Jirström's comparative analysis of the Green Revolution in Indonesia, the Philippines, India and Bangladesh and the earlier East Asian cases of Japan, Taiwan and South Korea, the following common features can be noted:[8]

1 State intervention was strategic for the investments in irrigation schemes and rural infrastructure, in fertilizer industry, and for the national agricultural research and extension systems. This holds for all cases, from the early Japanese development to the Asian latecomer, Bangladesh.
2 Administratively regulated markets are prominent in the Asian cases of agricultural development, as they were and are in the western ones we just discussed.
3 In all these cases agricultural development was family farm based; and the unimodal character of agrarian structures grew even more pronounced in the process.[9]
4 Price policies assuring profitability of family farming is a common feature and was an essential, although often neglected part of the Green Revolution, and a precondition for the spurts in production.
5 The cases discussed share a political goal, viz. self-sufficiency in food grains. This was important for regime survival, but unlike currently, it was also a goal promoted by the donors, especially the US.
6 Nationalism had an obvious role in motivating and legitimating agricultural development policies. In the case of Taiwan, the cold war and anti-communism played a similar role as an ideological driving force.
7 Foreign aid played an important part and for the donors it was motivated by strategic considerations during the cold war, but also informed by the neo-

Malthusian and anti-communist agendas (Perkins, 1997). These concerns motivated export of technology, crucial for making the Asian economies independent of food aid and import.

8 Finally, industrialization, although not discussed by the cited authors seems a common factor. In Taiwan, exceptionally dynamic agricultural growth led that in industry. There is no case of agricultural growth unaccompanied by industrial growth, with the possible exception of the Philippines (Mellor, 1995).

Some specific traits of the various cases discussed are worth mentioning. One is timing: East Asia, Japan and Taiwan are largely pre-Green Revolution cases; in the rest of Asia the movement towards self-sufficiency in rice started later. In South and South East Asia this had to do, not only with the breakthrough in seed technology, but also with the food crisis in the beginning of the 1970s, adding to the shock of the oil crisis. This also explains the divergent timetable in one East Asian case, i.e. South Korea where the Green Revolution was a drawn-out process, culminating in the late 1960s and early 1970s, in tandem with the development in South and South East Asia.

9 There is also a shift in finance policies at about the same time. After the delinking of the dollar from the gold price in the early 1970s, many countries turned to deficit financing as a means of driving agricultural development. This meant subsidies for farm inputs, remunerative farm gate prices and subsidised food prices, all at the same time. Understandably these policies fuelled at least a moderate inflation.

10 Thus the U-turn in price policies in South and South East Asia signifies a first partial break with the import substitution industrialisation strategies followed since de-colonization. Many authors have dated the break with import substitution industrialization to the 1970s (except in Taiwan and South Korea where it came earlier), but here we see that this break was antedated by the revamped agricultural development strategies. This leads Djurfeldt and Jirström to conclude that the shift to an export-led strategy of industrialization was preceded by a shift to import substitution in food grains.

11 In moving from the early phase in East Asia to South and South East Asia, agricultural development strategies become more top-down and less participatory. The balance between national and global institutions changed, with the Bretton Woods institutions and Consultative Group of International Agricultural Research (CGIAR) institutes playing a crucial role both in financing and in supplying specialised inputs to national programmes.

12 The characteristic features of the South Asian cases have to do both with the character of their states and with their social structures, but there are distinctive agronomic characteristics as well. While Green Revolution technologies broke through early for wheat in the Indian Punjab, Haryana and western Uttar Pradesh, the take-off for rice came only when the IRRI varieties had been crossed with national improved varieties in the late 1970s. Similarly, in

> Bangladesh the breakthrough came even later with improvements in small-scale irrigation technologies making it possible to expand the double-cropped area.

Both the Indian and Bangladesh states are far from the efficient machineries that we are wont to associate with development in East Asia and parts of South East Asia. In India, persistent poverty is largely explained by the impotence of the national executive in battling various sectional interests corrupting the food distribution system and targeting the most needy and discriminated parts of the population. India and Bangladesh also had a much weaker position of family (labour) farming, which seems another important factor accounting for their more sluggish performance. The same institutional factors probably account at least partly for the slower and later industrialisation in South Asia.

To quote Djurfeldt and Jirström's overall conclusion:

> The specificities notwithstanding, the model of the Asian Green Revolution that emerges is one of a market-mediated, small farmer-based, state-driven process. It is conditioned by geopolitical and institutional factors and part of industrialisation. However, it has no direct causal links to demographic factors. Finally, technology is not a driving force, but a necessary although not sufficient factor.
>
> (Djurfeldt and Jirström 2005: 60)

To conclude more generally on the agrarian ST, it is not an automatic, supra-historical economic process, but conditioned by political interventions and by country-specific and historical features. This is evident also when reviewing the post-Green Revolution phase.

From the Green Revolution to neo-liberalism

Epitomized by Milton Friedman and the Chicago School, by Margaret Thatcher's coming to power in 1979 and the Ronald Reagan Presidency from 1981, the neo-liberal era led to a major shake-up of development and other policies around the world. The Bretton Woods Institutions, the International Monetary Foundation (IMF) and the World Bank took it upon themselves to implement the neo-liberal principles enshrined in the Washington Consensus (Williamson 1989).

This led to the much criticized Structural Adjustment Programmes (SAP) (Gibbon 1992, Grindle 1996), especially ravaging in sub-Saharan Africa and in Latin America. The pressure for adjustment was less in India and the rest of Asia, mostly thanks to favourable balances of payment and lower debt. Coterminous with the SAP, the 1980s and 90s became a long period of stagnation agriculturally, again with the partial exception of India and other Asian countries. World market agricultural prices were rock bottom, largely due to extensive dumping of surplus products from the OECD countries, together with high fertilizer prices brought by high oil prices. This discouraged investment in agriculture and the dynamism brought by the Green Revolution petered out. These two decades can be described as lost for world agriculture.

Investments in agricultural research and development were relatively low in the 80s and 90s. Agriculture's share of donor budgets consistently went down, from a high in the early 70s to historically low levels, before the turning point in the 00s. Government priorities largely mirrored this. The progress made in tackling the global food problem with the Green Revolution was therefore difficult to consolidate. Again India and the rest of Asia is a partial exception: many of the not-so-low hanging fruits of the Indian Green Revolution were not picked until well into the 80s (Bhalla and Singh 2001), but thereafter relative inertia set in until the start of the new millennium.

Looking back on the neo-liberal era which admittedly did much harm to global human development, it must be conceded that neo-liberal economists did away with what previously was a scourge in the profession: the naïve view of the State as a benign and rational actor promoting development through planning, community development, agricultural extension etc. With the neo-liberals we got the terms "State failure" as well as "market failure." The sub-text is obvious: development is politically driven, but seldom by altruism and supreme rationality.

As if to mark the new era, around the turn of the millennium, global farm prices started to increase. The price rise came to a dramatic high with the Global Farm Price crisis in 2008.

World grain markets had been characterized by stagnant and even falling prices since the early 70s, when the world saw its last food price crisis. The trends turned in 2002, but were noted by non-specialists only in 2007 when rice, wheat and maize (corn) prices turned vigorously upwards. A year later, in 2008 a real crisis ensued. Rice prices went up from around 400USD per tonne early that year and reached 1000USD in April. Wheat prices similarly went from around 200USD in mid-2007 and reached almost 500USD in February 2008. Maize (or corn) was least affected, but prices almost doubled from 150USD per tonne in July 2007 to almost 300 a year later.

Dramatic consequences followed. Several capitals in the poor parts of the world, e.g. in Burkina Faso, Cameroon, Senegal, Mauretania, Côte d'Ivoire, Egypt and Morocco saw food riots with scores of people killed.

On 4 July 2008, the British newspaper *The Guardian* (Chakrabortty 2008) leaked a World Bank report (Mitchell 2008) that the Bank had tried to keep secret because it was critical of the then US President, George W. Bush. Since the United States is the biggest shareholder in the Bank, it was deemed too sensitive for the Bank to criticize the President. Thanks to the leak, the efforts to bury the report botched. Earlier that year G. W. Bush had pointed to a robustly growing demand in India and China as the main cause of galloping prices. The leaked report criticized the President for failing to mention his own government and its support of the production of biofuels from maize, which Mitchell showed was one of the main causes of the crisis.

Mitchell was a senior economist in the Bank. His paper went through the new trends in world food markets and made a detailed time series analysis of the various crops, which allowed him to conclude that biofuels production, from maize in the US and from rapeseed (canola) in Europe, was the main factor, leading to increasing world market prices for maize, and decreasing wheat areas in Europe, where wheat was replaced by rapeseed in crop rotations. Had not politicians in the US and the EU, without minding the consequences for the rest of world, supported the production of biofuels, directly or indirectly made from food crops, world stocks of maize and wheat would not have gone down to perilous levels. This again would not have left room for a bad harvest in Australia and a few other countries to affect prices. Similarly the explosion of rice prices was an indirect effect of the increase of wheat prices, so that this too was an effect, although indirect, of the subsidized production of biofuels in the US and in Europe. Spiralling prices were further accelerated by speculation and export bans in several producer countries (Mitchell 2008).

The above still holds and later analyses by other scholars have only slightly modified the original analysis by Mitchell. A noteworthy aspect is that the cause pointed to by George W. Bush, i.e. increasing demand for grain in several Asian countries, driven by economic growth in these countries, had only marginal influence on short-term international trends. More important was the fact that so much of the US maize production was and is destined to biofuels production, as is large shares of the oilseed production in the EU. It is difficult to escape the conclusion that policies to stimulate the first generation of biofuels, using food crops as feedstock, was and still is globally irresponsible. The second generation of biofuels, using other feedstock, will hopefully be less harmful both to the environment and for global food security.

World market prices began to fall in March 2008, but interestingly they did not fall back to the levels before the crisis. Many economists have predicted that the world will see and adapt to a long period of higher prices. At the moment of writing (early 2016) they have not been proven wrong. Higher prices have also led to new record levels of production, disproving the dismal prognoses of future production potentials proffered by neo-Malthusians like Lester Brown (Brown 1997). Since 2008, many players, politicians and investors have acted on the prognoses of higher price levels, leading to worldwide speculations in land, so called land grabbing (see among many others, Cotula, Vermeulen *et al.* 2009, Djurfeldt 2010, Friis and Reenberg 2010).

The new trends in global food markets, the break-down of the Doha Round, the nadir of the influence of the Bretton Woods institutions in development finance, all point to what in our view may amount to a new era in world development, i.e. what we could call the post-liberal era, presently to be discussed.

Post-liberalism?

'We live in a neo-liberal era'. This motto is unquestioned in some circles. For example many participants in the Indian debate regard the de-regulations of the Indian economy carried out from 1991 under the Rajiv Gandhi premiership with Manmohan Singh as the Finance Minister as 'neo-liberal'. Likewise, many radical participants in the globalization debate see the global order as a neo-liberal one (see for example McMichael 1995).

In the last analysis this is obviously a matter of definitions. We would argue that the blanket characterization of the Indian economy or the global order as neo-liberal is grossly misleading. In our view a more restrictive definition of neo-liberalism is more fruitful, for example the one proposed in Wikipedia:

"Neoliberalism is the resurgence of ideas associated with laissez-faire economic liberalism beginning in the 1970s and 1980s… whose advocates support extensive economic liberalization, free trade, and reductions in government spending in order to enhance the role of the private sector in the economy."[10]

According to Rodrik the Asian Crisis in 1997 marked the beginning of end of the neo-liberal era in development policies and of hyperglobalization (Rodrik 2011). The adjustment policies imposed by the IMF in countries like Thailand and Indonesia proved catastrophic and led to a determination among political leaders in many developing countries not to further expose themselves to the risk of similar quack treatments. Their counter weapon was accumulation of foreign exchange and financial assets. In the process both the World Bank and the IMF, despite the latter's self-critical evaluations, lost clout. They are no longer the dominant players they used to be in the developing world and they don't wave the neo-liberal flag as enthusiastically as earlier. The latest development in a chain of events is the launching of a BRICS development bank, launched by Brazil, Russia, India, China and South Africa.[11]

The Asian crisis largely by-passed India who around 1990 had had a balance of payment crisis, which led to the neo-liberal reforms mentioned earlier. Known as "neo-liberal" inside India, this is really a misnomer compared to what is meant by the same term in the rest of the world. More adequately in our view, M Singh's reforms were deregulations that did away with much of the old "license Raj." Most observers concur that they had a healthy effect on economic growth leading to almost double digit growth figures in the late 90s and early 00s. However agriculture was neither prioritized, nor did the growth in industry and services much stimulate the farm sector, which remained lethargic until global food prices began to rise around the turn of the century.

Rodrik sees the neo-liberal period between 1980 and 1997 as a consequence of the sabotage of Bretton Woods institutions by President Nixon and his Secretary of the Treasury, John Conelly when they scrapped the convertibility of the dollar to gold in 1971. The unilateral decision led to a global financial order with freely floating currencies. Until then, according to Rodrik, the Bretton Woods institutions, including the General Agreement on Tariffs and Trade (GATT) had served the world relatively well. They made possible a long period of economic growth, especially in the West, not ending until the oil crisis in 1971.

Initially the subsequent neo-liberal or globalization period had beneficial effects on economic growth, not so much in the west as in the rest of the world. It made possible the phenomenal economic growth of China and its massive poverty reduction and similar but less dramatic growth and poverty reduction in India and other countries in Asia and Latin America (Rodrik 2011).

The Doha process and the negotiations of a new "post-GATT" global trade regime seem to have reached a dead end with the collapse of the negotiations in Bali in the summer of 2014. This led to a further marginalization of the World Trade Organization (WTO) and a rising number of bilateral trade agreements between various countries, reinforcing Rodrik's argument that neo-liberalism and hyperglobalization is waning.

India asserted in Bali that it is her own sovereign right to regulate food security. If this will prove to drive or decelerate ST and if it will be beneficial to India's poor or not remains to be seen. We will return to this issue in the concluding chapters.

Structural transformation versus development

A friend commented: "Oh, you are studying structural transformation! How interesting: that's the core of development." We would like to take issue with that statement, because the two concepts differ in a fundamental way: structural transformation (ST) is a non-normative concept while, as we define it, the concept of development is fundamentally normative. Let us go into some detail with this.

As we defined ST in the beginning of this chapter, it has a simple and clear definition and, moreover, operationalizing it is straightforward, with two indicators: (1) the share of GDP originating in the agricultural sector and (2) the share of the total labour employed in the sector. If we agree on the definition and the operationalization, we can also agree on the degree of transformation, its pace historically and so on. We may disagree on the normative evaluation of the process; you may think it is good and we the reverse, or the other way round, while we all agree on the non-normative content of the concept, its application and its state in a given society at a given time-point.

Amartya Sen has convincingly argued that development is a fundamentally normative concept. In the Preface to *Development as Freedom* (2001) Sen writes that the "expansion of freedom is viewed… both as the primary end and the principal means of development" (ibid: xii). He thus argued against reducing development to the classical economic indicator, that is economic growth, which in his perspective is an instrument of development, although a very narrow indicator since it does not capture non-economic dimensions of unfreedom and freedom. He went on to discuss five distinct types of freedom: (1) political freedoms, (2) economic facilities, (3) social opportunities, (4) transparency guarantees, and (5) protective security (Sen 2001: 10). These are relatively easy to operationalize but we abstain from doing so here.

In his "The Idea of Justice" (2009) Sen argues that in principle it is possible democratically to agree, both on the normative question of what should ideally be the developmental impact of a process like ST and on the empirical question of what these impacts in fact are.

Accepting both these arguments implies that we can distinguish between the study of ST as a process, on the one hand, and its developmental impact on the other. We may also agree on its impact, but disagree on how to evaluate it. If the authors would argue that the agrarian ST on balance has increased the capability and freedom of Indian citizens, you might vehemently disagree.

There are certainly a lot of scholars and probably even more activists and citizens who would deny that agrarian ST has brought any kind of development, in the deeper sense of that concept (for example, Patnaik 1990, Shiva 1991, Sainath 1996).

We don't want to go too deeply into the normative developmental debate. In the empirical analysis we will keep to the classical indicator of development, that is income, and refrain from trying to estimate its impacts on health, education, democratic participation etc.

The Indian case in a comparative perspective

With regard to agrarian ST, Indian development policy fairly neatly falls in four phases: (1) the post-Independence planning period, investing in heavy industry and import substitution and squeezing agriculture. (2) The Green Revolution, which brought increased emphasis on agricultural policies, including investments in the national agricultural research system, succeeding in adapting imported high-yielding varieties of rice and wheat to domestic growing conditions and propagating them over vast areas. (3) The so-called neo-liberal reform period from the early 90s, which coincided with a period of low world market prices for food, spurring less interest and investment in agricultural development and, as will be shown later, retarding the agrarian ST. (4) Finally, as we have argued, the inception of what we call the post-liberal era and the world food price crisis from 2008 seem to have injected a new dynamism into agriculture and spurred the agrarian ST and, as we will see, re-established the distributional patterns of the agrarian transformation seen during the Green Revolution.[12]

Although the causal inferences cannot be made with the empirical material we are working with, the patterns we get in Models 2 and 3 fit with this periodization (see Chapters 6 and 7).

We bring with us one question from Chapter 1: Does the agrarian ST and especially the increasing competition for labour between agriculture on the one hand and industry and services on the other, lead to an increasing importance of family labour and therefore of family labour farms? What are its causal drivers, apart from ST? That is the second major research question which we will address in Chapter 6 of this book.

Before that, we will study how the ST is mirrored in the panel data we are analysing. More specifically: what are its drivers at household level? What are the causal forces, pushing or pulling households partially or entirely out of the agrarian sector? This is the topic of Chapter 5.

Finally, we will do an economistic analysis of the developmental impact of the ST in Chapter 7. The analysis is economistic in the sense that the only outcome variable we will go into detail with is the change in income per capita brought by ST.

First however, in Chapter 3 the concept of urbanization will be in focus and the specific nature of urbanization in India, which may explain some of the characteristic features of the ST in the country.

Notes

1 In a remarkable *volte-face* compared to the neo-classical perspective, the 2015 World Development Report from the World Bank is presented thus: "Whereas the first generation of development policy assumed that humans make decisions deliberatively and independently based on consistent and self-interested preferences, recent research shows that decision making rarely proceeds this way… paying attention to how humans think—*the mind*—and how history and context shape thinking—*society*—can improve the design and implementation of development policies and interventions that target human choice and action—*behavior*." World Bank Group (2015). *World Development Report 2015: Mind, Society, and Behavior*. Washington, D.C., World Bank.

2 Another possibility is by immigrant labour, as historically and currently in the US and the west, as well as in South East Asia and the Gulf countries (mainly absorbed by construction and the service sector).

3 Increasing dependence on imports can be a brake on structural transformation, as it has been in sub-Saharan Africa from the early 1970s to the early 2000s, World Bank (2007). World Development Report 2008: Agriculture for Development. Washington D.C., The Bank.

4 The following summarizes the analysis on pp. 14–22 in Bloom, D. E., D. Canning and J. Sevilla (2003). *The Demographic Dividend: A new perspective on the economic consequences of population change*. Santa Monica, CA, Rand. See also: Timmer, P. (2009). A World without Agriculture. The structural transformation process in historical perspective. Washington D.C., The American Enterprise Institute Press.

5 These are ordinarily defined as the ratio of agricultural to industrial prices. Timmer and Akkus calculate them from the sectorial GDP deflators in national income accounts data.

6 The reader may recall the Kuznets curve and the associated hypothesis that with economic growth inequality tends to rise at lower levels and to decrease again at higher ones, thus forming a reverse U-shaped relation. The hypothesis is commonly regarded not to have survived later research. Timmer and Akkus deal not with overall inequality, but inequality between the agricultural and non-agricultural sectors, which according to their model has this U-shape. Timmer, C. P. and S. Akkus (2008). The Structural Transformation as a Pathway out of Poverty: Analytics, empirics and politics. Working Paper no. 50. Washington D.C., Center for Global Development.

7 Even earlier examples are the Corn laws, according to Timmer (lecture, Department of Economic History, Lund University, December 2014).

8 The following draws heavily on Djurfeldt, G. and M. Jirström (2005). "The Puzzle of the Policy Shift: The early green revolution in India, Indonesia and the Philippines." *The African Food Crisis: Lessons from the Asian Green Revolution*. G. Djurfeldt, H. Holmén, M. Jirström and R. Larsson. London, CABI, Jirström, M. Ibid. *The State and Green Revolutions in East Asia*. Wallingford: 25–42.

9 Longitudinal data on rice farm size and farm distribution supporting this claim is provided through the World Rice Statistics compiled by: International Rice Research Institute (IRRI) (2004). World Rice Statistics, Area planted (or harvested) to modern varieties, selected Asian countries, 1965–1999. Luzon, IRRI.

10 See 'neoliberalism' in Wikipedia, downloaded 18 March 2016.

11 See for example: http://brics6.itamaraty.gov.br/media2/press-releases/219-agreement-on-the-new-development-bank-fortaleza-july-15, downloaded 08/01/2015.

12 The last statement contradicts what many scholars say about agricultural development since the late 90s, see for example Mohanty, B. B. and P. K. Lenka (2016). Neoliberal reforms, agrarian capitalism and the peasantry. Critical Perspectives on Agrarian Transition: India in the global debate. B. B. Mohanty. Oxford and New York, Routledge; Dhanagare, D. N. ibid. Declining Credibility of the Neo-liberal State and Agrarian Crisis in India: some observations. B. B. Mohanty. See the analysis and findings more in line with ours reported in Vakulabharanam, V. and S. Motiram (2011). Political economy of agrarian distress in India since the 1990s. *Understanding India's New Political Economy: A great transformation?* S. Ruparelia, S. Reddy, J. Harriss and S. Corbridge. London and New York, Routledge: 101–26.

3 Urbanization and agrarian change

A view from the margins

Srilata Sircar

As discussed in the previous chapter, Timmer (2009) is the latest among several scholars to view the process of urbanization as an integral component of structural transformation. Not unlike structural transformation, urbanization too has been imagined as a spontaneous process that is dependent on and responsive to market forces such as shifts in sectorial demands for labour, sectorial wage discrepancies, fluctuations in land rent and real estate valuations. (Harris and Todaro 1970, Venables 2005, World Bank, 2009, etc.). However, like structural transformation, the processes of urbanization, especially in the Global South, have been historically found to be shaped by direct state intervention in the form of urban policy and planning.

In this chapter we take a look at Indian urban policy, the aspects of the urban condition that it fails to address, and the close connections between the organization of agricultural production and the nature of urbanization. We argue that urban policy and agrarian policy need to be closely aligned in order to do justice to the unique experience of agrarian structural transformation in India. To do this, we first need to elaborate on the nature of the urbanization experience.

The first section summarizes the key features of national urban policy as reviewed by scholars like Shaw (1999), Mahadevia (2003), and Batra (2009). It also points out the shifting ontological basis of urban policy making, that runs parallel to political thought on agrarian policy. The second section draws attention to new and emergent forms of urbanization in smaller towns and settlement agglomerations, also framed as "unacknowledged urbanization" (Pradhan 2012) or "denied urbanization" (Samanta 2014). In this book we refer to this "under the radar" phenomenon as "grassroots level urbanization." The third section then proceeds to elaborate on the modes of organization of agricultural production, laying the foundation for the discussion in Chapter 5 about the classification of rural households and farm types. These three largely descriptive sections lay the groundwork for the concluding section that will comment on policy alternatives.

The aim of this chapter is to provide a microscopic insight into the conceptual elements that form the basis of the macro-level analysis that is carried out in the rest of the book. For this reason, a case study of a single census town is used as the communicative tool for introducing the core conceptual elements.

Urbanization and the Indian State

Much like the reviews of agrarian policy, comprehensive reviews of Indian urban policy in the post-independence period have also been organized in terms of distinct phases. Following Shaw (1999) and Mahadevia (2003), Batra (2009) has divided his appraisal of Indian urban policy into three phases. The first phase covers the period of the first three five year plans from 1951 to 1966. The second phase covers the fourth to the sixth five year plans from 1967 to 1989. The third phase covers the seventh to the eleventh five year plans from 1990 to 2005. I add here, an appraisal of the decade ensuing from 2005, concluding with the 100 smart cities project, which currently forms the mainstay of Indian urban policy at the national level.

The first phase of urban policy in India has been described as "ad-hoc" and "piecemeal" (Batra 2009: 9). The period was characterized by concern for the living conditions, especially of the urban poor, in prominent metro cities such as Delhi and Bombay (Mumbai). The proliferation of "slums" was seen as the key problem to be addressed and this was to be done through the adoption of Master Plans. The plans were instruments to implement a "strict spatial segregation of functions such as housing, commerce, industries etc." (ibid: 8) and were a direct replica of similar policy instruments from the West.

This phase also brought forth the conceptualization of "regions" and "regional development." This assumed greater importance in the second phase, which saw a pro-active shift towards dispersing populations to smaller urban centres, thereby aspiring to achieve "balanced urban growth." Thus during the second phase the state started to rise above individual urban centres and turned its gaze onto the larger urbanization patterns. The attempt to cultivate small and medium towns was executed in the form of strategic placement of industries and new economic activities. Due to this, the question of land use became paramount within the urban planning scenario. Its manifestations included urban land ceilings in metro cities, higher taxation of vacant plots in peri-urban areas to prevent speculative pricing, and taxes on land use conversion. At the same time, the focus on "high modernization" (Scott 1998, quoted in Batra 2009 : 14) dwindled and the Nehruvian efforts to radically re-make cities gave way to a milder tendency to "manage" cities in their existing forms. Thus "slum removal" turned into "slum redevelopment" and deviations from the stringent Master Plans came to be better tolerated.

The third phase is marked by two main developments – the introduction of private players in the housing finance market and housing provisioning, and the explicit acknowledgment of a link between macro-economic development and urban growth. The focus shifted away from regional development and the rhetoric returned to boosting economic activity where it was already concentrated i.e. the metro cities or the "engines of growth" (Government of India 1985). Following recommendations from the National Council on Urbanization (NCU) the future of urban growth was now planned to take place along nodes and corridors identified from among the existing urban centres. Although the line of regional development and balanced growth recurred from time to time, this responsibility was largely relegated to the state governments while the centre returned to the previous piecemeal approach. In keeping with this policy position the period witnessed a rollback on several erstwhile policy instruments, among which was the repeal of the Urban Land Ceilings and Regulations Act in 1999.

Two prominent manifestations of this change in the spirit of urban policy were the 74th Amendment Act of 1992 and the Jawaharlal Nehru National Urban Renewal Mission (JNNURM) launched in 2005. The creation of Urban Local Bodies (ULBs) under the 74th Amendment, with ward committees in all settlements with population above 0.3 million, was meant to decentralize urban governance. The bigger ULBs were expected to raise their own finances for infrastructure development, in collaboration with the private sector. The smaller ULBs were expected to work towards building capacity for the same. The underlying wisdom was that the centre did not possess the financial or administrative capacity to support the kind of infrastructure overhaul that the urban situation of the time demanded (Rastogi 2006).

The provisioning of funds was to be shared between the centre, the state and the ULB in varying proportions depending on the size-class of the urban centre. However the funds received from the centre and the state were meant to act as seed money to generate further financing from capital markets and private actors. The reforms had an explicit emphasis on promoting public–private partnerships, cost recovery through pricing of basic amenities, and a commitment to making land available to both domestic and foreign private developers. With this the urban policy came to be aligned completely with the larger macro-economic policy of liberalization, wherein the role of the state was reduced and its erstwhile commitment to the poor made susceptible to market forces.

Since the mid-2000s, the narrative of "global cities" and "megacities" has come to shape both urban policy and urban studies in India. In 2005 the Chief Minister of the state of Maharashtra, the late Vilasrao Deshmukh, stated in his election manifesto his intention to convert Mumbai from "Slumbai" to "Shanghai."[1] The statement immediately gained rhetorical currency in policy and development circles, with both supporters and detractors, and has continued to provoke responses in the form of opinion pieces, academic articles and even a 2012 feature film in Hindi. Under Deshmukh's regime Mumbai witnessed some of the most rapid and drastic slum demolition endeavours while he continued to legitimize them on various forums under the narrative of "ensuring quality of life comparable to the best of the international cities in order to put Mumbai on the world map as a global financial centre." This outlook may be seen as symptomatic of millennial thinking on urban policy across political party lines in India.

One of the outcomes of this dominant narrative is the rendering of cities as market entities that need to promote and sell themselves as viable destinations of capital investment. This is recorded to have widened and accentuated pre-exiting regional inequalities in terms of economic growth. Shaw (1999) has recorded the steady economic stagnation and eventual downfall of Kolkata in the post reform period, mainly due to its failure to attract private capital for infrastructure development and industrial growth. Ironically for the Trinamool Congress-led government of West Bengal that came to power in 2011, (riding on a popular unrest against the incumbent left party coalition, involving acquisition of agrarian land for industrialization), making the state into an industrial and economic hub by attracting private investment has been top of the agenda.[2]

This apparent contradiction is symptomatic of the prevailing climate in urban policy at the national level. In the same vein, I argue, it is possible to see the 100 smart cities project as a logical extension of this narrative, even though it is proclaimedly meant to accommodate the "burgeoning number of people" (Government of India 2014) migrating from rural areas. In December 2014 the Ministry of Urban Development released a draft concept note for developing one hundred "new cities" as "smart cities." "Smartness" is defined here in terms of competitiveness, which in turn is based on quality of life, employment and investment opportunities "comparable with any developed European city" (Government of India 2014: 4). In March 2015, *Business Today* published a cover story on the smart cities project in which Venkaiah Naidu, the Minister of Urban Development was quoted on how these "new cities" are to be selected for imparting "smartness." It would be on the basis of the "willingness of the city to be reformed and the willingness of the leadership to undertake reforms and bold action," he is quoted to have said.

Thus, as an extension of the "global cities" narrative, the smart cities project constructs some cities as more deserving of infrastructure investment and better quality of life, based on their commitment to cater to the demands of the global and private capital market. For instance the concept note available on the Ministry's website states that "A smart city cannot have only a few hours of water supply a day or electricity that goes off for several hours or the streets littered with garbage" (Government of India 2014: 9). The emerging implication is that services and amenities like water supply, electricity and sanitation which were once seen as the basic and universal constituents of urban provisioning, are now rendered exclusive and conditional. This also gives license to the state to withdraw from remaining urban centres while playing up the selected one hundred.

The four phases of urban policy summarized here resonate closely with the four phases of development policy (and its implications for the agrarian sector) outlined in the previous chapter. The first phase of heavy industrialization and relative neglect of agriculture was accompanied by a focus on planned slum removals in big cities. This implies that labour exiting from the agrarian sector was not adequately absorbed into the capital intensive industrial sector. The urban informal sector, which forms the safety network for displaced and underemployed labour from agriculture, was under pressure from urban planning that effectively rendered most existing lived experiences of the city "illegal." The second phase of development policy with its emphasis on the Green Revolution coincided with urban policy harping on balanced regional development. The contradiction in this is obvious; as the Green Revolution is widely acknowledge to have widened regional disparities in agricultural technology and productivity (Bardhan 1970, Rudra 1978, Das and Tripathi 2014). Chapter 7 of this book delves deeper into the varying outcomes of extending the Green Revolution to states beyond the original wheat-cultivating areas.

The third phase of urban policy, marked by falling investments in agriculture, was accompanied by privatization of housing finance and infrastructure building in the urban sector. The impact of this policy disposition is likely to have been most acutely felt by those seeking to exit agriculture and establish an economic foothold in urban livelihoods. The UNDP (Deshingkar and Akter 2009) estimated that there are roughly 100 million "circular migrants" in India, contributing ten per cent of the GDP. As later chapters of the book will demonstrate, "pluriactivity" has increased among all types of rural households but affects different groups differently. For the landowning households pluriactivity means formal sector employment for successive generations, while for landless labourers or small and marginal farmers it means circulating between seasonal agricultural work and insecure informal sector work in urban areas. These are the groups most vulnerable to the changing housing and infrastructure landscape of the urban centres.

The fourth and current phase is marked by greater dynamism for the agrarian sector, as later chapters will show. This could mean increased exit of labour from agriculture as warranted by the historical experience of structural transformation. The concurrent urban policy, in the name of accommodating the migrants, is solely focused on constructing elite hubs of exclusive, high-end living, in the form of the smart cities. Meanwhile, the public authorities responsible for providing low cost housing to low income groups have miserably failed to live up to their mandate.[3] It is probably the itinerant or "footloose labourers" (Breman 1996) who will build the smart cities through unacknowledged informal labour. But what unfolds beyond the glitz and glamour of metro cities and smart cities?

The question brings us to urbanization experiences outside of and away from the first and second tier cities.

Urbanization in the grassroots

Mayer and Knox (Mayer and Knox 2010, cited in Scrase, Rutten *et al.* 2015: 217) write:

> Different kinds of small towns, in different settings, … (are) often critical to not only their inhabitants but also to the economic and social cohesion of metropolitan regions and deep rural areas. Yet they are very often neglected in national policy…

The statement is of extreme relevance to India, especially at this particular moment of Indian urban history. The concept note on smart cities from the Ministry of Urban Development would have readers believe that no urban centres exist in India outside of the sprawling metropolitan regions of the megacities. Indeed, that is why it calls for the creation of "new" cities through state planning and private–public partnership. Scrase *et al.* (2015) have raised crucial questions regarding the nature of urbanization in India "beyond the metropolis" and the relationship between the "global modernity" of cities included in the "global economy" project, and the "regional modernity" of other urban centres outside of this economic network (ibid: 218).

Frequently, a population threshold of 100,000 to 500,000 is used to define and identify "medium towns," "second tier cities," or "Class II towns (Samanta 2014, Scrase, Rutten *et al.* 2015). However, the census criteria for being classified as "urban" is 5000 population, 400 per square kilometre density, and 75 per cent or more of the male workforce employed in non-agriculture. Thus, "small towns" in India can be much smaller than 100,000 or even 50,000 strong urban settlements and they seem to have fallen completely off the grid as far as national or even regional policy is concerned. The Integrated Development of Small and Medium Towns programme was announced in 1979–80 and was supposedly in effect until it got integrated into the Urban Infrastructure Development Scheme for Small and Medium Towns in 2005-06, which was ancillary to the JNNURM. How these schemes have fared is impossible to tell because they have never been evaluated or their impact assessed (Batra 2009, Scrase, Rutten *et al.* 2015).

What makes this subject particularly relevant at this point is the fact that in the Census of 2011, 2774 new settlements were classified as 'Census Towns' (CTs), a category of urban settlements in India, based on the three criteria mentioned above. To put this figure in perspective, the number of new urban settlements (across all size-classes) recognized by the census in the five decades preceding 2011 was 2541. Thus, the increase in the number of CTs between 2001 and 2011 has been more than the increase in the total number of all urban settlements between 1951 and 2001. This occurrence has been variously described as an "unexpected increase" (Pradhan 2012: 1) and a "phenomenal jump" (Kundu 2011). Census Towns as a category have existed since the first census operation in post-independence India, but these settlements remain excluded from the map of "small town" India; even for many of those who seek to contest metrocentricity. Studies focused primarily on CTs are very few and fairly recent (Kundu 2011, Samanta 2014).

As the upcoming sections will illustrate, CTs can be an appropriate site to understand how pluriactivity, integration into the non-farm economy, and the operation of family farms and combination farms relate to agrarian structural transformation-led grassroots level urbanization. Following the report of the Census of India, it may be argued that, these are sites where the process of land use and livelihoods transformation from agrarian to non-agrarian sectors has taken place in the decade between 2001 and 2011. These are the sites where structural transformation and urbanization can be palpably caught in action. However the limited amount of narrative material available from some of these sites suggests that this assertion is only partly substantiated and much complexity underlies the "emergence" of these "new" CTs. Before delving into the details of this, I summarize the work done by (Pradhan 2012) and members of the Subaltern Urbanization project in India, which constitutes the majority of scholarship on CTs at the moment.

Denis *et al.* (2012: 52) have described their use of the term "subaltern urbanization" as a literary device for discursive engagement in the tradition of the "global city." In their definition subaltern urbanization is "autonomous growth of settlement agglomerations (that may or may not be denoted urban by the Census of India) that are generated by market or historical forces, which are not (1) dependent on large traditionally important settlements or (2) 'planned' cities…" (ibid). The definition serves to distinguish subaltern urbanization as a phenomenon separate from the narrative of the megacities while also bringing forth the issue of official classification. The authors explain that their focus is explicitly on spaces away from the metropolis and on the extent of autonomy of the settlement "in the ability to affect its growth process and interact with other settlements, whether local or global." In their review of the patterns of urbanization in India, the authors find that "such vital small settlements" do in fact exist.

Pradhan (2012) further reveals that as many as 1625 of the new CTs recognized in 2011 had already met all of the necessary criteria back in 2001, but were overlooked for undetermined reasons. When the population threshold is reduced to 4000 (with the assumption that an increase of 1000 within ten years is inevitable) and the male non-agricultural employment criteria reduced to 60 per cent (instead of 75 per cent) the number of new CTs that already met the criteria in 2001 further increases to more than 2000. The findings of the subaltern urbanization project therefore lead us into a detailed exploration of life and livelihoods in the new CTs.

Census Towns, farm types, and the organization of agricultural production

Jhaalpahari[4] is one of the 526 new CTs recognized in the state of West Bengal in the Census of 2011. Located in the south-western district of Bankura, it is 25 kilometres (and a 20 minute train ride) away from the district headquarter Bankura Town. The spatial unit that is now denoted "urban" and listed as Jhaalpahari CT in the census, used to be previously listed as Jhaalpahari Census Village. However the actual built-up area of what is colloquially known as "Jhaalpahari town" extends far beyond the boundaries of the census unit. It covers parts of surrounding census villages and cuts across the administrative boundaries of three Gram Panchayats (GP)[5], the grassroots level institution for rural local governance.

This is a common occurrence in the case of several new CTs, as narratives from Garhbeta, Amlagora, and Singur would testify (Sircar 2016, forthcoming), (Samanta, 2014). The actual spatial extent of the continuous built-up area with urban characteristics supersedes the boundaries of the officially recognized CT in all of these cases. For the purpose of this chapter we use "Jhaalpahari" to mean the settlement in its entirety and not just the parts of it recognized as a CT. The choice of Jhaalpahari as a case to frame the discussion on the relationship between farm types and grassroots level urbanization is motivated in part by its relative obscurity from the mainstream narrative of urbanization in India. It is one of the smaller CTs (within West Bengal and nationally) with a little above 1000 recorded households. It is situated in a district that ranked 11th out of 17 in terms of HDI in 2004. Additionally Bankura is one of the least urbanized districts of West Bengal, housing only seven out of the 526 new CTs. Jhaalpahari is not adjacent to or in the immediate vicinity of any statutory town. The nearest place of prominence is the Block headquarters Chhatna, which is ten kilometres away and not designated urban.

Thus, Jhaalpahari is far removed from the global cities mould and is therefore not even in the running to be included in the smart cities project. It is a place that has fallen off the imagination of "urban India," even "small town India"; it is not the chosen landscape for the enactment of urban policy. Yet, one of the recurrent phrases that long term residents of Jhaalpahari use to describe their settlement is "a well-established commercial centre." This apparent contradiction is resolved by a cursory look at the economic foundation of the settlement.

Since the 1950s, Jhaalpahari has been home to a rice milling industry. In its best years, the industry comprised of twenty mills, which catered to all rice producing villages within a ten kilometre radius. It was also the centre of processing for rice cultivated in the neighbouring states of Bihar and Jharkhand. Rice processed in these mills entered the wholesale and retail markets at both local and regional levels, even making its way to the state capital of Kolkata, through mandatory levies imposed by the state government. In the recent past the industry has met with a serious crisis with the majority of mills closing down. In the terminology of this book, the erstwhile village of Jhaalpahari had for a long time been well integrated into the non-farm economy. In its current form, Jhaalpahari town is the hub of that non-farm economy of which the surrounding villages are also part.

At the time of this study in November 2014, only three mills were functional. Estimates from the mill owners placed the average capacity at 100–150 quintals per day, with each mill employing about 50 daily wage workers. The crisis was attributed to a combination of factors including the emergence of indigenous rice mill industries in the neighbouring states, the failure on the part of the mill owners to invest in technological modernization, and the absence of state support in the form of protective pricing or industrial subsidies.

Parallel to the rice mills, an oil milling industry has also had its base in Jhaalpahari despite no agricultural production of oil crops in the region. The establishment of this industry is attributed to the Marwari community, an itinerant trading community from the north-western state of Rajasthan that is well-known for its entrepreneurial spirit. The raw material for the oil mills is supplied by producers located in the northern part of the country, mainly Rajasthan and Haryana. The movement of raw and finished goods within and outside the region has therefore been a longstanding practice, despite having no explicit links to the global economy. At the time of the study, the local oil industry was also in crisis with 15 of the 20 mills temporarily closed down. This was unanimously attributed to the entry of bigger private players in the regional market. The local oil mill owners were, however, hopeful about the state of the industry. Being a less labour intensive industry than rice processing, they were waiting to procure capital to modernize their plants.

In the past five years a new form of economic activity had assumed importance in Jhaalpahari. The town had become a hub for wholesale and retail transactions in fresh vegetables and fruits. This was facilitated by its convenient rail connectivity since colonial times and the emergence of a young class of entrepreneurs who had not been absorbed into the formal service sector and did not wish to work as supervisors on their family farms. The daily vegetable market in the town brought together producers and traders from all the surrounding villages. The young brokers negotiated deals, ensured quality control, and facilitated exchange. This was the sector on which the future growth of the town was considered to be dependent. This aspect of the town's non-farm economy connects to the discussion in Chapters 5 and 7 about the exit of large landowners from the agrarian sector and the higher likelihood of these classes to be downwardly mobile in size of holding. Moreover, as mentioned in Chapter 8, small-size combination farms are increasing their involvement in much of the high-value crop production including vegetables and fruits, a process which in turn fuels the transformation of the markets in places like Jhaalpahari.

There was an unequivocal acknowledgement of the steady increase in population and density of built-up area that the town had witnessed over the past few decades. What needs to be noted here is that the growth of Jhaalpahari as a town had not taken place in a spurt during 2001 and 2011, but had been a gradual and consistent process spread over several decades. The agro-industries-based foundation of the town had been laid by gradual investment of agricultural profits into the secondary sector by successive members of the landholding elite. Some of the commonly cited attributes that residents considered as decidedly "urban" were the increased number of formal and public sector employees, the increase in the standard and prevalence of education, and the growing demand for urban amenities like street lighting.

The idea behind introducing the case of Jhaalpahari is not to extrapolate its socio-economic characteristics and generalize at a state or national level. This is quite impossible to accomplish, given the huge number of new CTs and the lack of transparency and consistency in the process of their identification (Pradhan 2012). What I wish to do here is to read the case symptomatically, for an understanding of the organization of agrarian production and the nature of grassroots level urbanization taking place under the radar. The first thing that this brief case description attempts to establish is the reality of grassroots level urbanization. The important economic linkages that a seemingly obscure settlement like Jhaalpahari manages to command, makes it clear that small towns as a phenomenon deserve national level policy attention. The second thing that the case indicates is the agro-dependent nature of this small town-based grassroots level urbanization. The movement of capital, labour and entrepreneurship from agriculture to industry in this case is neither linear nor neat. To discuss this further, we need to turn to a discussion of the different ways in which agricultural production is organized in the region, and indeed in India.

It has been widely noted that agricultural landholding in India, as also all other measures of property and wealth, is highly skewed along the lines of class, caste and community. (Dhanagare 1984, Karanth 1996, Thorat and Newman 2010, and Jodhka 2013). While the analyses in Chapters 6 and 7 of this book suggest that caste can no longer be treated as a reliable and easy proxy for class, it still remains an important factor to consider when studying the organization of agrarian production.

In the given agrarian setting, there are several different ways in which agricultural production may be organized. There have not been any comprehensive studies to document all the different kinds of production practices that are prevalent in India and/or how they have evolved over a period of time. Chapter 5 will take up a detailed and elaborate classification of farm types and rural households at a national level. In the following paragraphs I will describe three different modes of organization of agricultural production around Jhaalpahari, West Bengal and relate them to the accompanying urbanization experience.

A safe assumption to start with is that any given agrarian setting in India is marked by the presence of a dominant social group that owns a large share, if not all, of the agricultural land. This group often belongs to an "upper caste" such as the Bhumihar Brahmins or the Rajputs in Bihar. In some cases the group might be listed as part of the Other Backward Castes (OBC) or Scheduled Tribes (ST) or even Scheduled Castes (SC), although this is rare. In the case of Jhaalpahari, the landholding groups comprise of the Kundus and the Rakshits both of which are Tambuli castes, which is a part of the state OBC list. However the OBC classification does not take away from their dominant status within the particular context of agricultural production in the village, neighbourhood or vicinity. The dominant status is a function of customary and inherited landholding rights, and therefore an element of control over production practices. As several studies of caste relations have shown, dominant status in terms of landholding most often coincides with customary caste-based entitlements and extractions. However, having defined the notion of the dominant group, it is important to clarify that the ownership of agricultural land is not communal but private. Parcels of land are owned by individuals and passed on through rights of inheritance. Exceptions to this model are sure to be found, but the overall picture adheres to this generalization. Chapters 5 to 7 will illustrate that the trend at the national level over the past decades has been one of diminishing size of landholding for large landlords, with increasing prevalence of smallholder cultivation and combination farms. West Bengal being one of the intermediate states in terms of the rate of agrarian structural transformation, some of these trends might manifest themselves more emphatically in this region in the years to come.

In the first of the three observed modes of organization, the landholding family employs hired labour to carry out the actual agricultural work, while family members themselves assume supervisory roles. The agricultural labourers are hired on a daily wage basis, even if the same labourers are de facto tenants who work the same fields over several seasons, years, or even decades. As the family grows and landholdings get fragmented, successive generations move into formal sector employment usually outside of the agrarian setting, and presumably often in bigger urban centres. This is facilitated by the investment of profits from agriculture or proceeds from the sale of agricultural land into higher education. However, the movement of the landholding class away from the agrarian setting does not necessarily imply their movement out of agriculture per se. Their ownership of land and control over production practices is maintained through the continued physical presence of either an employed manager or a designated family member. Thus the emergence of pluriactive landowning households has made possible new forms of "absenteeism." The important thing to note here is that, despite the physical separation of successive generations of the family from the farm, the agricultural production continues to take place in the mode of a combination farm defined in the previous chapter. Often, the key motive behind production is not to maximize profit, efficiency or competitiveness, but simply to keep the production process going and maintain the landholding. Thus the face of landlordism is seen to be changing, as later chapters will further elucidate.

In the second mode of organization, the landholding pattern remains the same but instead of directly hiring labourers, the family engages in sharecropping. The intricacies of share cropping terms and agreements vary widely. One of the prevalent systems is for the landowner and the sharecropper to equally divide the cost of inputs such as the seeds, fertilizers, and irrigation. The sharecropper is then free to employ either family labour or hired labour for the actual cultivation process. At the end of the season, the harvest is divided in a pre-agreed ratio between the sharecropper and the landowner. In Jhaalpahari equal sharing of the harvest between landlord and sharecropper is most commonly agreed upon. However in other parts of the region, ratios varying up to 3:1 between landlord and sharecropper have been reported, depending on the quality of the soil, the nature of the crops cultivated, the number of cropping seasons and the overall power relations in the given context. In several cases the same sharecropper has been found to be cultivating a given piece of land under renewed agreements over periods of decades. In other cases, sharecroppers have been found to be cultivating different pieces of land every year or every season. An important factor to bear in mind is that share cropping agreements are almost without exception, verbal and customary contracts, and do not in any way represent security of tenure for the sharecropper. One of the factors to note here is the land reform measures introduced in West Bengal during the Left regime. Since 1977 Operation Barga has been implemented which seeks to register tenants to ensure security of tenure. Although the government estimate places the number of registered bargadars (sharecroppers) at about 2 million, Jhaalpahari is not one of the locations where this scheme has been particularly successful.

In the third mode of organization, the landholding family rents out its farms to tenant farmers who are responsible for all input investments and retain all profits after paying the designated cash rent to the landowners. In this case too, the same tenant farmer may be retained by the landowning family over an extended period of time, or the tenant for a given farm may change from year to year. In Jhaalpahari, this arrangement is adopted by landowners as a last resort of sorts. It is the option grudgingly adopted by those who have neither any willing family members nor the means or opportunity to hire managers to oversee the production process. One of the reasons behind the aversion towards this arrangement is the fear of "land usurpation" by long-term tenants. As part of

Operation Barga tenancies were made inheritable by a single living member of the deceased tenant's family.[6] This instilled a fear of permanent loss of control over leased out landholdings amongst the landowning class. The subject of land reforms continues to be a political hot potato at national and state levels. The issue has fallen out of prominence and it has now become nearly impossible to realize any measure of radical land reforms and, with decreasing mean size of holding, the historical opportunities for a classical type of equalizing land reform may be over.

In Jhaalpahari the sharecroppers and tenant farmers are traditionally drawn from the Scheduled Tribe community of Santhals. The 35 household strong Santhal settlement lies within a kilometre of the town's periphery. Although it is not connected to the town by an all-weather motorable road, a meandering ten-minute walk through the fields and groves brings one directly into the centre of the town. As a survey of all the households in this Santhal village revealed, sharecropping was a ubiquitous economic activity even if a large share of the household income was derived from non-agricultural employment, such as in domestic work. It was a common occurrence for the families to work as sharecroppers during the short and single crop season. In the remaining time, the male members worked on a daily wage basis at various establishments in the town while the female members took up short term assignments as domestic helpers for the landowning families. Work undertaken by the male members included loading and unloading trucks for the rice and oil mills in the town, assisting shopkeepers during peak business hours, unloading goods from freight trains, and other odd jobs involving manual labour.

The wage labour in agriculture was drawn on the other hand from the Scheduled Caste community of Bhuiyans, who also had a 40 household strong settlement adjacent to the Santhal settlement. This community was unanimous in asserting their inability to take up sharecropping or tenant farming due to the lack of resources for investment in agricultural production. Both men and women from this community worked as agricultural daily wage labourers during the sowing and harvesting seasons. In the remaining parts of the year, they sought short-term manual labour assignments in the district headquarter Bankura town. They were also dependent on employment provided through projects under the Mahatma Gandhi National Rural Employment Guarantee Act (MGNREGA) scheme although this was fraught with delays, insecurities, and political tension. Due to long-standing relations of patronage between the landowning households of the town and their Santhal tenants, sharecroppers and employees, the Bhuiyans did not see the town of Jhaalpahari as a possible source of employment despite its geographical proximity. Some of the respondents hinted at caste identities being at the centre of these conventional relations of labour.

Unlike States like Bihar, Uttar Pradesh and Rajasthan, from where circular migration of labour is well documented, the Santhals and the Bhuiyans of Jhaalpahari did not undertake such forays into distant metro cities. The historical or systemic reasons for this were not explored as part of this study. However it did emerge through interviews with male heads of households in the two settlements, that for both the Santhals and the Bhuiyans, Jhaalpahari was the standard commercial centre around which their socio-economic lives were organized. From everyday groceries to fertilizers and farm equipment, the Jhaalpahari market place was the go-to destination for both the communities.

From this account of socio-economic life in and around Jhaalpahari, a number of links between agricultural production and the nature of urbanization become apparent. The town of Jhaalpahari and the adjacent rural settlements are strongly inter-connected and interdependent. The residents of Jhaalpahari who have been building and upgrading their residential units leading to the expansion of the built-up area, are dependent on profits from their agricultural landholdings. These profits are earned through the labour provided by the Bhuiyans and Santhals. In fact, their landholdings and their perpetual stake in the agrarian sector is maintained by the caste-based arrangement of agricultural production. This arrangement is what allows parts of the profits from agriculture to be invested in education which may lead to formal sector employment or self-employment in bigger urban centres for successive generations of the landholding families. It also allows investment into the businesses in the town's commercial sector. Production and consumption in mid-level towns like the district headquarters Bankura, was also connected to the labour of marginal groups such as the Bhuiyans from the rural hinterland. Thus, these two relatively small settlements of the Santhals and the Bhuiyans held important links with urbanization at three different scales – the local, the regional, and the national.

As this case description makes evident, the strongest difference in the lived experiences of marginalized social groups such as the Bhuiyans and the Santhals, can be made by investment into small-town-based grassroots level urbanization such as in Jhaalpahari town. Urban service provisioning, strengthening of basic infrastructure such as roads, electricity, and drinking water, and improving opportunities for business and commerce in the emergent small towns are some aspects of urban policy that are most relevant in these settings.

Apart from the three modes of organization of agricultural production observed in Jhaalpahari, there can be a couple of other modes of organization that are relatively less prevalent but important nonetheless. In a previous study (Sircar 2012) we have encountered a system of agricultural production that involves landowners from outside of the dominant group. These are owners of smaller farms that are cultivated through a combination of hired and family labour. The hired labour is often from within the neighbourhood, the settlement, or the caste/community of the landowners. It is also common practice for landowners and their family members to be employed as daily wage labourers in similar sized farms owned by other families within the community.

In the same study, as also in multiple other studies, we have encountered the subsistence farmer. In the subsistence mode of agricultural production, landholdings are very small and the only labour employed is from within the family. Production is almost entirely for consumption within the household and not for sale in the market. Ignoring the connections of such farms and households to the non-farm sector gives a grossly misleading image of their livelihoods. Analysis of longitudinal and cross-sectional data for this book has revealed that such farms are very likely to be subsumed within the category of combination farms described in Chapter 5 and that pluriactivity is characteristic of their economic activities.

While these categorizations are based primarily on the nature of ownership and management of land, it needs to be pointed out that most of the agricultural production is made possible by the labour of landless agricultural workers, smallholders, and tenant family labour. Agricultural wages have traditionally been difficult to track and measure, not least because of their wide variations depending on the region, the crop, the season, the level of farm mechanization, the gender of the worker, and the prevalent levels of oppression and collective bargaining power. Nonetheless, the seasonal and circular movement of agricultural labourers to both spaces and productive activities outside of the agrarian sector is well documented, even if under-studied. The increasing occurrence of pluriactivity and competitive wages from non-farm work as revealed by analysis in later chapters hints at a move towards smallholder and combination farm-centred agrarian structural transformation.

Having recognized these possibilities and complexities within the organization of agricultural production in India, we now turn to the processes of urbanization that can emanate from these circumstances. The high incidence of circular migration and informal employment in the construction sector points to the role played by landless labourers, subsistence farmers and marginal farmers in the production of large scale cityscapes. At the same time, the exclusionary and elitist nature of these city spaces raises the question of where these labouring masses can seek refuge for a life of stability, if not prosperity. All indications point towards low-level urbanization in the margins of the urban landscape – the Census towns and other small towns in the fringes of the urban imagination of the nation.

The need to rethink urban policy

As established in the first two sections, the narrative of the global city or megacity is an exclusionary one. While the current urban policy of the Indian state seeks to divert all its resources to the reification of these selected sites as the face of urban India, these sites simply do not hold adequate economic opportunities or potential to accommodate the aspirations of the millions from the hinterlands. This is exemplified in the very presence and spread of grassroots level urbanization. As the third section demonstrates, subaltern urbanization takes place at close quarters with family farm-based agricultural production and is to a large exent driven by and also driving the agrarian transformation (see the subsequent chapters). It is therefore far more reasonable to develop an urban policy that is closely aligned to agrarian policy rather than one that bypasses agrarian considerations and focuses on handpicked hubs of privilege.

The complex and multi-faceted nature of family farming in India implies that the extent to which tenant farmers, sharecroppers and landless labourers are able to and willing to divert their labour into non-agricultural pursuits is determined by the opportunities and securities available in their immediate vicinity. Support to small towns and urbanization in the grassroots can create avenues for the absorption of this labour force into secondary and tertiary enterprises. This means that urban policy has to be integrated with policies addressing the rural non-farm sector, agro-based industries, and small and medium enterprises.

For the landholding classes, ties with the megacities have been longstanding. Better access to quality higher education and the aspiration of a formal sector white collar job are some of the factors that connect the rural landholding elite to the megacities. However this does not inevitably imply a complete severance of ties with the agrarian sector. The notional position of power and privilege that land ownership accords, keeps generations of the dominant landowning groups emotionally invested in their holdings. The diminishing size of the landholdings has served to dent the unequal power relations of agrarian production but the equation remains far from being balanced.

In conclusion, we argue that the shape of urbanization, when seen as the spatial concentration of people and productive resources in non-agricultural activities, is bound to be shaped by the exact contours of agrarian processes within a given local context. The exact terms of negotiations between landlords, tenant farmers, sharecroppers and landless labourers; and the competitive opportunities available in the non-farm sector determine at what pace labour is able to move out of agriculture. The productivity of the mode of organization and overall farm business cycles determine the extent to which agricultural profits are invested into non-agricultural enterprises. The successes of these enterprises in turn depend on state policy and support both to agriculture and to the very phenomenon of grassroots level urbanization.

In the light of these assertions, the current urban policy of the Indian State and the 100 smart cities project in particular, seem misguided at best and harmful at worst. Public funds from the centre and the State will be better utilized in fast-tracking the process of creation of ULBs for the existing CTs, building and maintaining urban infrastructure and amenities for these settlements, and nurturing the non-farm enterprises therein. This, coupled with a strong agricultural policy aimed at reforming the modes of production to make them more just and egalitarian, would constitute an adequate response to the experience of urbanization and agrarian structural transformation that have played out in the grassroots while the state has occupied itself with the dominant narrative of global cities. Much of what the present experience demands is a return to the fundamental goals of achieving balanced urbanization and pro-poor growth, with equity and justice being central concerns.

Notes

1 See http://indiatoday.intoday.in/story/vote-bank-politics-cm-vilasrao-deshmukh-halts-mumbai-slum-demolition-drive/1/194322.html

2 See http://www.firstpost.com/business/economy/bengal-as-investment-hub-mamata-to-head-for-uk-to-woo-investors-2342478.html

3 See for example analysis of low income housing provisioning by the Delhi Development Authority in Bhan, G. (2009). "This Is No Longer The City I Knew:

Evictions, the urban poor and the right to the city in millennial Delhi." *Environment and Urbanization* and Bhan, G. and K. Menon-Sen (2007). Swept off the Map: Surviving eviction and resettlement in Delhi. New Delhi, Yoda Press..

4 Name changed to protect the identities of the respondents.

5 Gram Panchayats or Village Panchayats are the lowest level of the three tier rural local governance bodies under the Panchayati Raj Institutions (PRIs) introduced through the 73rd Amendment Act of 1992.

6 See West Bengal Land Reforms Act 1978 and Roy, D. (2012). "Caste and Power: An ethnography in West Bengal, India." *Modern Asian Studies* **46**: 947–74.

4 What you might like to know about regression

This book is written for social scientists and other interested readers. As such you might not be familiar (enough) with the regression techniques which will be used in later chapters. This section aims to improve your knowledge and understanding of regression, statistical and econometric modelling.

Regression

First about the terminology: economists refer to *econometrics* as models derived from economic theory and testable with statistical data. *Statistical modelling* is a broader category, referring to techniques used to model statistical data. This type of modelling need not be theory-driven as econometric models should, but nothing prevents it from being so. The models in this book are designed to test some hypotheses about the Indian agrarian structural transformation derived from the discussion in Chapters 1 and 2. Thus they are theory-driven but differ from econometric models in neither being mathematized nor derived from an abstract body of theory, but rather from what sociologists would call middle-range theory (Merton 1968: 9–10, Portes 2010, Ch 1–2).

Regression is thus a tool for causal analysis of quantitative data: the idea is to reveal causal links between a dependent variable (y) and a set of independent variables (x) by a technique which has been called *quasi-experimental,* or *statistical control* and is a major analytical device for the non-experimental sciences.

Path models help to understand regression models. Figure 4.1 on the next page is a simple path model.

In Figure 4.1 the dependent variable (y) is rendered as a function of an independent variable (x), which however is not the sole determinant of (y). This is symbolized by the ellipse containing the symbol "Res," standing for *residual*, an aggregate of other variables also influencing (y). Other variables than (x) influencing (y) are of three kinds referred to as *omitted variables*, random errors (*noise*) and non-random errors (*bias*).

Ordinary least square regression

Statistical modelling is a large body of techniques, but the most common ones are regression models. The most widespread form of regression is ordinary least square

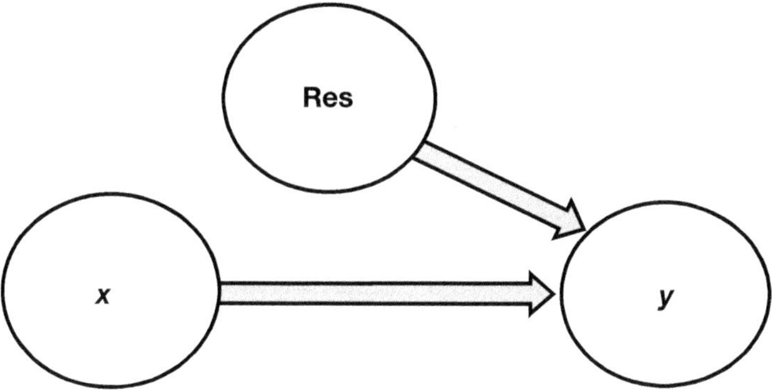

Figure 4.1 Simple regression path model

(OLS). It is used when we have a dependent variable (y) that is a scale, ideally ranging between negative and positive infinity ($\pm\infty$). Take a concrete example like the one used by Pearson who pioneered regression: son's body length can be modelled as a function of father's body length, (forgetting for the moment in these gender sensitive times both daughters and mothers). Presumably tall fathers would beget tall sons, but not always. In other words we regress son's body length on that of the father with the aim of estimating the strength of the causal link between the height of father and son. In equation form, a regression model for this case would look like this:

$$y = f(x) + e \qquad (1)$$

$$y = \alpha + \beta + e \qquad (2)$$

Where:

y = the dependent variable, here son's body length

f = function of some form (here linear)

α = constant or intercept

β = regression coefficient

x = independent variable, here father's body length

e = error, often also written as u for "unmeasured."[1]

Thus Equation 1 above can be read as stating that the dependent variable, son's body length (y) is a function of the independent variable, father's body length (x). This is graphically illustrated in Figure 4.1 above.

More specifically as in Equation 2, (y) is a function of a constant (and the product where (x) is the independent variable and is the regression coeffient plus an error term (e), also referred to as the "residual" ("Res" in Figure 4.1).

We can think of body length as a normally distributed variable, i.e. one having the famous bell shape. Ordinary least squares (OLS) presumes that the independent variable is normal, but as often in statistics this can be taken as *approximately normal* since the techniques tolerate some deviance from normality, especially in large samples.

If we were to estimate this model from a body of data, provided there is no human development leading to sons being on the average taller than fathers or a major humanitarian crisis having the opposite effect, we would expect the average body length of sons to be equal to that of their fathers. This implies that the regression coefficient is expected to be unity (β=1). If on the other hand sons were on the average taller than their fathers, say by five per cent, we would get (β=1.05). But even in the first case, with no difference in mean body length, we would not expect a son to be of the exactly the same length as his father. On the contrary we would expect him to be either shorter or taller. This in turn is due to the far from perfect correlation between the two variables. Lacking other information the best guess we can make of a son's body length is that it equals his father's. This is obviously not a very good prediction because there is an error (e) in the prediction that is due to the correlation between the two variables being some distance from unity.

Before we continue we need one more equation:

$$\hat{y} = \hat{\alpha} + \hat{\beta} x \tag{3}$$

where

$\hat{y}$ = the expected value of the dependent variable ("y hat") as estimated by the model.

To continue the argument, if the regression coefficient is estimated ($\hat{\beta}$) to be equal to unity, the estimated value of the dependent variable is:

$$\text{if } \hat{\beta} = 1, \text{ then } \hat{y} = x + \hat{\alpha} \tag{4}$$

So what is $\hat{\alpha}$? Setting $x = 0$ in Eqn 4 gives $\hat{y} = 0$. Thus ($\hat{\alpha}$) is the expected value of ($\hat{y}$) when $x = 0$. As our database is unlikely to contain any fathers with body length equal to zero, any value of ($\hat{\alpha}$) thrown up by the model has a mathematical interpretation but usually no theoretical interpretation.

Returning to Equation 2 the whole idea of regression is to find a value of ($\hat{\alpha}$) *and* ($\hat{\beta}$) that minimizes the error (*e*) in the prediction of (*y*). That is, in mathematical terms we have to find Min(y–$\hat{y}$). In OLS regression this is done by finding the value of (α and β) that minimizes the sum of the squared distances between the observed values of the dependent variables (*y*) and the predicted values ($\hat{y}$). This is the same as minimizing the error term (*e*) of the prediction.

The precision of the model or of the prediction is measured by the coefficient of determination (R^2), which varies between zero and unity and which can be interpreted as "the proportion of the variance in the dependent variable (y) that is due to variance in the independent variable (x)." The coefficient of determination (R^2) can also be taken as measuring the "goodness of fit" of the model. In practice we would never get ($R^2=1$), which would imply a deterministic relation. This is because in social science we hardly ever deal with deterministic relations, but with stochastic variables.

Since statistical modelling usually is done with sample data, regression models contain sampling errors. Using our example, this means that even if we expect son's body length on the average to equal father's, due to random variation, the value of the regression coefficient will never equal unity as the hypothesis says, but deviate somewhat from unity. Therefore we test the coefficient ($\hat{\beta}$) with Student's t. If the t-value is sufficiently large to be statistically significant we conclude that the hypothesis that average body length of fathers and sons would be equal does not hold, perhaps because human development has caused an increase in the average length of sons. Before testing the regression coefficient ($\hat{\beta}$) we should however test the goodness of fit of the model by submitting the coefficient of determination (R^2) to an F-test. If the model survives this, it is considered to catch non-random variations in the data and can potentially be used for causal analysis.

Extensions

We need to go into three extensions of simple regression: (1) multiple regression, (2) functional forms other than linear and (3) multilevel models. They will be dealt with in the following.

(1) Multiple regression is a seemingly straightforward extension of simple regression:

$$y = \alpha + \beta_1 x_1 + \beta_2 x_2 \ldots + e \qquad (5)$$

Where:

y = the dependent variable, as before

α = constant or intercept

β_1, β_2 = regression coefficients

$x_1 x_2$ = independent variables

e = error, as before.[1]

Figure 4.2 is a path diagram with three independent variables, and is the analogue of Figure 4.1 (p. 59), the difference being three independent variables, instead of one. Bowed arrows have been added to mark the correlations, or *collinearity*, as the correct term would be, between the independent variables. Collinearity is usally present in some degree, but should not be too high, as this may lead to biased estimates of the regressions coefficients.

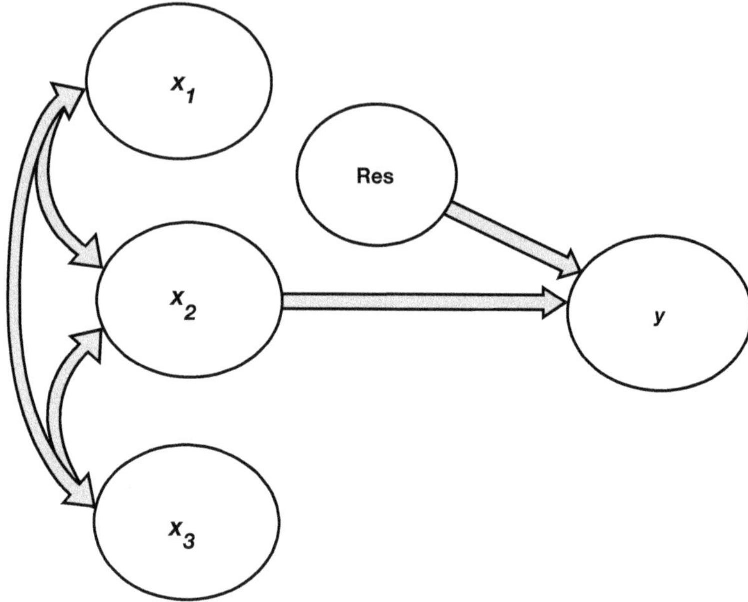

Figure 4.2 Path diagram of regression model with three independent variables

The strength of regression models is exactly that they can deal with several independent variables, i.e. with "multi-causality" and, if there are no errors or bias, estimate the influence of each one of them, independently of the others. This is what is meant by statistical control or quasi-experimental methods. It explains why statistical models are so useful to social science: they allow strict causal attribution, which is often impossible by other less stringent methods.

(2) *If we let go of the assumption that the functional form (f) of the model is linear it opens up a range of possible statistical models*

An important case is when the dependent variable (y) is binary, i.e. taking the values of zero and one. The world is full of binary outcomes, like yes or no, poor or non-poor etc. It was therefore a great bonus to science when statisticians and economists developed first "probit" and later "logit" models. The former are models of the probability of an outcome dependent on a vector of independent variables (x_1x_2 etc.). Logit, or logistic binary regression has gradually replaced the coarser probit models. In this technique we model the natural logarithm of the odds of an outcome. In statistics the odds ratio of an outcome is defined as the probability (p) of an outcome divided by the probability of its non-occurrence:

$$odds = \frac{p}{p-1}$$

Odds vary between infinitely low and infinity (∞). If you take the natural logarithm of the odds you get the logit, which has the attractive property of varying between ±∞. In logistic regression, however, the logic is not the same as in OLS where the aim is to account for as much as possible of the variation in the dependent variable (y) by means of the independent ones. There is no real counterpart to the coefficient of determination (R^2) in logistic regression. Various measures have been proposed, for example Nagelkerke's R^2, but although often it is said so, it cannot be interpreted as a measure of explained variance. Instead the aim is to account for as much as possible of the information (as opposed to random variation or noise) in the data. There are various ways of testing this, for example the Wald test, a variant of the Chi Square test which is used to test if a model accounts for a statistically significant amount of information. If it does not, it should be discarded. If the Wald test is significant, it is worth examining the *t*-tests of the regression coefficients (denoted as β as in OLS regression).

Logistic regression can be extended to ordinal or nominal outcomes, a method we will use in this book.

(3) The last type of regression analysis to be introduced here is "multilevel models"

This is ideal for the type of data we will be using where the primary unit of data collection is the household and where, as a consequence of sample design, households are clustered in villages, which in turn are clustered within blocks, districts and States. This means that the total variance in a dependent variable can be broken down into four components: variance due to differences between households, between villages, blocks, districts and States.[2] To put it differently, since the mean of the dependent variable (or the proportion of ones in a binary logistic model) is likely to differ between villages, part of the total variance is due to inter-village differences and part to differences between higher level units.

To round off: regression is a powerful technique to perform causal analysis of statistical data. It does not make the causal analysis for you, on the contrary. Interpretation and causal attribution is not the job of the statistician, but of the analyst using sociological, geographical or other theories to interpret the results. The many pitfalls involved will be evident as we go into our own modelling exercises in later chapters.

Notes

1 For simplicity we have avoided indexing the variables y, x and e. Conventionally these are rendered y_i, x_i and e_i where the index i denotes an individual case and where the index varies from 1 to n (n = the sample size).

2 For logistic models we usually do not define variance between primary units (here households).

5 Drivers of agrarian transformation

We discussed the Weberian methodology of ideal types and definitions of capitalist and family farming in Chapter 1 and of structural transformation (ST) in the following one. Chapter 3 provided an insight into the interaction between the agrarian ST and the development of third tier urbanization in India. We will now proceed to examine the main hypothesis of this book saying that the agrarian transformation in India is likely to lead to an increasing predominance of family labour farms (see "The competitive advantage of family farms" on pp. 12–14).

We have arrived at the heavy empirical part of this book, i.e. the tests of the family labour farm hypothesis and the description of the Indian agrarian transformation more generally. First we describe the process of transformation historically, by means of census and other macro level statistics, starting in the early twentieth century. While the historical analysis provides an account of the speed of the process it does not give much insight into its consequences for agrarian society. For the latter we have to rely on survey and panel data.

Historical and macro level analysis

In Timmer's analysis of the ST, discussed in Chapter 2, a crucial indicator is the share of agriculture in the total GDP compared to the share of agricultural labour in the total workforce. The graph in Figure 5.1 shows the latter historically and for India.

Around 1900 the share of the agricultural work force in the total was between 0.67 and 0.68, with an upward trend continuing until 1921. The share first fell to reach 0.67 in 1931 when it turned upwards again. Remarkably, a corresponding figure was reached again only in the 1990s. Amazingly, according to this indicator, the agrarian ST stood still for about 60 years, to take off only in the 1990s. We take this finding with us into the analysis of panel data.

In Figure 5.1 horizontal lines have been inserted to emphasize what appears to be epochal shifts in the time series: (1) the period up to the end of World War I when the share of the agricultural work force increased, indicating a reverse trend in the ST; while (2) the trend line turned down after the war, a period usually regarded as somewhat of a golden age for Indian farmers with good prices for cotton, groundnuts and other cash crops in the 1920s (Baker, 1984, see also Kumar

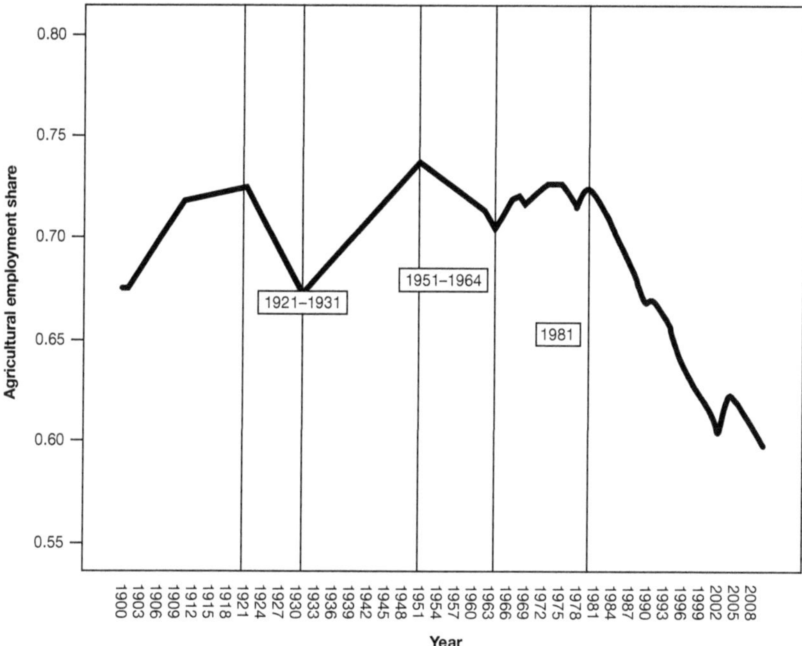

Figure 5.1 Share of agricultural employment in total, time series 1900 to 2008
Source: (anonymous undated) and Mitchell, B. (Wingender 2014)

and Desai 1983: 613 and 893). (3) The Great Depression in the 1930s and World War II also appear as retrogressive periods, with the share of agricultural work force in the total increasing rather than the reverse. According to the graph, (4) the period after the War and Independence and until 1964 was a period of progressing ST, which ended with what seems to be (5) a structural stagnation during the Green Revolution from 1965 to 1981. After that year (6) ST seems to have resulted in a long period of shrinking shares of agricultural labour in total employment from higher than 0.70 at the start of the period to less than 0.60 at the end. It continued to fall and even seems to have accelerated after 2008, as is indicated in Figure 5.2 overleaf.

Recall the discussion of Arthur Lewis in Chapter 2 (pp. 30–31). According to Lewis' theory, during the initial period of industrialization and capitalist development, labour is pulled out of the agrarian sector without harming production or productivity because it is surplus to production in what he terms, the "traditional" sector. Assuming a closed economy as Lewis did, when surplus labour in the traditional sector is exhausted, further exodus of labour is harmful to production. To avoid scarcity of food in the "capitalist" sector (again with Lewis' terminology), the productivity of agricultural labour must increase, either through new crop technologies (like during the Green Revolution) or through mechanization.

The long period of ups and downs in the share of agricultural employment, from 1900 to 1981 shown in Figure 5.1 (p. 65), according to the theories of ST of Lewis,

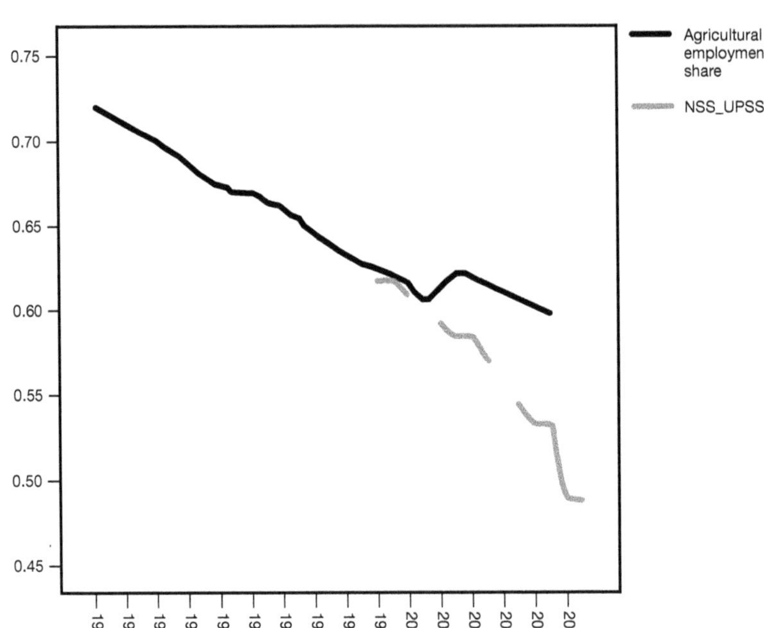

Figure 5.2 Agricultural employment share from 1981 to 2011 according to national accounts and according to National Sample Survey 1999 to 2012

Source: National Sample Survey (NSS), various rounds. Usual Primary and Subsididary Status (UPSS)

Timmer and others, is thus a sign of stagnation rather than dynamic process. Dynamism in those terms is apparent only after 1981 when the share of agricultural labour in the total workforce consistently decreased. Does this mean that India reached a *Lewis turning point* (LTP)[1] in the early 1980s? Reddy *et al.* have investigated this and show that in the 80s India must have been far from the LTP. According to these authors, currently some States are on the verge of passing the turning point while others are lagging:

> …among developed states, Kerala, Tamil Nadu, Himachal Pradesh, Haryana, and Punjab are on the verge of the LTP with high structural change, low poverty, and high wage rates. Andhra Pradesh, Maharashtra, Gujarat, and West Bengal with their rapid economic growth have the potential to reach the LTP but their non-inclusive development with low development of the rural non-farm sector have resulted in low wage rates and high rural poverty. States such as Odisha, Madhya Pradesh, Uttar Pradesh, and Bihar will take a much longer time to reach the LTP although wage rates and the non-farm sector show increasing trends.
>
> (Reddy 2015: 65)

According to the authors quoted, India as a whole is still some distance from a Lewis Turning Point. To investigate why and how we need other types of data than we have used so far. The ARIS REDS and HDPI-IHDS surveys allow checking for whether India or different States in the country have reached a Lewis Turning Point. Moreover, the panels allow us to check the drivers of the transformation and its consequences at household and village level.

Data sources

ARIS REDS is unique in being both nationally representative and covering a long period of India's modern history. Organized by the Government of India and supported by Ford Foundation, the first surveys called Agricultural and Rural Industries Surveys (ARIS), were taken in 1969 and aimed to cover the areas over which the Green Revolution was being rolled out. In subsequent years, up to 1971, the surveys, now called Rural Employment and Development Surveys (REDS), were expanded outside the original areas so as to be nationally representative. The data contain a weighting variable that provides nationally representative point estimates. It becomes increasingly problematic to use these weights due to attrition, especially in the later survey rounds that were undertaken in 1982, 1999 and 2006. We therefore prefer to use the unweighted data, so that statistics describe the sample rather than the rural population, from which it was drawn. We have not detected bias or other problems arising from this.

The 2006 round of REDS is problematic though. First of all, keys for matching households participating in both the 1999 and 2006 rounds have been partially lost, so that several States are not at all or poorly represented: Madhya Pradesh, Himachal Pradesh, Bihar, Jharkand, Chattisgarh and West Bengal. Furthermore, surveyors have allowed negative incomes so that, 2006 being a poor year for farming, income data maybe representative for that year, but cannot be used to study trends over time.

Two more variables that are central to our analysis cannot be used. There are detailed data on castes and caste names given by the respondents, covering over 70 pages in the code list, but with no effort made to classify these into caste groups, which is the variable we need. Furthermore, data on irrigation are problematic, with village mean proportion of area irrigated varying between 45 and 55 per cent. From the other surveys we can group villages into three categories based on the per centage of area irrigated as dry (below 25 per cent), intermediate (between 25 and 75 per cent) and wet (over 75 per cent irrigated). With REDS 1999–2006, all villages end up in the intermediate category, which is plainly wrong.

Fortunately we were able to replace REDS 1999–2006 with two nationally representative surveys containing the data we need: the Human Development Profile of India (HDPI) taken in 1994/95 and India Human Development Survey (IHDS) with data collected in 2004/05. The latter included the HDPI households and the resulting panel covers almost the same period as REDS 1999–2006. Given the problems in the latter and the excellent data quality in HDPI-IHDS we prefer using the latter.

In all these surveys interviewees have been heads of households, usually men. Data contain demographic particulars about all members of the households, details about farming, land owned and cultivated, land leased out and in, incomes and income sources including employment both in farming and outside. They do not contain data on input of family or hired labour; neither do they contain number of days of employment of agricultural labour, only incomes from such labour. Few if any nationally representative surveys contain data on family and hired labour days, which would have been eminent for our purpose.[2]

For more details on the data sources, see Appendix 1.

Inter-sectorial mobility

Above we used indicators of ST for macro data: share of agriculture in GDP and share of agricultural labour in the total labour force. Such indicators are evidently not suitable to micro data only covering the rural and agrarian population, not the urban non-agricultural one. Our first task therefore is to develop other indicators.

Theoretically, ST involves movement of labour from the agrarian to the industrial and service sector. In our case we have data on households at the beginning of a period that we call t_0 and at the end of it (t_1). We can systematically compare the status of households at these points in time.

Usually we count with three possible relations to agriculture, a household can either be: (1) a cultivator, i.e. cultivating some land, owned or leased; (2) an agricultural labourer working for wages on another's land; or (3) a landlord household, i.e. leasing out but not working on its own land. A fourth possibility is of course to be (4) a non-agrarian household, not having any of the above relations to agriculture. Among the ones mentioned the only exclusive or non-overlapping relation is the fourth one, i.e. being a non-agrarian rural household. The other three can be combined in various ways, either by different individuals within the same households and even by individual members of the household. This complicates operationalization. A further complication is that households and individual members can combine farm sources of income (being cultivators, wage labourers or non-cultivating landowners) with non-farm ones. We call this "pluriactivity," a concept we will return to below (see the theoretical discussion on page 16 ff. above.

Since ST involves movement of labour wholly or partly out of the farm sector, a possible index of the process is the exit of individuals or entire households from the sector, i.e. mobility in terms of three relations, leaving cultivation, leaving agricultural wage labour, or ceasing to lease out land. One complication is of course that such movement need not be out of the farm sector; it can equally well be within the sector, for example when a cultivator is proletarianized and becomes a landless agricultural labourer. Moreover things get complicated because these movements can be partial and individual rather than characteristics of entire households.

We will first be looking at change in cultivator status, i.e. exit from and entry to the farm sector, which in terms of our data boils down to being a cultivator at t_0, or not and being so at t_1, or the other way round. This gives rise to four possible combinations:

Table 5.1 Cultivator status at t_0 and t_1

	Cultivator status at t_1	
Cultivator status at t_0	*Yes*	*No*
Yes	Remained a cultivator	Exited cultivation
No	Entered cultivation	Remained a non–cultivator

Remaining a cultivator or a non-cultivator is obviously less an interesting outcome than changing status, i.e. going from being to not being a cultivator, or the other way round. Of these two outcomes, the rate of exit from cultivation of the sample over the period t_0 to t_1 is obviously the most interesting and a prime index of ST. If you compare the rate of exit between different periods, you will get an index of its pace, if it is stagnant, accelerating or possibility decelerating. Thus, the rate of exit from the farm sector is the process we will be mainly studying in the rest of this chapter. Note that exit from the farm sector need not imply exit from the agrarian sector and entry into the industrial and service sectors. Movement from farm to other parts of the agrarian sector is not the main problem here, although we will touch on it when discussing pluriactivity and multi-sectorial livelihoods.

Operationalizing the family labour farm

The family farm hypothesis is difficult to reliably approach by means of macro statistics.[3] While the prevalence of family managed farms is relatively easy to estimate (see Chapter 1), family labour farms are problematic because their operationalization requires detailed data on farm labour input by family and by non-family workers. Lacking this, we use a so-called manifest variable, which is the opposite of a latent one.

We loosely define the statistical concept of a latent variable as a variable which is "out there"[4] and for which we are looking for a manifest variable, i.e. a variable possible to define by the data at hand (Loehlin 2004, Skrondal and Rabe-Hesketh 2004) and which can serve as an indicator of the latent variable. More precisely we need a categorical latent variable, among the categories of which an indicator of the latent category of a family labour farm would be crucial.

We call this latent categorical variable "farm type," in which there are three categories: (1) the family labour farm, which depends on family labour in cultivation as well as in management; (2) the large farm or estate that may be family managed but depends on hired labour (or possibly tenants) for cultivation; and (3) the smallholder–labourer farm in which the cultivator in addition to work on his own farm also works as an agricultural wage labourer on other people's farms. The latter is the operationalization of the "combination farm," which we defined in Chapter 1 (see page 16). The smallholder–agricultural labourer category is obviously only meaningful in an economy with a large agricultural wage labour force, and therefore suits the Indian case.

The family labour farm hypothesis (see Chapter 1) makes us expect an increasing prevalence of family labour farms, brought about by higher rates of exit in the other two categories: large farms dependent on hired labour and smallholder–agricultural labourers.

Farm types are nested within a classification of the entire rural population, which we will come back to. First we need to discuss in detail the operationalization of farm types. A common proxy for farm type is size, usually operationalized in terms of area cultivated, although income or turnover would be more meaningful. The latter type of data is not easy to come by and in Indian farm economy studies we would moreover expect a great deal of unreliability, since respondents are wont to underestimate their incomes.

In Indian macro statistics, for example in the Agricultural Censuses, scale is converted to farm type by means of size groups: "marginal farmer" means a farmer cultivating up to 1 hectare or 2.5 acres; similarly a "small farmer" means a farmer cultivating more than 1 hectare and up to 2 hectares (5 acres) etc. Since, as we argued in Chapter 1 (p. 6), farm size is a heterogeneous variable, for analytical purposes this operationalization is not very meaningful and the further ST grows, the less is it so.

In the Indian context, family managed farms are the rule, and the sampling criteria for ARIS REDS make them 100 per cent of that sample (see Appendix 1 for details on the data sources). Within the sample there are both own and tenant farms, a distinction we will return to in the next chapter.

We need to distinguish between the three latent farm types, i.e. types of cultivating households, and do so with reasonable reliability. Furthermore we must classify non-cultivators. Avoiding the definition of smallholders in terms of area is easy: households cultivating some land and in which some members work for agricultural wages will be called *smallholder–agricultural labourers.* This type of smallholders cannot feed themselves and their families from their own cultivation, but have to go for "coolie work," as the Indian term is. We therefore take it that their own or leased holdings are too small in area or economic terms to provide them the correspondence of a wage.

When discussing smallholders, it must be remembered that agricultural labour, or "coolie work," is at the absolute bottom of the agrarian social order. Scheduled Caste, or low caste workers, with or without land, do coolie work. Such work is considered undignified and those who get the chance would be expected try to get away from it although escape is not easy with the stigma attributed to these groups. We assume that with a proceeding ST the odds of exiting the segmented agricultural labour market would improve.

Landless agricultural labourers are traditionally considered even worse off than smallholders combining own cultivation with coolie work. At the early stages of the ST, their ambition presumably would often have been to save up (for example by seasonally migrating to work outside the village) to buy some land in order to gain a safer foothold in the agrarian economy; but as the transformation progresses to higher levels, they are more likely to aim for a non-agrarian future, outside the village. For a Scheduled Caste man or woman such a future would also promise an escape to a more dignified life than that of the agricultural coolie (cf. the discussion in Sharma 2005, especially page 970 and, Jodkha 2015).

Singling out the smallholder–agricultural labourers and the landless labourers is relatively easy. With the present data it is more difficult to distinguish farmers who are dependent on hired labour from those that are dependent on family labour. Data on the exact input of hired as well as family labour is not at hand, so operationalization must build on other criteria. One way to proceed is to use the variable criticized above, i.e. size of farm, but with the special objective of looking at the largest farms. Everything else being equal, they should contain many units dependent on hired labour.

Since predominance of large farms differs a lot between villages, it may be wise to expand beyond villages to blocks or districts. We have chosen the latter and will be looking at the largest farms in the district.[5] We can easily sort out the 5, 10 or 20 per cent cent largest landholdings and provisionally regard them as more likely than others to be dependent on hired (or tenant) labour. We have found the latter limit to work best and we thus use a broad definition of large landowners implying a more narrow operational definition of family farms.

Having sorted out the smallholder–agricultural labourers at the bottom of the cultivator's hierarchy and the largest farms at the top, we get the family labour farms as a residual category. Cultivating households in which no member works for agricultural wages and who do not belong to the 20 per cent of the largest farms in the district, is the manifest category, which hopefully functions as a reliable enough indicator of the latent category of family labour farms.

The farm types defined so far do not encompass all the variations since they was drawn from the rural population, which contains many non-cultivating households. Thus we need to put the farm types within a typology of households in the rural population as whole.

Table 5.2 Classification tree for agrarian households

Sample frame: Rural Population		
1) Non–agrarian population: (Only households with no relation to agriculture (as cultivators, labourers or landowners) are classified here)	2) Agrarian population:(Households with some relation to agriculture are classified according to the below)	
	a) *Types of cultivating households or farms*: i) *Large estates dependent on hired (or tenant) labour* ii) *Family labour farms* iii) *Smallholder – agricultural labourers*	b) *Types of non–cultivating households*: i) *Landlords, owners of large estates, dependent on tenant (or hired) labour* ii) *Landless agricultural labourers* iii) *Petty landlords*
	Note: Categories (a.i) and (b.i) have been merged into one called 'Large estates', allowing these to be cultivated by hired labour or by tenants, or a mixture of these forms	
Cross–cutting dimension: Degree of pluriactivity, or share of non–agrarian income		

To get an exhaustive classification of the agrarian population we add another two categories, first *petty landlords* who do not belong to the category of owners of large estates, who own but do not cultivate any land and who do not work as agricultural labourers. In the present context a residual category is the *non-agrarian households*, with all their income from outside agriculture (except petty[6] lessors of land).

In this rather elaborate classification, one category, *owners of large landholdings* or estates contains both cultivators and non-cultivators and thus an individual member household can either stay stable, exit or enter cultivation during a period. Therefore we use owners of large estates as a reference category,[7] with which the odds of entry and exit for all other categories of farms and households can be compared.

Irrespective of types, farming households as well as landless agricultural labourers vary in their dependence on non-farm income. To capture this we need to add another conceptual dimension, criss-crossing the farm typology, i.e. pluriactivity.

Pluriactivity

It is easy to define pluriactivity at an individual level: a farmer or a labourer is pluriactive if he or she has got more than one source of income. Here we are interested in households and in inter-sectorial livelihoods, so we define pluriactivity as households having incomes from inside as well as outside the farm sector. One obvious indicator is the share of household income originating from outside the sector. For the earlier periods we will be using another variable, however, i.e. having gone pluriactive over the period studied. At the household level this variable is binary and for a given period would be equal to unity if, at the beginning of the period the household had no non-farm sources of income and if, at the end of the period, they had some such sources.[8]

During the early stages of ST we would expect pluriactivity to be negatively correlated with exit from the sector. At that stage a multi-sectorial livelihood may instead have paved the way for an entry into the sector, for example by using savings from work outside the sector to invest in land and in farming. India had long-standing patterns of labour migration, for example to tea plantations in Sri Lanka, the Nilgiris, Assam, Darjeeling etc. where labourers were often aiming to save enough to return to their native villages and set up a farm there.[9] In the current stage of transformation we would rather expect pluriactivity to be positively correlated with exit from the agrarian sector. Once an individual or a household is established well enough in a non-agrarian livelihood, they may find it easier give up the foothold in the village, and in cultivation. This hypothesis is easy to test with the ARIS REDS and HDPI-IHDS data. In later waves we would expect higher rates of exit from cultivation and higher correlations among households between the rates of exit and of having gone pluriactive. For non-cultivators, as for example landless labourers we would expect lower rates of entry into cultivation when opportunities outside the agrarian sector improve, as they presumably do as the ST proceeds. Regression techniques are suited to handling this kind of multidimensional complexity. We can statistically control for their respective effects by entering both variables into the regression: (1) having gone pluriactive during the period studied and (2) farm and household type. Statistically controlling for one dimension allows us to assess the effect of the other dimension on the dependent variable.

Recalling the hypothesis from Chapter 1, the driver of a reinforced position of the family labour farm sector in the farm sector as whole is the wage level of agricultural workers, in turn driven by increasing demand for unskilled labour in the non-farm sector and increasing wages. Hypothetically this creates a "labour problem" for large estates dependent on hiring labour. Indirectly it would also affect lease rates, for example making it more difficult to find sharecroppers. Competition for labour not only drives the exodus of labour from the farm sector, but also induces labour shedding in the large farm sector in the form of mechanization, for example. Moreover, it encourages exit from farming by owners of large landholdings. Being able to substitute hired with family labour gives an advantage to family labour farms in this scenario, making the odds of exiting hypothetically lower for family farms than for large estates.

The smallholder–agricultural labourers are in a different situation, since they earn both from higher wages and should be able to substitute family for hired labour. It is not given *a priori* whether they would have higher rates of exiting than family farmers though.

All these tendencies are moderated by the relative opportunities in the non-farm sector, for smallholders as well as for others. For owners of large estates opportunities for investment in the non-farm sector and earnings from these may for example help to retain their holdings despite increasing labour costs. Similarly for family labour farms: pluriactivity may be an interesting alternative to increasing the input of family labour on one's own farm. Combining labour or other resources in own farming and off the farm is an interesting possibility, which as we will see, joint families could be able to draw on.

Descriptive data

The question is what panel data say about the process we are studying. Remember that during the period 1965 to 1981 according to macro statistics, there was no clear tendency for the share of agricultural employment to decrease (see Figure 5.1 on page 65). Since this reflects net mobility, there should have been an underlying pattern of sectorial exit and entry, so that they balanced each other during the period, a pattern which is not discernible in repeated cross-sectional data. The 1970–81 period is covered in the first wave of ARIS REDS. The subsequent period in ARIS REDS is 1982–1999 and in HDPI-IHDS 1994/95 to 2004/05. Table 5.3 on the next page looks at the picture given by the repeated cross-sections, as well as the corresponding panels.

Table 5.3 firstly shows the proportion of the sample that were cultivators in the respective waves. We see a small decline between 1971 and 1982, a somewhat steeper decrease from the latter year to 1999. The HDPI-IHDS data are comparable,

Table 5.3 Mobility between farm and non–farm sector between ARIS REDS and HDPI–IHDS waves and in panels

a) Survey sample means		*Cross–section (year)*			
		ARIS REDS		HDPI–IHDS	
		1971	*1982*	*1994/95*	*2004/05*
Household cultivating some land, per cent, cross–sectional data		72%	70%	66%	63%
b) Panel means		*Panel period*			
	1971–82	*1982–99*	*1999–2006*	*1994/95–2004/05*	
Average yearly rate of exit	0.17%	0.33%	0.85%	0.25%	

Data source: Surveys mentioned. Data are unweighted and thus valid for the sample but not for the population

although the rate of exit appears lower in these. When inserting the sample data in a time series graph, an interesting pattern, mirroring macro level data appears (see Figure 5.3 below).

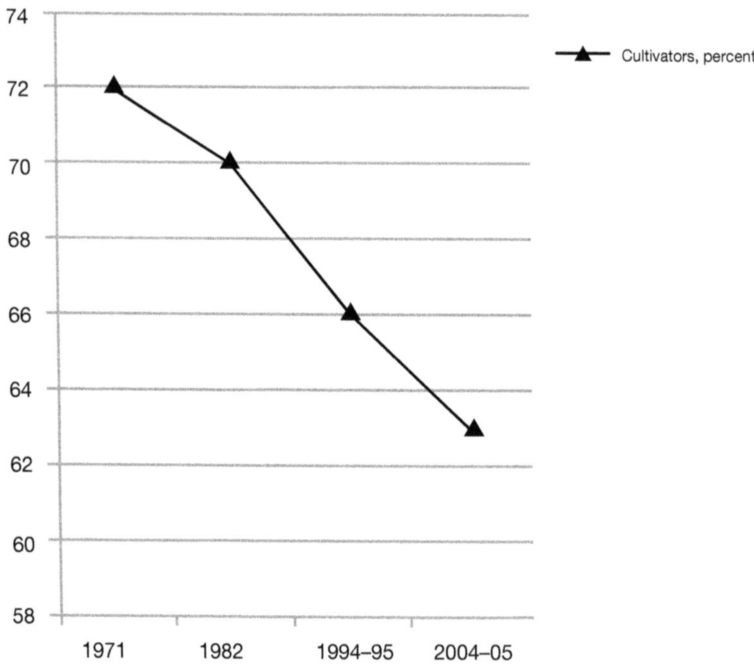

Figure 5.3 Cultivators, per cent by year of survey

Data source: ARIS REDS and HDPI-IHDS surveys

Note: The biased figures from REDS 1999 and 2006 are not included

The development over time in the rate of exit seems quite smooth judging from the graph above. If there was a dip between 2004 and 2006, as observed in the macro data (see Figure 5.1 on page 65), it is not visible in our micro data. This obviously depends on the choice of time points to be measured.

To summarize the patterns emerging, in the first ARIS REDS period 1971–82, i.e. the early phase of the Green Revolution, the net movement out of the sector was modest (see Table 5.3 on page 74). The trend picked up to reach an average of 0.33 per cent during 1982–99, but this higher rate does not tally with that reported by the HDPI-IHDS, which is 0.25 per cent for the period 1994/95 to 2004/05. In line with macro data discussed in the beginning of this chapter then, ST seems to have stalled in the 1980s and 90s. Still the accelerating trends seem clear. In the second and third periods exodus from the farm sector turned from a trickle to a small brook. It may have turned to a stream after 2005, but this is not reflected in the panel data.

The drivers of exit from the agrarian sector

We turn next to the drivers of the increasing exit from the farm sector and its consequences for agrarian structure. Given our emphasis on family labour farming, we are especially interested to know if that farm type strengthened or weakened its position in the process (see Table 5.4 below). The first driver to be discussed is pluriactivity and the increasing importance to livelihoods of the non-agrarian economy.

According to ARIS REDS data the rate of going pluriactive was even higher during the early period from 1971 to 1982 than in the later one, when it went down to 1 per cent of the sample (see Table 5.4 below). There are two ways to interpret this: either the livelihood opportunities within the farm sector improved after 1982 (perhaps due to the Green Revolution), or alternatively the opportunities became poorer outside the sector, or both. From the mid-90s, coinciding partly with a period of high growth for the non-agrarian economy, the rate of pluriactivity went up considerably.

Both these data and the rate of exit from farming, already discussed, point to a substantial acceleration of the ST of the farm sector from the mid-1990s.

Farm type

The concept of farm type was discussed above, but without presenting data on the prevalence of family labour and other types of farms.

Table 5.4 Gone pluriactive since start of the period

	Panel period		
	1971–82	*1982–99*	*1994/95–2004/5*
Gone pluriactive since the start of the period	6%	1%	13%

Data source: ARIS REDS and HDPI–IHDS surveys

Table 5.5 Farm and household types, per cent by cross–section

	Cross–section, year			
	1971	*1982*	*1994/95*	*2004/05*
Large landowner among 20% largest in District	13.6	4.4	22.3	10.3
Family farmer, narrow definition exluding 20% largest landowners in District	56.0	60.1	29.4	21.8
Smallholder – agricultural labourer	2.1	5.9	16.5	24.6
Landless agricultural labourer	12.9	8.8	15.3	21.3
Petty landlord, landowning household not cultivating any land, earning no agricultural wages	6.6	6.5	–	–
Non–agrarian household	8.8	14.3	16.4	22.0
Total	100.0	100.0	100.0	100.0
Summary statistics				
Proportion family farmers, of all cultivators including smallholders (%)	58.1	66.0	45.9	46.4

Data source: ARIS REDS and HDPI–IHDS surveys

The prevalence of farm and household types fluctuate in an unexpected way over time, which we take to reflect unreliability in the data. Figures seem good enough for non-agrarian households with a steady increase over the years, so that on the mean almost a quarter of the village population is classified as non-agrarian in 2004/05, up from less than 10 per cent in 1971. The apparent vanishing of the petty landlords in the last two rounds is not credible however and is due to definitional problems in the data. The proportion of landless agricultural labourers dips in 1982, possibly due to widespread entry into cultivation during the early Green Revolution, but equally possible a reflection of data problems. The ensuing increase in the proportion of landless labourers from 1982 would seem more credible. Its strong growth is an indication that the family farm hypothesis and the associated hypothesis of widespread exit of landless labourers from the farm sector might not hold in the Indian case. We will come back later to the likely causes of this development.

Like the landless labourers, the smallholder–agricultural labourers category shows a steady and marked increase over the years, from a minute proportion in 1971 to almost a quarter at the end of the period. Since family farmers and large landowners are separated by statistical fiat, it is not safe to draw any conclusion of the prevalence of the former. But the combined group shows a steady decline over the years with approximately a 40 per cent reduction from 1994/95 to 2004/05. This obviously reflects the increased prevalence of smallholder–labourers and of landless labourers, again an indication that the family labour farm hypothesis may get into difficulties when confronted with data.

Note finally that the combined group of cultivators, including the large landowners, the family farmers and the smallholder– agricultural labourers show a consistently decreasing trend over the years, which obviously mirrors the increase of the non-agrarian population, as well as the increased proportion of agricultural labourers.

Joint family

Family structure may be both a determinant and an effect of livelihood strategies. For a family farm, augmenting labour resources by avoiding partition and keeping the family together is a sensible strategy, especially in the absence of mechanization on a Western scale. By such means farmers can avoid depending on hired labour and can compete with large farms reliant on such labour. We operationally define a joint family as a household containing more than one married couple, as opposed to a nuclear family containing only one couple. Our hypothesis is that a joint family structure formed during the period studied will promote stability of family farms and thus be negatively correlated with the odds of exit.

The above argument leads to the first building stones of a regression model with three independent variables: pluriactivity, farm-household type and joint family. We will not estimate that simple model; and the actual model is unfortunately not that simple. Besides some technical variables, which we will presently introduce, we need two characteristics at village level, i.e. ecotype and the degree to which the village is drawn into the non-agrarian economy. Furthermore we include education. But we begin with caste.

Caste groups

Caste obviously has to be included in the analysis: Distinguishing between five broad groups of castes, Brahmins and Other Upper Castes, the Scheduled Castes (SC) and Tribes (ST), the so-called Other Backward Castes (OBC), and Others (including Muslims, which with some local exceptions is a small group in rural society), we get a clear but far from perfect correlation between caste and the type of household and farm (see Table 5.6 on page 78).

A Chi^2-test shows significant differences in this table (0.1 per cent significance). The most marked are: (1) Not unexpectedly, a strong overrepresentation of Brahmins and other Upper Castes among large landowners and a corresponding underrepresentation of these castes among smallholders and landless agricultural labourers; (2) a strong overrepresentation of Scheduled Caste among smallholders and agricultural labourers; (3) a similar pattern among Scheduled Tribes, with the difference that these are underrepresented among non-agricultural households as well; (4) Other Backward Castes (OBC) are over-represented among smallholders and agricultural labourers, much like the Scheduled Castes. The OBC are also slightly underrepresented among non-agricultural households. These are mostly well-known facts (see for example Vakulabharanam and Motiram 2011: 119–22, and Jodkha 2015). But how have these characteristics developed over time?

As shown in detail in Appendix 4, Table A4.3, statistics from the various survey sample rounds indicate that: firstly, the control of the 20 per cent largest

Table 5.6 Household and farm type by caste group, 1982

Household and farm type	*Brahmin and Upper Castes (%)*	*Scheduled Caste (%)*	*Scheduled Tribe (%)*	*Other Backward Caste (%)*	*Other (%)*	*Total*
Large landowner, among 20% largest in District	56.5	5.6	3.2	28.2	6.5	100
Family farmer, narrow definition, exluding 20% largest landowners in District	39.7	9.3	5.0	33.3	12.7	100
Smallholder – agricultural labourer	12.4	19.8	10.2	48.0	9.6	100
Landless agricultural labourer	17.0	28.9	10.8	35.0	8.3	100
Non–agricultural household	40.4	14.4	4.3	21.5	19.4	100
Petty landlord, agrarian household not cultivating any land, earning no agricultural wages	40.7	12.2	7.1	20.8	19.2	100
Total	36.7	12.8	5.9	31.0	13.6	100

Source: ARIS REDS 1971–82 panel

landed estates in each district by Brahmins and Other Upper Castes hovered around 50 per cent from 1971 to 1999 and, according to figures from 1994/95 and ten years later may then have gone down to around 30 per cent. It is an open question what has happened to the landed properties as such, if they have been leased out or sold off, whole or in parcels to members of other caste groups. Secondly, Brahmins and other Upper Castes were also strongly represented among family labour farmers, or slightly below 40 per cent in 1971 and 1982, and somewhat less (below 30 per cent) in both 1994/1995 and ten years later. The share of OBC among family farmers was slightly above their share of the rural population, or around 34 per cent, but this per centage increased to around 40 per cent respectively in 1994/05 and the survey round after that. Thirdly, the proportion of Scheduled Caste in the category smallholders– agricultural labourers was over 30 per cent in 1971, but declined since then and fluctuated around 20 per cent. So here SC lost out, one would guess mainly to members of OBC households. Fourthly, the proportion of SC among landless labourers fluctuated around 30 per cent from 1971 to 1999 and may have increased to almost 40 per cent after that. Fifthly, Scheduled Tribes continue to be underrepresented among non-agrarian households in rural India. OBC finally constitute about 30 per cent of the non-agrarian households, which is roughly equal to their share of the rural population.

All this seems to indicate that the development revealed by Athreya *et al.* in their case study of the old Tiruchy District in Tamil Nadu (1990, Chapter 4), although not unique, has been less prominent in the rest of the country. In Tiruchy

District, the old mainly Brahmin landlords have to a large extent left agriculture and sold off their properties. Not surprisingly this seems less true for the country as a whole. Like in Tiruchy OBC households appear prominent among those who have taken over whole or parts of the old estates.

Ecotype and irrigation intensity

We try to capture irrigation development in our notions "dry" and "wet" agrarian ecotypes (developed in Athreya, Djurfeldt *et al.* 1990, Ch 3). The operational definition used here is that villages with less than 25 per cent of their cultivated area under irrigation are classified as "dry"; and villages with more than 75 per cent of area irrigated are regarded as "wet," leaving an "intermediate" category with 25 to 75 per cent of area under irrigation. Representing this we get the following data on irrigation development in ARIS REDS villages (see Figure 5.4 below).

While the per centage of dry villages was above 40 per cent in the 1969–70 sample, the per centage had more or less halved in 1999. After that, according to HDPI-IHDS estimates, irrigation intensity seems to have gone down in some villages, mirrored in a decrease of intermediate villages. Wet villages similarly increased from about 30 per cent of all villages in 1969–70 to more than 40 per cent in 1999, and according to HDPI-IHDS the trend continued after that.[10]

As is well known, the early phase of the Green Revolution was associated with heavy investments in expansion and consolidation of canal irrigation. Much of the steam went out of this when the low hanging fruit had been picked and the

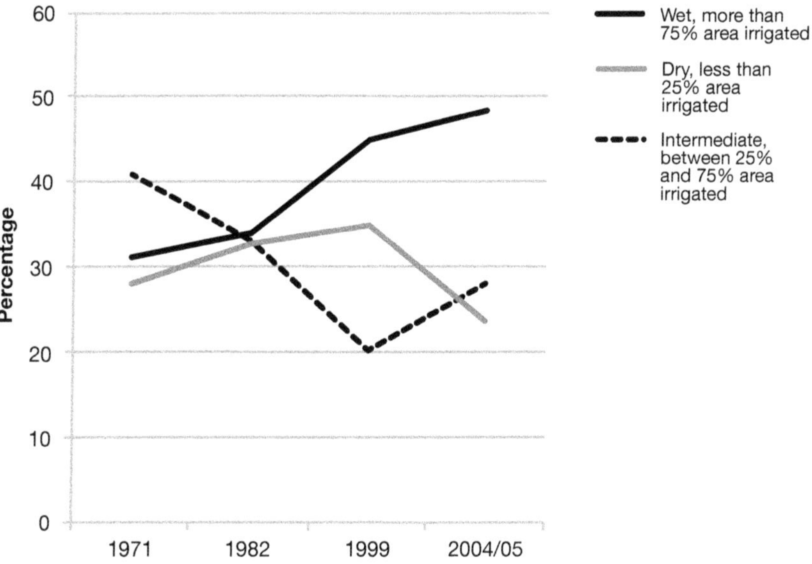

Figure 5.4 Classification of villages by degree of irrigation, by panel wave, per cent

Source: ARIS REDS and IHDS data

criticism of big dams and canal irrigation grew stronger during the 1980s. Decreasing public investments in irrigation, however, led to a boost of private investments in minor irrigation, especially in wells and pumps. This seems to have taken mainly two forms, (1) conjunctive well irrigation in canal and tank irrigated land, drawing on fairly easy-to-reach subterranean aquifers in the areas served by major and usually State-owned irrigation works; and (2) deep wells in rainfed lands, drawing on less easy-to-reach and sometimes non-renewable aquifers (Shah, Singh *et al.* 2006).

Would or could the differential expansion of irrigation have any effect on rates of exit and entry in intensively versus extensively irrigated villages? This is hard to say. Foster *et al.* (2004) have argued that investors in rural industries and services tended to be attracted to dry villages where labour costs, due to less competition for labour, would tend to be lower than in wet villages. This should turn up rates of pluriactivity, but how would it have affected rates of exit and entry? Since many other factors are involved, it is not clear what the net effect on rates of exit or entry would be. We keep the issue open and refrain from formulating a definite hypothesis on this.

Education

Previous research shows that education is important for the life chances of individuals, when exiting the agrarian sector (see Prowse, Prowse and Chimhowu for an overview). Does it also influence decisions to change status in cultivation, so that educated persons are more likely to opt out? To answer this question too, operationalization is crucial. We have found that in order to trace the influence of education, a cutting point seems to lie at levels of education below and above primary school level, presumably because an education lower than that may not be much of an asset when exiting farming. We refrain from giving sample statistics on education, which are similar to widely known macro data.

Control variables: partitioned household, age of head of household

Panel data models routinely include the age of the respondent. This is because with each round the panel members grow older and any change in the dependent variable may be due to ageing, rather than to structural transformation in our case.

ARIS REDS and HDPI-IHDS have comparatively long wavelengths, which is why many respondents pass away between the waves. One way to augment panel longevity, especially when dealing with household data, is to replace deceased members with their descendants. This was done in the second and third rounds of ARIS REDS as well as in the HDPI-IHDS panel. Including all descendants in the analysis evidently increases the number of households included in each round, but we used the alternative of sampling descendants. To control for the effect of replacing original members of the sample with a sample of descendants we introduce a descendant household dummy in all equations. As long as this variable is not statistically significant, being a descendant does not change the propensity to exit from or enter to farming.

Methods of controlling for spatial diversity

Levels of structural transformation obviously vary between States, from the poorest and most stagnant, to the most dynamic ones. With the multi-level modelling strategy adopted here (see Chapter 4, page 60 and Appendix 2), we can control for spatial diversity by estimating so-called "random effects,"[11] or shares of variance between States, districts and villages. Nothing prevents us, however, from also introducing village-, district- or State-level variables as fixed effects. So for example, it seems that the mean share of non-farm income at village level is an important determinant of household level characteristics like the propensity to exit farming. We hypothesize that the higher the derived village mean non-farm income, the higher the odds for exit of individual households. In other words, once the ST has set in at village level, there is a propensity for the process to run faster than in villages where it has not yet taken off.

Using change in cultivator status as an indicator of exit from farming and entry to cultivation

We do not want to model cultivator status as such, but the movement out of and into that status. One way of doing this is by means of an autoregressive model. This type of model captures change in a variable, in this case cultivator status, by introducing an autoregressive component in the model. In this case, we have cultivator status at the end of a period, say 1971 to 1982 as the dependent variable (y_{t1}), with cultivator status at the beginning of the period as the autoregressive component (y_{t0}). By thus controlling for cultivator status at the start of a period, the dependent variable (cultivator status at the end of period) can be made to capture change in status.[12] This again means that the regression coefficient (b) for another independent variable, say joint family, measures the influence of joint family on the odds to have exited (for cultivators) or entered cultivation (for non-cultivators) over the period.

Model specification

We now have a model with cultivator status at the end of a period as dependent on the variables mentioned above, i.e.:

- having gone pluriactive since the start of the period
- farm and household type at the start of the period, with owners of large estates as reference category (as discussed above)
- caste group (Brahmins and Other Upper Castes, Scheduled Castes and Tribes, Other Backward Castes and Others)[13]

- irrigation development or ecotype (dry and wet, with the intermediate ecotype as reference category) at the start of the period
- joint family at the end of the period
- education of head of household (dummy = 1 when the head of household has studied at least to primary school level), at the start of the period
- partitioned household at the end of the period
- age of head of household, at the end of the period, logged
- cultivator status at start of period (i.e. the autoregressive component)
- mean village share of non-farm income, at the start of the period and
- random effects for village, district and State.[14]

As mentioned before, the dependent variable is the logged odds of being a cultivator at the end of the period. Controlling for cultivator status at the start of the period, this denotes two outcomes, one for cultivators (exiting) and another for non-cultivators (entering). A mathematical specification of the model is found in Appendix 2.1 and detailed results in Appendix table 3.1. Readers, who want to study these, can take a break in reading now. For others, a somewhat simplified account is given in Table 5.7 on page 83.

Since the number of cases per independent variable is quite high (100 and above), we do not take account of significance levels above 1 per cent (denoted by one asterisk in the table above), but require at least two asterisks. Statistically significant associations (at 1 per cent level or less) are thus marked with arrows in the table above. Upward-pointing arrows denote a positive association with exit and entry, downward-pointing ones negative associations. By comparing the results between periods, we get an impression of the development over time. We will discuss separately the results for cultivators (the odds of exit) and for non-cultivators (the odds of entry to cultivation).

Controlling for age and partitioning of households

Starting with the control variables, and thinking of households that were cultivators to start with, we see that partitioning had a significant effect only in Period 1 (1971–82) when there was a negative association with exit. In other words, even if a 1971 household had been partitioned, there was a tendency for the descendant household to keep cultivating land and by implication usually to stay in the village. This pattern is not repeated over time. In later periods descendants in partitioned households became as likely to leave cultivation as to stay, relative speaking. Even if there is no evidence of the association turning from negative to positive, this is still a clear indication that, despite traditional laws stipulating partible inheritance, fathers are becoming less prone to divide their holdings and sons more prone to leave agriculture.[15] This is obviously an indication of ST gaining pace from the early 1980s.

The age of the head of the household at the end of the period shows another pattern. During the first two periods there was no association between age and the odds of change of status, while during the third period the association turned

Table 5.7 Model 1 Entry and exit to cultivation

Parameter	*Panel 1, 1971–82*			*Panel 2, 1982–99*			*Panel 3, 1994/95–2004/05*		
	B	*Sig.*		*B*	*Sig.*		*B*	*Sig.*	
Constant	–1.41			–2.56	**	↘	1.81	***	↗
Autoregressive component: Cultivator status at start of period	–1.78	***	↘	–0.37			–2.07	***	↘
Ecotype									
Intermediate ecotype	0.40			0.01			0.09		
Wet ecotype	0.15			0.19			0.20		
Household partitioned since start of period	–1.26	***	↘	0.03			0.00		
Age of HH, logged	0.19			0.34			–0.30	**	↘
Caste groups									
Brahmin and other Upper Caste	0.08			–0.21			–0.41	***	↘
Scheduled Caste	0.38			0.47	*		0.25	*	
Scheduled Tribe	0.09			–0.17			–0.25		
Other Backward Caste	–0.06			0.15			–0.20		
Farm type, large farmer, among 20% largest landowners in District									
Family farmer, narrow definition	0.87	***	↗	0.45			0.40	***	↗
Smallholders – agricultural labourer	2.19	***	↗	1.25	***	↗	0.66	***	↗
Landless agricultural labourer	1.36	***	↗	2.26	***	↗	0.12		
Non–agricultural household	0.93	***	↗	1.71	***	↗	0.00		
Petty landlord	0.00			1.16	***	↗			
Gone pluriactive since start of period	0.04			–0.48			–0.01		
Joint family, at the end of period	–0.80	***	↘	–0.72	***	↘	–0.91	***	↘
Head of household studied beyond primary level, dummy	–0.22			0.21			–0.21	***	↘
Proportion of non–farm income, village level mean	0.97	***	↗	1.10	***	↗	1.40	***	↗
No. of cases	2844			2731			10255		
Missing (%)	43			45			1		
–2*Loglikehood, null model	3203.41			3477.22			13165.10		
–2*Loglikehood, full model	1456.96			2687.60			9106.94		
Chi2, p–value of	0.00	***		0.00	***		0.00	***	

Source: ARIS REDS data

Note: Constant" denotes $\hat{\alpha}$ i.e. the estimated α. Similarly "B" denotes the estimated regression coefficients ($\hat{\beta}$). Arrows denote positive and negative associations so that an upward pointing arrow indicates a positive correlation with exit/entry, while *, ** and *** denote 5 per cent, 1 per cent and 0.1 per cent level of significance significantly negative. Thus, from no association in the earlier periods we get a negative one from the mid or late 90s, meaning that the older the head of the household, the higher the odds that he (because it is usually a "he") would remain in cultivation. This can be taken to be an effect of ST with the new pattern being that the older generation tends to keep control of farm management, perhaps because the likelihood is lower that there is a younger generation to take over.

It has to be kept in mind that this effect of age is independent of the effect of other independent variables.[16] Thus we keep separate the effect of partitioning, already discussed, which used to be for descendants to stay in cultivation and by implication in the village, and the effect of age of head of household, which changed from zero to negative, meaning the older people are more likely to stay in cultivation and postpone the partitioning of the holding.[17]

Having looked at the control variables, age and partition, it is time to get a grip over other drivers of the ST.

Integration of the village in the non-farm economy

We first look at the level of ST of the village economy, as operationalized by the village mean share of income from non-farm sources (see Figure 5.5 below).

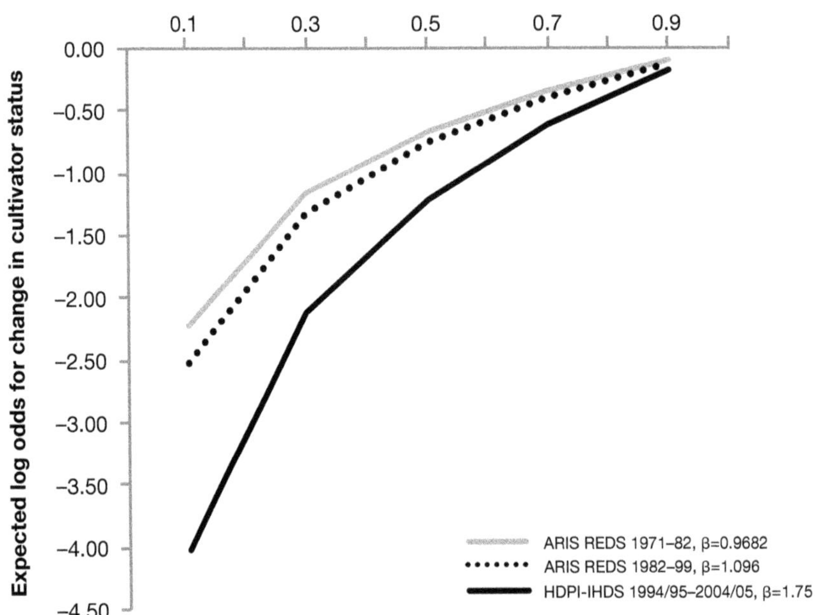

Figure 5.5 Odds for exit/entry to cultivation by village mean share of income from non-farm sources, expected values by survey panel

Data source: ARIS REDS and HDPI-IHDS surveys

Note: Expected values are calculated from the estimated models (see see Appendix Table A3.1). Note that the regression coefficients for village level mean share of non-farm income are reproduced in the legend

The regression coefficients (β) in Figure 5.5 indicate how much the odds for exit/entry can be expected to change for a given value of the independent variable (in the Graph x = 0.1, 0.3, 0.5, 0.7, 0.9). The increasing values of the regression coefficient, from 0.97 in the first period to 1.75 in the last one indicate generally increasing odds, as is to be expected during the ST. All three lines tilt upwards, i.e. in all panels the odds for exit increased with the village mean share of income from non-farm sources. Lines are increasingly tilted, not so much between the first two periods, as between the second and third one. The interpretation seems given: differences are increasing between villages that are weakly and highly integrated into the non-farm economy and the pace of ST is going up, especially in villages highly integrated in the non-farm economy. Thus we see an increasing pace of the agrarian ST and, as this result also implies, growing spatial inequalities.[18]

Household level of integration in the non-farm economy

Village-level integration in the non-farm economy obviously has a counterpart at the household level. In other words, households may be either highly pluriactive with important sources of livelihood and income outside the farm, or heavily dependent on the farm. While the non-farm share of household income could be used as an indicator here, we have opted for another indicator, which works equally well, at least for the earlier periods. This is a time-dependent dummy, called "gone pluriactive," taking the value of unity if the household was exclusively relying on farm income at the start of a period and had gone pluriactive at the end.

For none of the periods is there any association between "gone pluriactive" and the odds of exit/entry. This should mean that the entire effect of pluriactivity is caught by the village-level variable discussed in the preceding section.

Irrigation intensity and ecotype

Whether irrigation intensity has any influence on the level and pace of ST is not given. There are reports that dry villages and regions are more attractive to investors in rural industries, which would speak for a faster integration in the non-farm economy in the dry ecotype (Foster and Rosenzweig 2004, Lindberg, Athreya *et al.* 2011, Lindberg, Athreya *et al.* 2014).

However, there is no evidence in these data sets to support such a hypothesis. As illustrated in Table 5.7 on page 83 there is no association at all between ecotype and the odds for exit/entry. Thus the hypothesis about higher level and pace of ST in dry villages receives no support at all from this exercise, maybe because that effect is caught by the other village-level variable, e.g. mean proportion of non-farm income.

Joint family

We started the modelling exercise using a joint family dummy at the start of a given period and got no significant associations. Scrutinizing the time dimension, there is no need for assuming that joint family formation precedes strategies for exiting or entering cultivation. On the contrary, formation of a joint family may be a strategy for using family labour power to remain in farming, or the reverse, viz. as a resource when taking up cultivation. Instead of joint family at the start of period, we here test the role of having formed a joint family during the period.

The result is a very clear pattern, with a consistently high and statistically significant *negative* association between being a joint family at the end of a period and the odds for a household to have exited (compare to Table 5.3 on page 74). For non-cultivators, having become a joint family thus hampers entry to cultivation, maybe because pluriactivity is a more attractive option.

The regression coefficients for the joint family dummy lie between 0.7 and 0.9 in all panels. Taking the exponents of this, this again means that a joint family who were cultivators had between 2 and 2.5 times higher odds of having exited at the end of a period than other types of families, especially nuclear ones. It is difficult to escape the conclusion that the agrarian ST in India has weakened the role of joint families, a finding mostly going against the stereotypes.[19]

Education

Many observers would assume that individuals with higher education would be more likely to exit cultivation and less likely enter into it. Again we prefer to be open on the issue. To start with we worked with a literacy dummy, which however turned up little in terms of significant associations. When we switched to a primary education dummy, taking the value of unity for household heads who had completed primary school at the start of the period studied and zero otherwise, we arrived at some interesting results. In the ARIS REDS data we still saw little association but in the HDPI-IHDS panel we get a strongly significant and negative association between primary education and the odds of exit for cultivators.[20]

This is interesting because it says the opposite of what many theories of education would suggest. A somewhat speculative interpretation would be that Indian agriculture is becoming professionalized; in order to be a successful entrepreneur in farming there is an increasing need for some level of education. The corresponding interpretation for non-cultivators is that primary education would lower the odds of entry. Intuitively and not surprisingly, going into farming is an unattractive option to them.

Farm type

We have come to a pivotal part of this chapter, viz. the test of the family farm hypothesis. This is the hypothesis that along with the agrarian ST, family labour farms would strengthen their position, both *vis-à-vis* large landed estates dependent on hired labour and versus smallholder–agricultural labourers. The stronger position of family labour farms would partly be a consequence of the upward pressure on wages, resulting from a competition for labour with the industrial and service sectors.

The family labour farm hypothesis is operationalized by means of farm type. To repeat, this is a nominal scale containing the three positions: (1) large landowners, (2) family farmers, (3) smallholder–agricultural labourers. In order to cover the entire sample, the farm typology is complemented with three non-cultivator household types: (4) landless agricultural labourers, (5) non-agrarian households and (6) petty landlords. Owners of large estates who may or may not be cultivators are here the reference category. This means the regression coefficients for other types should be read as comparing the odds of entry/exit for a given category compared to the reference category. When looking at cultivators we compare with large landowners cultivating some of their land; while in the case of non-cultivators, like landless labourers, we compare with owners of large estates who lease out all their land. The latter is a small category in the last period, which as we will see creates some complications. (Consult Table 5 2 on page 71).

The results appear an almost deadly blow to the family farm hypothesis. Except for one panel, ARIS REDS for 1982–99, family farmers have seen higher odds of exit than large landowners. Disregarding the non-significant one for 1982–99, the regression coefficients range between ($0.4 < \hat{\beta} < 0.9$), which taking the exponents means that family farmers have had between 1.5 and 2.5 times higher odds of exiting agriculture than large landowners. The only period when this tendency weakened somewhat was during the second phase of the Green Revolution, when it spread beyond the original wheat areas in Punjab and Haryana to rice in the rest of India, i.e. from 1982 onwards in our data. After that period the tendency seems to have resumed with stronger tendencies for family farmers than for large landowners to opt out of agriculture.

The results for smallholder–agricultural labourers are comparable but even stronger and hold for all three periods. The regression coefficients vary between periods, with β-values ranging from 2.19 during 1971–82 and 1.26 during 1982–99 and a weaker value for HDPI-IHDS of 0.66. Thus, the odds of exit for smallholders appear even higher than for family farmers and much higher than for large landowners. Contrary to the family labour farm hypothesis it seems large landowners are entrenched in farming, while family labour farms are less so. However, when looking in the next chapter at the distribution of operated area, we will modify this conclusion.

Caste

An obvious question to ask is what consequences the above results have for the odds of the several caste groups to change cultivator status. Here we use Other Castes to compare the odds for entry/exit for Brahmins and Other High Castes, Scheduled Castes and Tribes (SC, ST) and Other Backward Castes (OBC). As usual Table 5.7 on page 83 shows the results. Interestingly, in two first periods, there were no significant differences between the Caste Groups in the odds of entry to or exit from farming. This changed in the third period when Brahmins and other Upper Castes had lower odds of entry/exit (mostly exit) than the reference category of Other Castes. This also goes against expectation, which says that the Upper

Castes who run family-managed farms, rather than family labour ones, would be tending to lose out. Again, as we will see the study of mobility with size-classes of operated area will modify this conclusion.

More on entry to the farm sector

Above we have mainly discussed the odds of exit from the farm sector. Let's look also to the opposite movement, i.e. entry to the sector. This is relevant for non-cultivators and mainly for landless labour households and of course for non-agrarian ones. There are two conceivable ways for them to enter cultivation, either by purchasing land, or by leasing it. One can assume that the former is relatively rare among landless labourers whose capacity to save enough to buy land is limited. On the other hand, their possibilities of leasing land would largely depend on what is on offer and on the lease conditions. We note the highest odds for entry for landless agricultural labourers during the second ARIS REDS period, from 1982 to 1999, when the logged odds were 2.26 higher than for large non-cultivating landowners. During the period before that, they were somewhat lower but still high ($\hat{\beta} = 1.36$). The 1994/95–2004/05 panel indicates that the coefficient was much lower from the mid-90s onwards ($\hat{\beta} = 0.12$). This is a statistically significant decline with lower odds of entry for landless labourers pointing both to increasing competition for labour with the non-agrarian sectors and perhaps also to less land entering lease markets, at least in the small parcels that we assume would be interesting for landless labourers to lease.

Regional disparities

Below is a table giving the variance shares according to level and period. The conclusion already drawn that regional disparities are increasing is reinforced by the increasing variance between States, which does not reach statistical significance until Period 3, when on the other hand between-State variance became more than half of the total. This conclusion also implies that variance within States become less with time. The latter is mirrored in the between-district variance for Period 3, which was considerably lower than that for the first two periods. The ground for drawing the conclusion that State policies become more important for what happens at State level is undeniably weak, but these results do point in that

Table 5.8 Share of variance in Model 1, according level and period of panel

Random effects:	*Panel 1, 1971–82*	*Sig.*	*Panel 2, 1982–99*	*Sig.*	*Panel 3, 1994/95–2004/05*	*Sig.*
State	0.25		0.04		0.42	**
District	0.31	**	0.28	*	0.14	***
Village	0.22		0.42	***	0.24	***

Source: ARIS REDS and HDPI–IHDS

Note: *, ** and *** denote 5 per cent, 1 per cent and 0.1 per cent levels of significance. SE = standard error direction. It is more difficult to draw any definite conclusions from the trends in the between-village variance, which as seen from the figures in the above table, takes an inverted U-shaped distribution between the periods, with the highest value for 1982–99 mirroring the low between States variance in the same period. We refrain from suggesting an interpretation for this result.

We will instead look at the hypothesis advanced by Reddy *et al.* (2014, 2015) that some States have reached a Lewis Turning Point (LTP), while others are lagging (see page 66). Figure 5.6 consists of three graphs showing the State-wise residuals for the three periods and the LTP status for different States, i.e. results in line with those of Reddy *et al.*

There are too few cases (i.e. too few States) to make any statistical tests of the differences between States and rank in terms of residuals in the above graphs. For Period 2 moreover and due to the high attrition, there are several states missing. But a pattern seems to emerge, viz. that backward States, marked with large black triangles, lie closer together in the third period than earlier and with ranks above the mean meaning lower ranks of exit than others.

Conclusions

Keeping to what was established above, we can conclude that there is solid evidence of an agrarian structural transformation in India, which unsurprisingly seems to gain in pace and be quickest in villages that are already highly integrated into the non-agrarian economy.

The macro data presented in the early parts of the chapter indicate that the pace of transformation quickened since the period covered here, making way for new levels and modalities of transformation, possibly changing some of the above results.

The other hypothesis developed in the first two chapters of this book, about agrarian structural transformation leading to an increasing predominance of family labour farms, does not do well in these tests. If anything, family labour seem to have lost position in Indian farming, with large landed properties dependent on hired labour strengthening theirs, until the last panel period when rates of exit did not differ significantly between large landowners and family labour farms. The explanation for this is not to be found in the data, but will have to be conjectural. A possible explanation is that until 2004/05, competition for labour between the farm sector and the service and industrial sectors was not hard enough to induce labourers to leave farming and to create an upward pressure on wages. This could also explain the growing proportion of landless labour households throughout the period.[21] Thus there is so far no solid evidence in our data of a development akin to what has been documented for other periods and parts of the world, of large landowners leaving the farm sector. Instead we witness a strengthening of what we have called the smallholder–agricultural labourers who, according to cross-sectional data grew to nearly 25 per cent of the rural population in 2004/05 (see Table 5 1 on page 69).

This again has consequences for another surprising result of the above, viz. that unlike what many believe to be the case, Brahmins and Other Upper Castes were

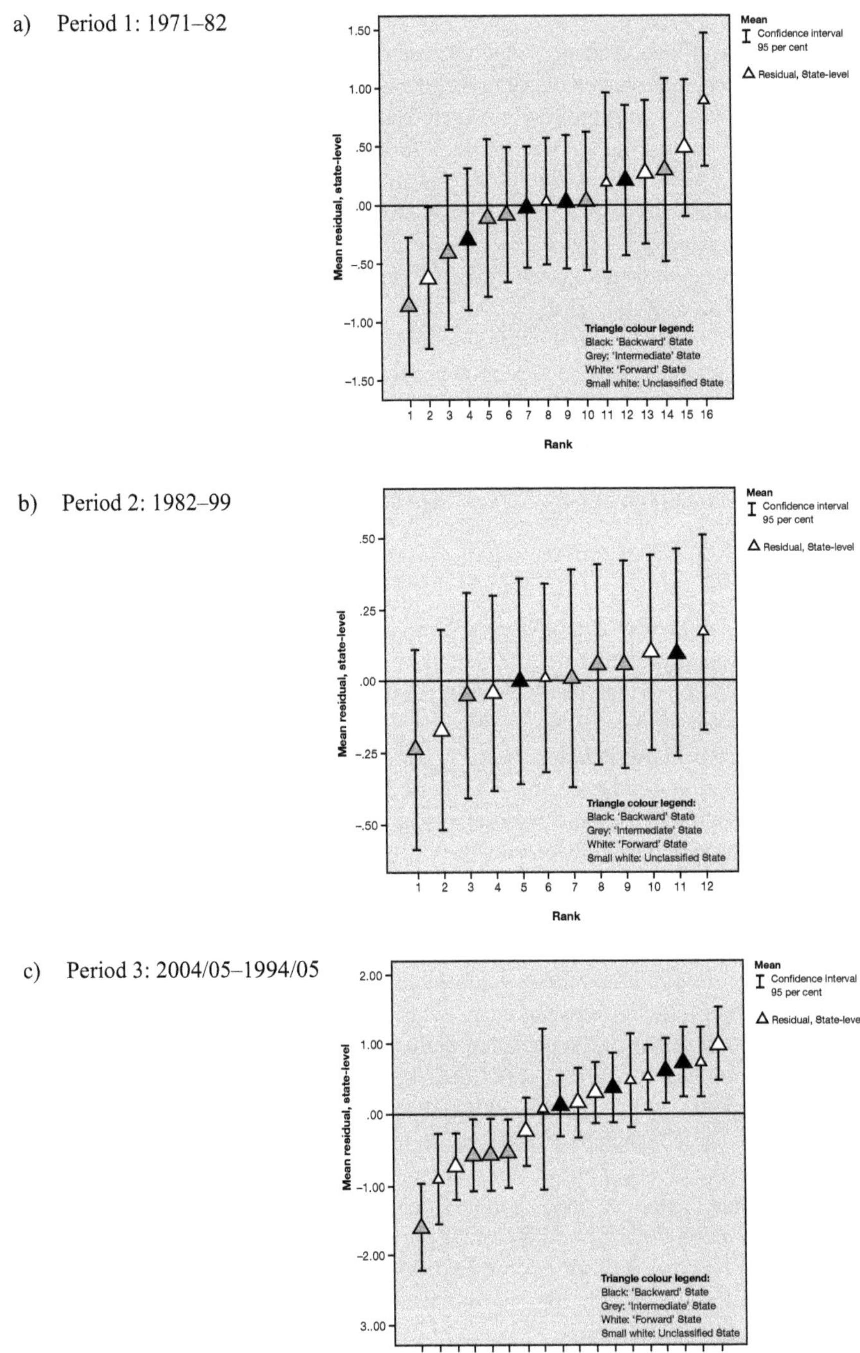

Figure 5.6 State-wise residuals for Model 1, Periods 1, 2 and 3

not leaving the sector at a faster pace than others. On the contrary, at least until 2004/05, these castes have apparently retained a grip over their landholdings, but as we will see in the next chapter, their holdings seem to have become considerably smaller over time, undermining the lordship based on feudal-like institutions, which these aristocratic castes used to enjoy. Although they still keep a considerable foothold in the sector they have not succeeded to retain their top-notch positions within a market-dominated, democratic setup.

Does this mean that the family labour farm hypothesis is entirely irrelevant in the Indian setup? As we will see in the next chapter, this may be to

Notes

1 A Lewis Turning Point is aptly defined in Wikipedia as a "term used in economic development to describe a point at which surplus rural labor reaches a financial zero. This in turn typically causes urban wages to rise dramatically. Upon reaching the Lewis turning point, a country or state usually experiences a labour shortage which leads to a rise in agricultural and unskilled industrial real wage[s].This usually continues until a labor surplus can be reached once again. Typically, reaching the Lewis turning point also causes an improvement in the wage bill and the functional distribution favoring labor." https://en.wikipedia.org/wiki/Lewis_turning_point downloaded March 10, 2016.

2 The village surveys conducted over a long period by ICRISAT in Hyderabad, Andhra Pradesh previously included input of family and hired permanent labour (but not daily hired labour), but questions on this were removed from the latest rounds and are therefore not very useful for our purposes Rao, Y. M., K. R. Chand, V. Kiresur and M. Bantilan (2011). Documentation of Second-Generation Village Level Studies (VLS) in India (2001/02–2004/05). Patancheru, 502304 Andhra Pradesh, India, ICRISAT, International Crop Research Institute for the Semi-Arid Tropics..

3 As discussed in Chapter 1, scholars have attempted to estimate the preponderance of family farms worldwide by means of the Agricultural Censuses that are taken worldwide. See above p. ix and pp. 5 ff.

4 Which is real in ontological terms, as defined for example by Bosc, P.-M., J. Marzin, J.-F. Bélières, J.-M. Sourisseau, P. Bonnal, Bruno Losch, P. Pédelahore and L. Parrot (2015). "Defining, Characterizing and Measuring Family Farming Models." *Family Farming and the Worlds to Come*. J.-M. Sourisseau (ed.). Dordrecht, Springer. See also: Bhaskar, R. (1975). *A Realist Theory of Science*. Brighton, Harvester Press, Bhaskar, R. (1989). *Reclaiming Reality: A critical introduction to contemporary philosophy*. London, Verso.

5 Except owners of less than 10 hectares, who occasionally turn up among the 20 per cent with the largest holdings in a district.

6 Petty since the large landlords possibly receiving major land rents are classified as belonging to the agrarian population.

7 See Chapter 4 for a definition of this concept in regression analysis.

8 If this variable is coded as =1, the reference category, coded = 0, would contain two subsets: (i) those remaining "monoactive" and (ii) those ceasing to be pluriactive, i.e. specializing in farming. In the following we will not distinguish between categories (i) and (ii).

9 In their small sample in Tiruchy District Athreya *et al.* found some such cases in the early period (before 1979) while they found none in the later one (from 1979 to 2004).

In the first period of ARIS REDS there were some cases of entry into cultivation, while they are practically absent in the later rounds. A few cases can be found in the much larger HDPI-IHDS sample.

10 The ARIS REDS statistics are unweighted. The problematic 2006 wave of ARIS REDS contains only wet villages and has not been used here.

11 In statistics, random effects as opposed to fixed ones denote effects, the variance of which is assumed to contain no contribution from sampling error.

12 For details on how this is done see Appendix 2.

13 Caste group is time constant, so period need not be specified.

14 Since this model has a binary dependent variable (being a cultivator or not), it is not meaningful to include household level variance as random effect.

15 For a parallel finding for Tiruchy see: Djurfeldt, G., V. B. Athreya, N. Jayakumar, S. Lindberg, R. Vidyasagar and A. Rajagopal (2008) "Modelling Social Mobility in Rural Tamil Nadu." DOI: Lund University Publications: http://luur.lub.lu.se/luur?func=downloadFile&fileOId=1267070

16 Technically, drawing this conclusion requires a *non-biased* model with residuals being approximately normal. See the residual analysis in Appendix 3.

17 For non-cultivators, the same result implies that the odds for entry into cultivation by any member of the household diminish with increasing age of the head. For landless labour households, this could again reflect a lower supply of tenancies.

18 Scholars seem to be quite unanimous on this point: regional inequalities have been increasing in rural India, at least since the 1970s. See for example Kar, S. and S. Sakthivel (2007). "Reforms and Regional Inequality in India." *Economic and Political Weekly* 42(47): 69–77, Nagarajan, H. K., K. Pradhan and A. Sharma (no year). "The Curse of Location: Investigating links between income mobility, migration and location premium." New Delhi, NCAER, Puja, D. and H. K. Nagarajan (no year). "Spatial Inequality among Indian Villages: Do initial conditions matter?" New Delhi, NCAER.

19 Mukherjee's classical article on the issue shows that joint families were more prominent in small towns than in villages. Mukherjee, R. (1963). "Urbanization and Social Transformation in India." *International Journal of Comparative Sociology* **4**(2): 178–210. Kolenda stressed the regional and sub-regional variations in family patterns: Kolenda, P. M. (1968). "Region, Caste, and Family Structure: A comparative study of the Indian 'joint' family." *Structure and Change in Indian Society* (47): 339. See also Caldwell, J. C., P. H. Reddy and P. Caldwell (1984). "The Determinants of Family Structure in Rural South India." *Journal of Marriage and the Family* 46(1): 215–29.

20 This is a different problem to the one investigated by Foster and Rosenzweig working with the ARIS REDS data. Theirs was "the effects of exogenous technical change on the returns to schooling, the effects of schooling on the profitability of technical change, and the effects of technical change and school availability on household schooling investment" Foster, A. D. and M. R. Rosenzweig (1996). "Technical Change and Human-Capital Returns and Investments: Evidence from the Green Revolution." *The American Economic Review* **86**(4): 931–53.

21 With a small dip in 1982 (compare to Table 5.7 on page 83).

6 Volatility in land distribution

Having investigated exit from the agricultural sector in the previous chapter, we concluded that the structural transformation (ST) in rural India not only goes on, but increases in pace and moreover that the inequalities growing between villages and regions are weakly or highly integrated into the non-farm economy. These results support one of the main hypotheses of this book. On the other hand, we get less clear-cut support for our hypotheses on the effects of ST on agrarian structures. The entry/exit model points to a weakening of family labour farms at the same time as large landowners are more resilient. There may have been a break in trends in the latest period studied, but this is not firmly established. What is clear however is that smallholder– agricultural labourers as well as landless labourers have grown in terms of their share of the agrarian population.

From a structure increasingly dominated by family labour farms we would expect tendencies towards a unimodal land distribution, i.e. with most farms concentrated in the middle of the size distribution. Increased unimodality is one characteristic of comparable cases in the west as well as in East Asia (see pp. 22 ff. above). This means that with the ST of the agrarian sector, everything else equal, we would expect volatility in the size distribution and a movement away from bimodality and towards unimodality. Expressed in terms of our main hypothesis on farm types, we would predict large landowners to lose land and smaller-sized family labour farms to augment their share of the cultivated area, if not of the owned one. This is of course contrary to what many observers believe to be the case: inspired by Leninist or classical economic theories about farming getting dominated by "factories in the field," they foresee a bimodal agrarian structure rather than a unimodal one (Das 2014 is one exception). However our "unimodality" hypothesis did not gain much support in the previous chapter, so in the current one we remain open to the exact development in terms of size-classes.

The smallholder–agricultural labourers is an operationalization of the combination farmers discussed in Chapter 1 (see page 16). What would we expect in terms of mobility in size-class in their case? It is more difficult to formulate a precise hypothesis, since pluriactivity gets in the way. Ever more pluriactive livelihoods make it possible for smallholders to retain their landholdings, subsidized by off-farm earnings, which progressively stem less from agricultural labour and more from non-agrarian sources.

But the effects of pluriactivity are profound also for other farm types. For large landowners' households, increased wage bills, as an effect of competition for labour with the non-farm sector, may be offset both by earnings from non-farm sources and by savings from such sources, not consumed but invested in labour-saving machinery like tractors, threshers and irrigation pumps.

Family labour farmers depend on pluriactivity too. Remembering that their advantage lies exactly in their supply of non-wage labour, the earnings of family labourers may increase if that labour is also pluriactive and contributing cash earnings towards consumption, as well as farm investments.

All in all and on a general and theoretical level the bimodality of the size distribution inherited from British rule, characterized by many small farms and a small proportion of large farms, would thus be expected to change towards an increasingly unimodal one. As we have seen in Chapter 1, this pattern held for a number of Western and other countries including almost the entire region of East Asia. Will it hold also for India, or will this hypothesis need modification in the face of empirical evidence? In view of our hypotheses the results of the panel data we are working with are indeed encouraging.

Before coming to the relative distribution of land, we will briefly look at the absolute distribution.

The mean area cultivated, and obviously also the one owned to a large extent is driven by India's still high population growth. Means have decreased throughout the period, with the exception of the period 1982 to 1994/95, when they went up. This result should obviously not be taken at face value and indicates the noise level in the data.

These distributions are obviously skewed with a tail to the right, implying first that the modes are close to the means rather than the medians. Presuming unimodality, the modal farm sizes seem to hint at smallholder rather than family labour predominance.

But relative distributions are better studied by means of Lorenz curves and Gini indices. The graphs shown in Figures 6.1 and 6.2 contain relative distributions first of owned and then of cultivated area.

Above are the Lorenz curves for distribution of owned area according to the four survey rounds. Such a curve gives the per centage-wise distribution of land among, in this case, deciles of households. If land had a completely equal distribution, we would expect a curve lying close to the diagonal marking equality. The further removed from the diagonal, the greater is the inequality.

Table 6.1 Owned and cultivated area, hectares by period. Mean and standard error (within brackets)

	Cross–section			
Area:	1971	1982	1994/95	2004/05
Owned	4.29 (0.12)	3.29 (0.07)	4.82 (0.06)	2.86 (0.21)
Cultivated	4.06 (0.10)	4.13 (0.08)	6.02 (0.06)	0.59 (0.03)

Source: ARIS REDS and HDPI–IHDS surveys

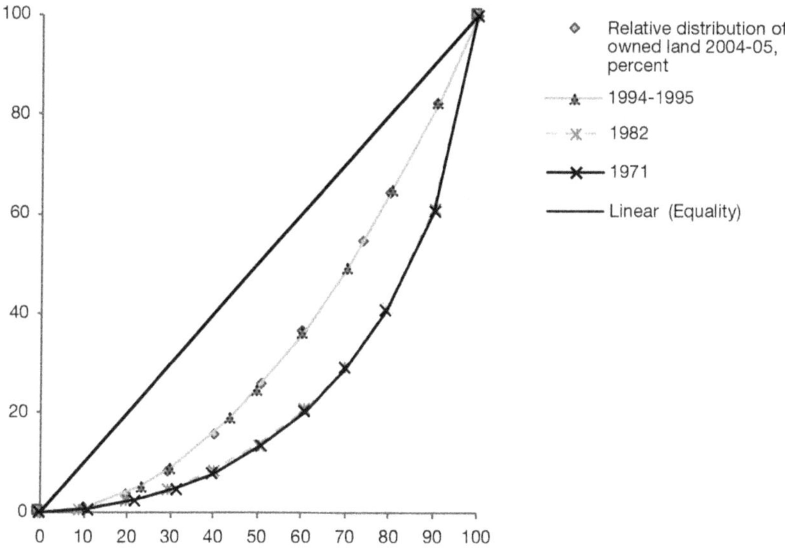

Figure 6.1 The distribution of owned area by cross-section (Lorenz curves)
Source: ARIS REDS and HDPI-IHDS surveys

According to our data, a massive reduction of inequality occurred between 1971 and 1982. After that period the level of inequality seems to have stayed more or less constant and in the above graph the curves for the later rounds are indistinguishable.

One could have worried that a marked difference between ARIS REDS and HDPI-IHDS data could be due to differences in method between the surveys, but this explanation for the reduced inequality need not worry us, since the major difference is between the first round of ARIS REDS and subsequent rounds.

Scholars working in the tradition of Lipton, Hazell and others who have stressed the smallholder friendliness of the Green Revolution (Lipton and Longhurst 1989, Hazell and Ramasamy 1991) would perhaps not be surprised by this apparent reduction in inequality. But recall the phases of the Green Revolution in India with its first phase occurring for wheat in the 1970s and then mainly in Punjab, Haryana and parts of Uttar Pradesh, while the second phase mainly involved rice and occurred from the 1980s and onwards (Bhalla and Singh 2001). Most researchers would date the end of the Green Revolution to some time in the 1990s. These facts seem at odds with an explanation attributing the reduced inequality entirely to the Green Revolution. Explanations must be sought elsewhere and it remains to be seen if the detailed analysis later in this chapter will provide any clues.

The relative distribution of cultivated area looks somewhat different than that of owned area. See the graph in Figure 6.2.

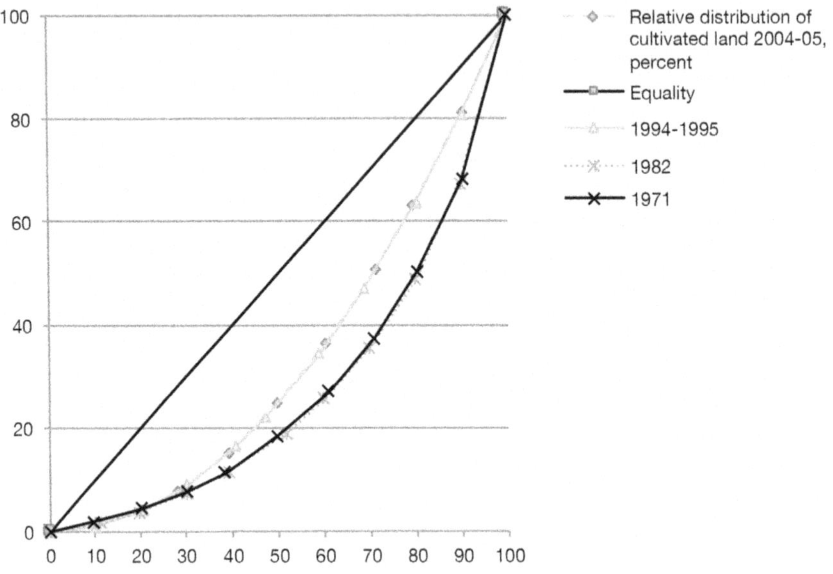

Figure 6.2 The distribution of cultivated area by cross-section (Lorenz curves)
Source: ARIS REDS and HDPI-IHDS surveys

The Lorenz curve for distribution of cultivated area in 1971 completely overlaps that in 1982, but then a jump in inequality took place until 1994/95. Recalling the results of Model 1 in the previous chapter, this apparently reflects the setback for the equalizing effects of the Green Revolution which occurred in the 1980s. In that chapter we got the opposite effects on farm types compared both to the earlier period and compared to expectations. In the 1980s large landowners consolidated their holdings, rather than opting out as our hypothesis predicted.

The above figures thus contradict much received wisdom about the effects of ST on the distribution of cultivated land. These visual impressions are supported by the Gini coefficients in the Table 6.2.

The Gini indices were stable from 1970 to 1982, but then fell steeply after that. During the last two periods, from 1994/95 to 2004/05 we thus see a marked deconcentration in the relative distribution of both owned and cultivated areas. This is a remarkable finding, which requires both validation and explanation.[1]

Table 6.2 Gini indices for owned and cultivated area, by period

	Owned area	*Cultivated area*
1970	0.42	0.42
1982	0.41	0.42
1994/95	0.28	0.30
2004/05	0.26	0.21

Source: ARIS REDS and HDPI–IHDS surveys

Concluding from the above, we are dealing with distributions characterized by sharply decreasing farm sizes and, parallel to that, decreasing inequality as well. It follows from this that, in terms of mobility of individual households, most cultivator households would be downwardly mobile, at least when comparing the land sizes of descendants to those of their ancestors. We would also expect low rates of upward mobility, and less stability in size-class.

These expectations are borne out in Table 6.3, but again the 1982–99 period represents a setback, or a reversal of trends. During this second period of the Green Revolution, focused now on rice rather than wheat, rates of stability and also of upward mobility were higher than ever, reflected in a much lower rate of downward mobility than before or after. During the end of the 1990s patterns of mobility returned to those seen inthe 70s, but grew even stronger (see Table 6.3 below).

When comparing the rates of mobility between periods in the above table, one must keep in mind the difference in duration of the periods compared. The second and the third periods are of comparable duration and should, other things being equal, have comparable rates of mobility. This is the case for upward mobility, but not downward, which seems to have increased considerably. The same is the case for stability. The period in-between is of much longer duration and, since much mobility occurs at generational shifts, should have lower rates of stability, which is not at all the case: Given the duration of the period, 1982–99 shows remarkable stability, the lowest rates of downward mobility, and the highest upward mobility. The first part of this period overlaps with the second period of the Green Revolution, while the second saw the so-called neo-liberal reforms of the Manmohan Singh Ministry. What happened during that period which could explain these patterns? We will return to that question later.

Model 2: Mobility between size-classes of cultivated area

We can now pose the question of what factors influence the probability of being downwardly or upwardly mobile in size-class of cultivated area. Formulated this way, the problem can be addressed with a multinomial logistic regression model (see Appendix 2).

Irrigation intensity

The expansion of irrigation in India affected the ecotypes differently. In an earlier phase, the government invested much in expansion and improvement of canal irrigation systems, while later more was invested, to a large extent privately, in the

Table 6.3 Mobility in size-class of operated area by panel period, row per cent

Period	*Downward*	*Stable*	*Upward*	*Total*
1971–82	52.1	42.5	5.4	100.0
1982–99	41.8	46.3	11.9	100.0
1994/05–2004/05	89.1	5.4	5.4	100.0

Source: ARIS REDS AND IHDS surveys

expansion of well irrigation, a development, which we believe benefited mainly the dry and the intermediate ecotype. The latter led to a concentration of investments in irrigable soils and a comparative neglect of rainfed ones, which in turn must have caused a great deal of volatility in size-class of area. Thus we would expect higher mobility in the dry ecotype during the second period.

Integration of the village into the non-agrarian economy

Of the various indicators of integration of the village into the non-agrarian economy we have tested, the village mean proportion of non-farm income seems to work best and can be used to test a hypothesis about the effect of "deagrarianization" at village level on mobility in size-class of cultivated area. The effect would depend upon an intervening variable, viz. the propensity for households to reinvest earnings from non-agricultural sources in agriculture. Given the profitability of such investments we would expect high level of integration into the non-agricultural economy at the village level to be positively associated with low mobility among the size-classes of cultivated area.

Farm types

A main hypothesis to be tested by means of Model 2 is that mobility among size-classes of cultivated area is leading to downward mobility in size-class of area on the part of large landowners dependent on hired labour. We derive this from our overall hypothesis saying that competition with the non-agricultural sector for labour leads to an upward pressure on wages, which in turn hits most those who cannot compensate for this by increasing inputs of family labour, i.e. the large landowners dependent on hired labour.

Mirroring the above, our second hypothesis states that family farmers are expected on average to be less downwardly mobile in size-class of area. The corresponding hypothesis on rates of exit from cultivation in the previous chapter did not survive testing. Keeping this in mind we may have to revise our expectations on the mobility of family farmers.

What about the lowest class of farmers, i.e. the smallholder–agricultural labourers who combine own cultivation with labouring for wages? Our hypothesis is related to what we discussed in the previous sections: during the first period there was some movement into cultivation by labourers with accumulated savings acquiring land, but possibly not enough to compensate for the counter-tendency, i.e. the exit of smallholder–agricultural labourers stimulated by higher earnings outside the agrarian sector. As we found out from Model 1, there was considerable exit among smallholders during the first Green Revolution period, a tendency that weakened in the second period from 1982 to 1999. Hypothesis 3 follows from this, viz. that the odds of smallholders–agricultural labourers to be stable in size-class would increase from the first period to the second one. Thinking of the overall growth of the smallholder–agricultural labourers a revised hypothesis on the mobility chances of smallholders compared to those of family farmers would be that the upwards odds of mobility would be higher for the former than for the latter.

Caste groups

Recalling the results of Model 1 for caste group, we found few significant differences, except for relatively lower odds for the Brahmin and Other Upper Caste group to exit cultivation in the third period. Given that the regression coefficients in Model 2 refer to a reference category, that is the odds of stability, we would expect Brahmin and Upper Caste households to have higher odds of being stable or upwardly mobile in size-class of cultivated area in later periods.

Joint family

In view of its pooled resources, economically as well in terms of labour, one would expect a joint family to have comparatively higher odds of stability or upward mobility in size-class of cultivated area compared to nuclear or incomplete nuclear families. This tendency could be moderated by pluriactivity, however. In the Tamil Nadu case we found a tendency for pluriactive joint families to have invested in farming, increasing their propensity to have been upwardly mobile. This mechanism would not come into play if opportunities appear better for investments of labour or capital in non-farm sources of income. Thus we have to be open with regard to the influence of joint family in the all-India context (Djurfeldt, Athreya *et al.* 2008).

Age and partition

As regards age of head of household, we would expect different patterns to emerge in situations where it becomes increasingly difficult to manage a farm relying entirely on hired labour. If this is the case, and controlling for partition, our hypothesis is that the older the head of the household, the less likely it is that he (because it is normally a "he") would have been upwardly mobile since the start of the period. Moreover, this tendency should have been strengthened during the later Green Revolution period 1982/99 and also the third period (1994/95 to 2004/05), making for higher negative regression coefficients in Period 2.

However, the logical content of the variable partition is not the same in Period 1 as in Period 2. When in 1982, households previously interviewed were revisited, the interviewers were instructed to go to the same house and interview the current head of household, given that he was, either the same person as in 1971 or a descendant of the latter. If the latter was the case it is recorded in a separate variable (b04015). In 1999, on the hand, the interviewers were again instructed to visit the same house as in 1982, but if it was occupied by a descendant of the 1982 head of household, to locate and interview all the descendants. We in our turn have sampled one of these descendant households. Different procedures for selection make it difficult to compare the size of the regression coefficients for the two periods. Leaving aside comparability and given partible inheritance, one would expect that on average the descendants in both periods would have been downwardly mobile in size-class of cultivated area.

Fitting Model 2

It turns out that Model 2 is not easy to fit. While both Modesl 1 and 3 can easily be fit with the MLWin programme, the iterative procedure did not reach convergence in the case of Model 2. This is due to the dependent variable being nominal with three categories of mobility between size-classes of cultivated area: "downward," "stable" and "upward" movement. Of these categories upward mobility is not frequent and moreover becomes increasingly rare over time. The model further contains three categorical variables (ecotype, caste group and farm type) together with a number of binary variables or dummies. If one were to inspect the many combinations of the dependent and the independent variables one would find many empty cells that make it difficult for the algorithms to function and the iterative estimation to converge. This problem is aggravated by the low and decreasing upward mobility. In Appendix 3 we reproduce three non-converged models with a warning that the results must be treated with caution.

In order to achieve more reliable results,[2] we chose to work with what is known as Hansen–Hurwitz estimators (Christman 2002). This is a technique where you reweight cases so that the skew distribution of the outcome variable is removed. We thus generate a dataset where the outcomes (downward, stable, upward) are equally frequent. It has been shown that with this technique it is possible to establish statistically significant associations, with the right sign, but with possibly biased estimators. If you moreover fit the model in two steps, first running the full model with all independent variables discussed above and, in the second step remove variables which are not significant in the first step, you will get a reasonably good fit. It has to be remembered though that the estimates of regression coefficients may be biased. This makes it especially hazardous to compare regression coefficients between periods.

In Figure 6.3a–e on pages 101 to 104, results from the Hansen–Hurwitz estimation of Model 2 are presented in simplified form.

Modelling results

Looking at the results of Model 2 in Figure 6.3, note that the number of significant effects is highest in Period 3. This is because the HDPI-IHDS panel contains more cases than the two ARIS REDS panels. Moreover, the model for Period 1 seems the poorest one, with no significant fixed effects for upward mobility and with only two for downward mobility. This is probably due, both to the low number of cases in the panel, again due to difficulties in matching households for the 1982 – 99 panel, and also because of lower data quality.

The first step in interpreting the above results could have been to compile a list of variables that show no significant regression coefficients for any period. There are no such variables, but at the same time it is apparent that many variables appear only once, viz. in the Period 3 model. It is convenient therefore to first discuss the results for this period, with appropriate reference to the models for the earlier periods.

Farm types

Beginning with Period 3 the results on downwards mobility shows a rich model with many statistically significant effects, among them for smallholder–agricultural labourers. Together with the family farmers they face significantly lower risks of being downwardly mobile. These results tally nicely with our hypothesis that family farmers would be more stable in size-class of holding. So here, unlike in Chapter 5, the family labour farm hypothesis gains strong support from the data.

A similar result was established by Deininger *et al.* (2009) and constitutes strong support for the family farmer hypothesis, but with one important reservation: the resilience to downward mobility is high, not only for family labour farms, but also for smallholders. We have previously presented evidence that the opportunity of entry to cultivation of landless labourers is high, at least during the two first periods, as was also shown by Deininger *et al.* (2009). This considerably softens the blow that the family farm hypothesis received in the last

Figure 6.3a–e Regression coefficients for Model 2, by panel and for downward and upward mobility[3]

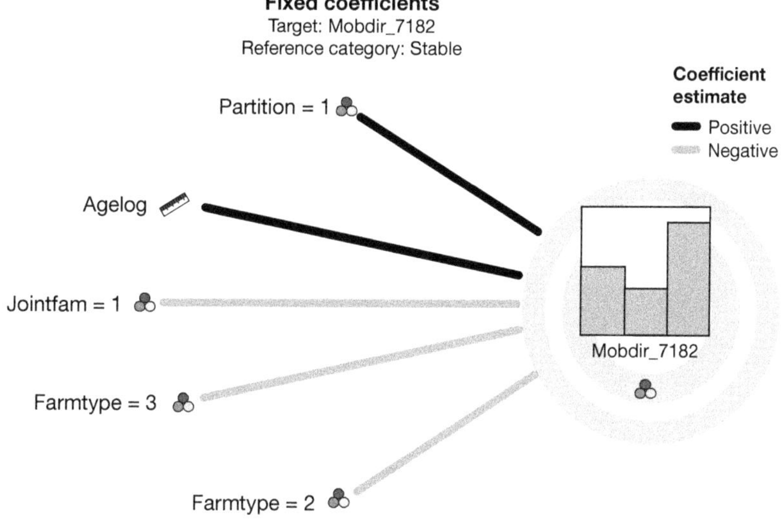

Figure 6.3a Period 1, downward mobility

Note: From the top the variables are statistically significant: partition,age of head of household, logged, joint family at start of period, dummy, smallholder-agricultural labourer dummy and family labour farm dummy

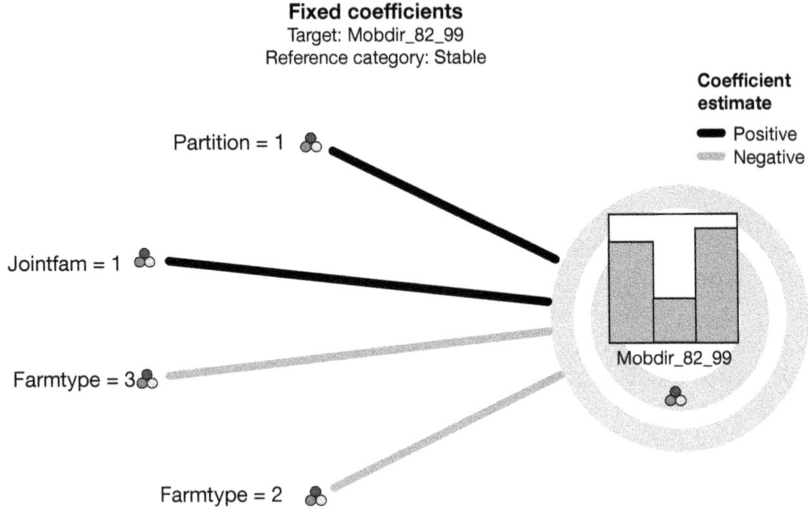

Figure 6.3b Period 2, downward mobility

Note: From the top: partition dummy, joint family dummy, smallholder-agricultural labourer, family labour farm

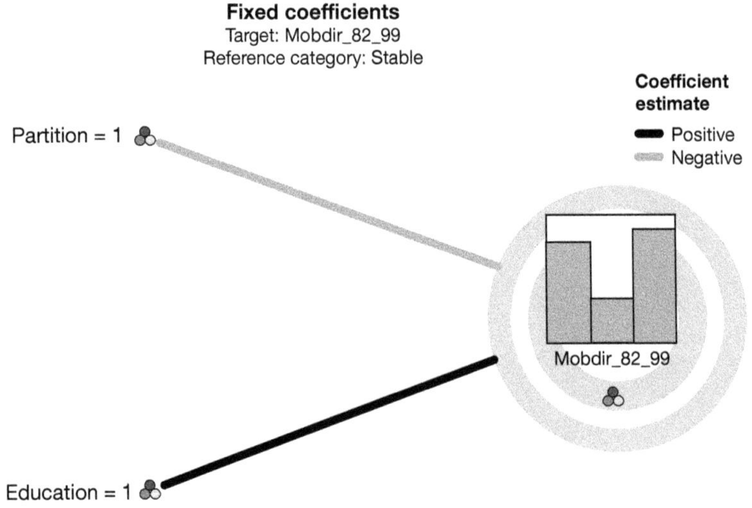

Figure 6.3c Period 2, upward mobility

Note: From the top: partition dummy, education dummy

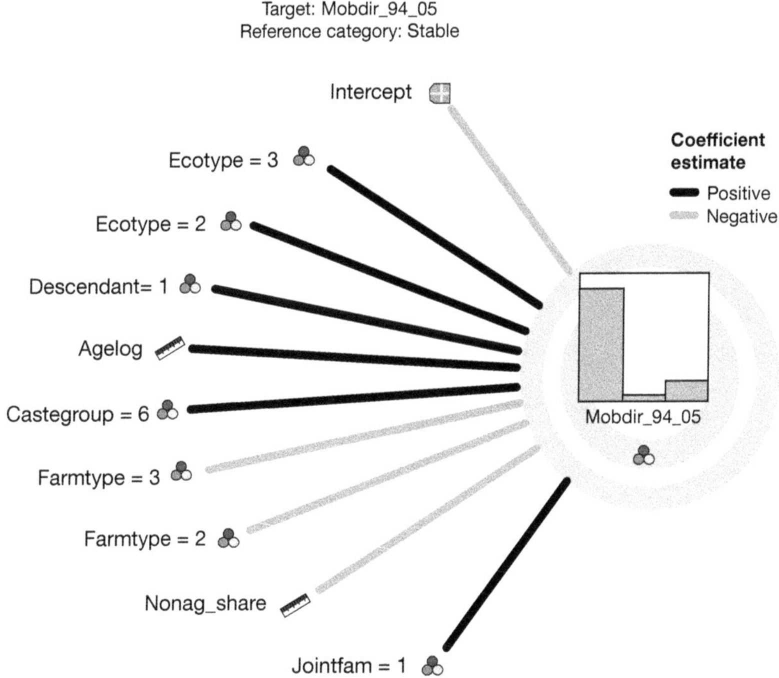

Figure 6.3d Period 3, downward mobility

Note: From the top: wet ecotype, intermediate ecotype, descendant dummy, age of head household, Other Backward Caste, smallholder–agricultural labourer, family labour farm, non-agricultural share of household income and joint family

chapter. However, our expectation that the tendency for family farmers to have become more resilient during the second phase of the Green Revolution and also afterwards cannot be reliably tested here, because the possible bias in the Hansen–Hurwitz estimators prevents testing the difference between regression coefficients for different periods.

What about the smallholders? For the last period the fixed effect for smallholder–agricultural labourers' downward mobility is significant and negative meaning that the odds for a smallholder to move downwards in size-class are quite low. It would be wrong to call this a surprising finding. Since smallholders generally cultivate small areas they can hardly move downwards in size-class. In practice their options are either to remain stable, move upwards, or exit cultivation.

Can this result be reconciled with the finding in Model 1 in Chapter 5 that smallholders had significantly higher odds of exit from the farm sector than the reference group of large landowners? Admittedly, their odds for exit seem to have gone down over time with a significantly steep fall between Periods 1 and 2.

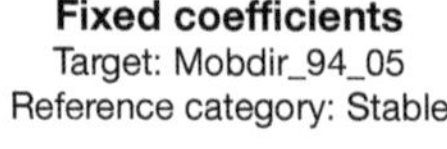

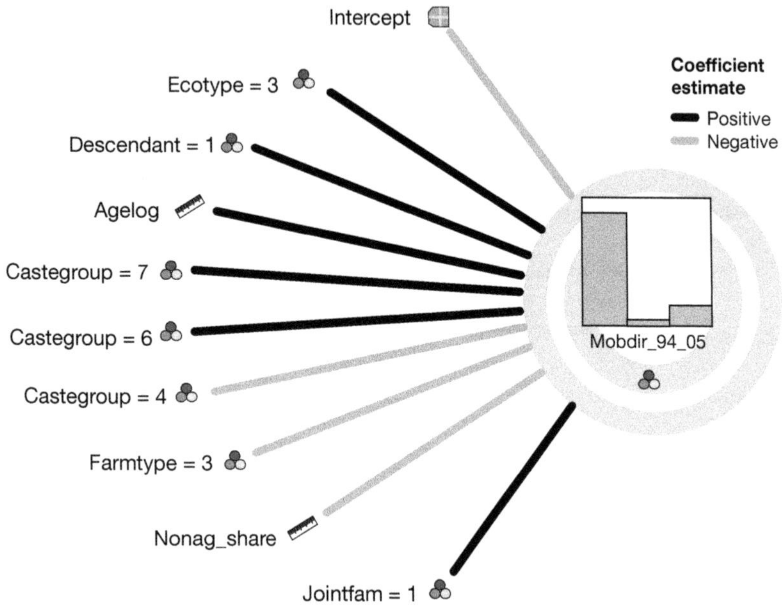

Figure 6.3e Period 3, upward mobility

Note: From the top: wet ecotype, descendant dummy, age of head of household, Other Caste, Other Backward Caste, Scheduled Caste, smallholder–agricultural labourers, non-agricultural share of household income, joint family

Moreover, in the last period, 1994/95–2004/05 their logged odds are 0.66, with the exponent = 1.95, which means that they were almost twice as likely to exit as the large landowners. In other words although they seem to have become more resilient over time, they are still less resilient than the large landowners, as we will discuss next.

In line with our hypotheses, large landowners have higher odds of downward mobility in size-class than family farmers and smallholder–agricultural labourers. We will argue that this result does not contradict the finding from Chapter 5, according to which large landowners are less likely to exit cultivation than other types of farmers. They have an option that smallholders lack: they can dispose of parts of their land and move downwards in size-class. Moreover such mobility can be combined with increasing investments in the land remaining under their own management. Remembering that during the second period, the Green Revolution was much driven by private investments in minor irrigation, it merits pointing out that high levels of such investments are possible to reconcile with stability and even downward mobility in cultivated area for large landowners. Since as a result of investment in irrigation, capital intensity may increase in well-endowed lands, the overall capital intensity of the farm may increase without an increase in area.

This interpretation can also be reconciled with the descriptive statistics pointing to the increasing proportion of smallholders and also of agricultural labourers in the rural population.

Caste groups

There are several statistically significant fixed effects for caste groups in the last period. This holds for downward as well as upward mobility (see Figure 6.3), i.e. during the post-Green Revolution phase. Three caste groups: Other Caste, Other Backward Caste and Scheduled Caste had higher odds of upward mobility in size-class than the reference group of Brahmin and Other Upper Castes. At the same time Other Backward Castes had higher odds of downward mobility than the reference group.[4] One can read this either as indicating less discrimination of lower castes in the farm sector, or as a secondary effect of Brahmins and Other Castes disposing of land making room for other caste groups to acquire land evacuated by the former. This interpretation can be reconciled with the finding from Chapter 5 that Brahmins and Other Upper Castes had lower propensity to leave the farm sector compared to the reference group, which in that model is 'Other Castes'.[5] They tend to stay in the farm sector while being downwardly mobile in size-class of cultivated area.

Ecotype

So far in the analysis we have seen few effects of ecotype. With its higher number of cases, Model 2 is a partial exception. As shown by Figure 6.3, the fixed effects of downward mobility in the wet and the intermediate ecotype were significant and positive while for the latter ecotype, the odds for upward mobility also appear somewhat higher than for the reference ecotype, i.e. the dry one. Of the most recent period then, this implies not only higher downward mobility in the wet and intermediate ecotypes, but also a significant number of upwardly mobile households in the former. The evidence is not overwhelming, but in the most productive tracts, there may be a counter tendency to the overall fragmentation, i.e. some consolidation of holdings. Since villages in the wet ecotype seem to be more integrated into the non-agrarian economy than others, we suggest that this may be because households in wet villages more often use non-farm income to strengthen their foothold in agriculture. Differently put, pluriactivity should not be seen merely as a short-term interlude preceding total exit from the farm sector. On the contrary, pluriactive households use their off-farm incomes to make it possible to remain in cultivation.

The fact that we get no significant results for ecotype in the two first periods should not be taken to mean that there were no such differences. As has been discussed above, lower number of cases together with low reliability of the indicator is a more plausible explanation for the null results.

Joint family

We get significant associations for the joint family variable in all three periods, but the pattern is not entirely clear. In the first period, there was a significantly negative association of joint family with downward mobility. In the first phase of the Green Revolution (or before it in most parts of the country) joint family formation was a way of decreasing the odds of downward mobility. If our results are right, the pattern reversed during the second phase of the Green Revolution when we see a positive association between downward mobility and joint family formation. There are many ways of interpreting this, one being that joint families during this period used their more abundant labour resources for going pluriactive rather than for labour investment in farming. The shifting profile could have to do with the different roles of labour and capital inputs discussed earlier, viz. that in the early phases of the Green Revolution investments of labour in the application of yield-increasing technologies were profitable, but at the second phase of the Green Revolution in the 1980s, focus came to be on private investments in irrigation, making it possible to expand the cultivation of the new varieties. In the most recent period, the pattern reverted to the one obtaining in the first one, i.e. with lower odds for joint families to move downwards in size of holding, but also a significant tendency in the other direction. An interpretation is that some joint families used off-farm earnings to strengthen their position in farming. With this movement, according to our interpretation, joint families lost the advantage they previously had.

Partition and age of head of household

As we noted earlier, the two different ways of recording partition in 1982 and 1999 makes interpretation difficult. The results in this model seem non-surprising though. Finding that the descendant dummy has a profound impact on mobility chances is not strange given that major changes, both in cultivator status and in land size tend to occur in connection with generational transfers.

Beginning with the third period, there is significant positive association between the descendant dummy and the odds of being upwardly mobile. In other words, descendants had higher odds of moving upwards than households that remained under the same head. This is in contrast to the previous period, 1982–1999 when the association was negative. It is possible to reconcile this with our hypothesis of an increasing tendency of household heads to avoid partitioning their property and instead hand it over undivided to one heir and, perhaps at the same time, subsidize a non-farm career for his other children.

If this interpretation is accepted, it is interesting that, with the ST, the pattern seems to have changed so that for descendants the odds of upward mobility in size-class turn positive in the third period. Given higher rates of exit in the 90s and 00s, we would expect higher odds of landed resources being handed over undivided to the succeeding generation.

Higher risks, both of upward and downward mobility imply lower likelihood of stability for descendants. In itself this is not unexpected since major changes in size-class of holdings as well as changes in cultivator status can be expected in connection with generational shifts.

Head of household's age, finally, is unrelated to downward mobility chances in both the first and the second period, while in the final period the odds for both upward and downward mobility get higher with a higher age of the head of household. One way, although probably not the only one, to read this is that if generational transfer occurs at a younger age for the older generation handing over, it provides room for the younger ones to take over earlier in their career. This interpretation would also be compatible with the higher odds for upward mobility for those who take over.

Pluriactivity

As with several other independent variables, non-agricultural share of household income yields significant results only in the third period. Here the pattern on the other hand is very clear: households with higher shares of non-farm income have higher odds of upward mobility and lower odds of downward mobility. The interpretation of this is fairly straightforward. Non-farm incomes are often used to boost household resilience in farming. Supposing that non-farm incomes tend to increase with the ST, this would imply that this process tends to promote stability and even upward mobility for the households involved.

Integration into the non-farm economy

Looking on the other hand at the integration of the village into the non-agrarian economy, preliminary runs of Model 2 did not throw up any significant fixed effects, which simply means mobility risks cannot be shown to have been different between highly integrated villages and others. Again the patterns of entry/exit to the farm sector studied in Chapter 5 prove different from the patterns of mobility in the agrarian structure. While the odds for exit of cultivating household from the farm sector increase with higher integration of the village into the non-farm sector, a comparable effect is not seen in the mobility between size-classes of cultivated area.

Conclusions

An interesting pattern emerges from the results on mobility in size-class, especially when the findings on changes in cultivator status made in the previous Chapter are kept in the picture. First note that the level of integration of the village into the non-agrarian sector (a proxy for the level of ST) could not be demonstrated to have any effect on mobility in size-class. Similarly, while in Model 1 (Chapter 5) we got no significant differences between ecotypes (an indicator of irrigation intensity), neither did we get any such results for the first two periods with Model 2 (in this chapter). We have already vented doubts on the validity of this, doubts reinforced by the fact that Model 2 displays significant fixed effects for the last period, 1994/95 to 2004/05. Albeit thin, there is some evidence of two-directional mobility in the wet ecotype, with higher levels of both downward and upward mobility. It is tempting to see this as an effect of the agrarian transformation unexpected by many: households tended to use pluriactivity and non-farm incomes to reinforce or improve their foothold in farming and not always or necessarily as a stepping-stone to exiting from the sector.

The reader may recall that in Chapter 5, with the results of Model 1 in hand, we spoke of an "almost deadly blow" to the family labour farm hypothesis. The epithet "almost deadly" must be qualified in terms of the findings from this chapter. Studying the drivers of mobility in size-class, with a recent and partial exception for the wet ecotype, we found what must be judged a tendency towards uni-modality, not centring on the family labour farms as our hypothesis predicted but towards smallholder–agricultural labourers, or combination farms in the terminology used in Chapter 1. Kept together with the finding from the last chapter of an increasing share of landless agricultural labourers in the rural population, this means that the ST of the agrarian sector points to a smallholder–agricultural labourer pattern, where large landowners dispose of land (compare Das 2014), acquired not so much by family labour farms, as by smallholders, or combination farmers. In that sense we discern a pattern according to which India may be approaching those obtaining in East and South East Asia (Rigg, Salamanca *et al.*

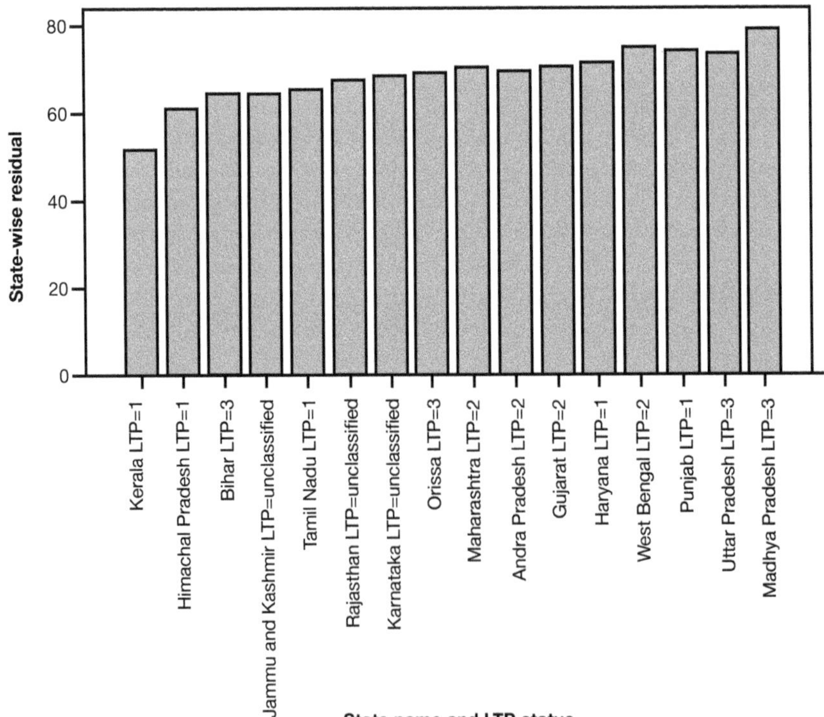

Figure 6.4 State-level residuals by State, 1994/95–2004/05
Source: HDPI-IHDS surveys

2016). This is also a blow to the family labour farm hypothesis, whose time has not yet come, if it ever will. India after all may be more a place for combination farms than for family labour farms.

Regional disparities

In the previous chapter our findings on State-wise residuals tallied well with Reddy *et al.* (2015) and their grouping of States in three groups depending upon the proximity to 'Lewis Turning Point' (see page 89). A parallel pattern is not visible in the State-wise residuals for risk of downward mobility in size-class of holding (see Figure 6.4 on page 108).

As can be seen above the various types of States ("advanced," "intermediate," "backward" and those unclassified do not form clusters in the graph in the same way they did in Figure 5.6. If we take States as "containers" of policy and marked by their stage of ST, neither policy nor level of ST (advanced, intermediate, backward) seem to affect patterns of mobility in size-classes. Yet, the volatility in land distribution seems to be affected by other drivers than policy, creating another type of spatial variability. As we saw above, irrigation or ecotype seems to affect volatility in land distribution. The wet ecotype seems to be the least volatile and we saw indications that pluriactivity among households in that ecotype serve to bolster their resilience in farming. At the other extreme the dry ecotype seems to have the highest volatility. This would produce a spatial pattern, less following administrative divisions than the shades of green, brown and red, which distinguish irrigated from rainfed agrarian landscapes.

Notes

1 Using National Sample Survey (NSS) data, Sharma covers the period from 1953 to 1982, including only one overlapping with ours, i.e. the one between 1971–72 and 1982. During that period the Gini index for own area, excluding landless households declined marginally from 0.6749 to 0.6703. The trend is compatible with our findings, but the level of the index is obviously not. The main reason for this is that we use deciles, while Sharma used the size-classes of the Agricultural Census. This makes the Gini indices incomparable. The Agriculture Census 2011 reports that the average size of operational holding declined from 1.23 hectares in 2005–06 to 1.15 hectares five years later. Similarly, large holdings above 10 hectares decreased from 0.85 per cent in 2005/06 to 0.70 per cent in 2010/11, and with their per centage of area down from 11.82 to 10.59 respectively. See page 6 in: Sharma, H. R. (1994). *Distribution of Landholdings in Rural India, 1953–54 to 1981–82: Implications for land reforms.*
2 Inspired by Björn Holmquist and Sultana Nasrin.
3 Only coefficients significant at 5, 1 or 0.1 per cent level. The reference category is "Stable in size-class of cultivated area."
4 This should be held together with the higher odds for upward mobility of the OBC implying that this group is less stable in size-class than others.
5 Note that the reference caste group is different in Model 1 (Other Castes) to Model 2 (Brahmins and Other Upper Castes).

7 Relative change in income

In this chapter we will have a brief and maybe somewhat narrow look at the welfare and equity consequences of the process of agrarian structural transformation (ST). We will touch on a vast area of research and debate, viz. Indian poverty and its persistence, especially in rural areas. Those who are interested in the general debate should consult well-known standard works (e.g. Datt and Ravallion 1998, Mehta and Shah 2001, Kapur and Shah 2003, Bhalla, Karan *et al.* 2006, Mahendra Dev and Ravi 2007, Himanshu 2008, Ravallion 2008, Datt and Ravallion 2010, Dhamija and Bhide 2011).

Our primary indicator in this exercise will be household income. At this point many readers might object, saying to themselves that everybody (including the present authors) knows that income is a problematic indicator and that poverty measurement usually builds on household expenditure rather than income. Even if it is preferable, the latter method is not handy with the present data, especially as regards the earliest survey. Given the present data we cannot be more sophisticated, and use for example multidimensional poverty indicators (Alkire and Foster 2011, UNDP 2015).[1]

Recognizing the unidimensionality of the income indicator and its chronic unreliability, especially in measuring income for the wealthy sections, we stick to it for want of better alternatives. A definite advantage here is that data are available throughout the period studied. Using the agricultural labour price index as a deflator, which is the conventional method,[2] we get estimates of real income for all survey periods. We can also compute Gini indices from the distribution of income among deciles of households.[3]

Table 7.1 Mean self–reported household income per capita and Gini indices by cross–section in 1982 and 1994–95 prices

	Cross–section			
	1971	1982	1994/95	2004/05
Mean, current prices	4189	9970	16615	53922
Mean, 1982 and 1994/95 prices	9588	9970	16615	20777
Mean change/year		0.36%		1.73%
Gini index	0.26	0.26	0.19	0.19

Source: ARIS REDS and HDPI–IHDS surveys

Over the first 11 years between the first rounds of ARIS REDS, mean income in real prices increased 3.98 per cent, which translates a mean increase of 0.36 per cent per year. From 1994/95 to 2004/05 mean income grew faster with 1.73 per cent per year. However, our concern is not with income and neither with change in income (although the log change is the dependent variable in Model 3). We are interested in the drivers of change. The latter may come to the fore even with reliability problems in the data.

Inequality of self-reported income remained low throughout the period studied. The Gini index remained constant between the two first survey waves; and between the two last ones with indices at 0.26 and 0.19 respectively. This is almost certainly understating the inequalities compared to other indicators and other methods of measuring them (Rama, Béteille *et al.* 2015).

Can these figures be taken at face value? They cannot, at least not as estimates of what happened in the population of rural India as a whole. As pointed out elsewhere, our estimates are not population estimates, but sample means. What happened in the country is better brought out, for example in Deaton and Drèze's article (2002), according to which inequality increased in the 1990s.

On this point, it seems that our panel data is biased and it is good that population data exist to correct for unfounded conclusions. In the following we work with income change over a period as the dependent variable, using more or less the same independent variables as in the previous chapters and adding household size as a control variable, effectively making the models measure changes in real income per capita. The main idea is not to measure this in a better or alternative way, but to elicit the drivers of socio-economic change.[4] For details on the model and estimation see Appendix 2.

Hypotheses and results for Model 3

As is necessary with household panel data, we control for age of head of household (a scale) and also for partition (a dummy). Moreover, introducing size of household (a scale) as an independent variable makes income changes comparable between households.

Village integration into the non-agrarian economy

As in previous models, our primary indicator of the integration of the village into the non-agrarian economy is the village mean proportion of income from non-farm sources. In line with the ST hypothesis we expect income changes to be higher in villages which are more integrated into the non-agrarian economy. Moreover, accelerating transformation should be reflected in higher regression coefficients in the later periods.

Farm type

With regard to farm type, our general hypothesis is that with the structural transformation, high dependence on hired labour, upward pressure on wages and technical change in agriculture, large landowners would face relatively impaired conditions of production and thus also relatively lower increases in income. Thus we would expect that during the first Green Revolution period 1969–71 to 82, large landowners would have lower odds of increasing their income than family farmers, whose reliance on family labour turned into an advantage in the process. In the later phase, 1982–99, when the Green Revolution entered its second phase and spread over wide areas of the country, we would have expected the same distribution profile. But results from Models 1 and 2 indicate that the distribution profile in Period 2 worsened indicating that the hypothesis might not hold.

What about the smallholder–agricultural labourers? As often pointed out, Green Revolution technologies were to a large extent divisible (the now classical source is (Lipton and Longhurst 1989, but see also Lipton 2005). This would give some advantage to family labour farms, as would upward pressure on wages hitting large landowners. Another classical hypothesis about the Green Revolution, especially in its early stages is that it brought advantages to agricultural labourers, because the demand for labour increased, so that for example, higher harvests demanded more labour to be reaped and threshed. Thus we would expect that during the first period and possibly also later, the incomes of landless labourers would increase relative to the other groups.

Pluriactivity

As operationalized here, pluriactivity is crosscutting farm type meaning that multiple sources of income are prevalent among all sections of the agricultural population. The first question to ask is how increasing pluriactivity relates to change of income. It is well known that when going pluriactive people often end up in the informal non-farm sector where incomes are low and often with dismal and exploitative conditions of work (Breman 1985, Breman 1996, Harriss-White, 2009; Harriss-White, 2011). This obviously does not imply that going pluriactive under such conditions would not render increased incomes to the households concerned. A test of this is if the regression coefficient for the variable "gone pluriactive during the period" comes out significant and with a positive sign.[5]

Ecotype

Regarding the ecotypes, according to the finding by Foster et al (2004), Foster, 2004 industrial investments tend to be attracted to low wage areas. Such a process could dampen the advantages of the irrigated tracts and make for small differences in income change between ecotypes.

In previous chapters we got few significant results for ecotype. This may depend on data quality and the methods used. We estimate village ecotype from the mean irrigation intensity of individual farms. So far we have not attained much in terms of significant associations, except in Model 2, Chapter 6 where in adddition to high odds for downward mobility in all ecotypes, we traced a somewhat higher tendency to consolidate holdings in the wet ecotype compared to the dry one.

compared to the dry one (see page 105). The failure to get results for earlier periods may be due to a large number of villages with a small number of respondents each giving high standard errors, which in turn makes it more difficult to attain statistical significance. The larger number of cases in HDPI-IHDS makes it easier to establish significant results for ecotype, which we saw in Model 2, where we spotted a significant difference in volatility of movement among size-classes of cultivated area. So we remain open with regard to the role of ecotype in Model 3.

Joint family

In the Tamil Nadu study referred to earlier (Djurfeldt, Athreya *et al.* 2008), we detected a positive association between joint family and income change, which we interpreted as an increasing advantage of this type of family in a transformed agriculture. As earlier we use joint family at the end of the survey period as an indicator in order to test if this is more generally applicable.

Education

Literacy should be an increasingly important asset (see Foster and Rosenzweig 1996), who used the same data as we use here. We test the importance of education by introducing "head of household completed primary education" in the model and expect a positive sign if head's education brings benefits in terms of increased incomes to their households.

Caste groups

As we have seen in the previous models, caste groups do not always turn up the expected correlations. We traced the reasons for this to the low correlation between caste group and farm type. This implies that caste cannot be seen as an indicator of class defined in economic terms. Thus, and since we control for farm and household type, we have no explicit hypothesis on correlations between caste groups and income change. But we will see to what extent the far from complete emancipation of lower castes has effected a change in their income compared to other groups.

Model results

According to the Table 7.2, the integration of the village into the non-agrarian economy had an income increasing effect but only in the 1994/95 to 2004/05 period.

We cannot demonstrate that, during the early phases of the ST, the integration of villages to the industrial and service economy had any positive effects in terms of income. During the last period, the pattern changed. The regression coefficient then was 0.28 with an exponent value of 1.32. This implies a strong effect. With a 1 per cent increase in village integration into the non-agrarian economy, we expect household income to increase over 30 per cent during the period.

Table 7.2 Model 3: change in income over survey periods

Parameter	*Panel 1, 1971–82*			*Panel 2, 1982–99*			*Panel 3, 1994/95–2004/05*		
	B	*Sig.*		*B*	*Sig.*		*B*	*Sig.*	
Constant	1.13	***	↗	–0.33			–0.22		
Ecotype									
Intermediate ecotype	–0.05			0.09			–0.12	**	↘
Wet ecotype	–0.11			–0.05			–0.07		
Partitioned	–0.10	**	↘	0.01			–0.20	***	↘
Age of HH, logged	–0.20	***	↘	–0.01			–0.02		
Household size at the start of period, logged	–0.34	***	↘	0.05	***	↗	–0.24	***	↘
Caste groups									
Scheduled Caste	–0.20	***	↘	–0.07			–0.07	*	
Scheduled Tribe	–0.08			–0.05			–0.07		
Other Backward Caste	–0.10	*		–0.15	*		–0.04		
Other castes	–0.09			0.02			–0.03		
Farm type, large farmer, among 20% largest landowners in District									
Family farmer, narrow definition	0.31	***	↗	–0.23	*		0.44	***	↗
Smallholders – agricultural labourer	0.30	**	↗	–0.33	**	↘	0.36	***	↗
Landless agricultural labourer	0.27	***	↗	–0.53	***	↘	0.89	***	↗
Non–agricultural household	0.46	***	↗	–0.47	***	↘	0.81	***	↗
Petty landlord	0.51	***	↗	–0.45	***	↘			
Gone pluriactive since start of period	0.05			–0.11			0.33	***	↗
Joint family, at the end of period	0.38	***	↗	–0.52	***	↘	0.55	***	↗
Head of household studied beyond primary level, dummy	–0.02			0.01			0.04		
Proportion of non–farm income, village level mean	0.23			–0.01			0.28	***	↗
No. of cases	2835			2754			10562		
Missing (%)	43			45			12		
Deviance of null model	7024.43			4702.44			29015.86		
Deviance of full model	6343.57			4348.18			27049.00		

Table 7.2 Continued

Parameter	*Panel 1, 1971–82*		*Panel 2, 1982–99*		*Panel 3, 1994/95–2004/05*	
	B	*Sig.*	*B*	*Sig.*	*B*	*Sig.*
Chi^2	29.60	***	15.40	***	85.52	***
Random effects by level	Estimate		Estimate		Estimate	
State	0.06	*	0.11	*	0.04	*
District	0.08	***	0.00		0.06	***
Village	0.08	***	0.08	***	0.08	***
Household	0.50	***	0.68	***	0.86	***

Source: ARIS and HDPI-IHDS data

Note: For a detailed version see Table A3.3. "Constant" denotes the estimated ($\hat{\alpha}$.) Similarly "B" denotes the estimated regression coefficients ($\hat{\beta}$). Arrows denote positive and negative associations so that an upward pointing arrow indicates a positive correlation with exit/entry, while *, ** and *** denote 5, 1 and 0.1 per cent level of significance. Results are after removal of 8 outliers in period 1, 18 in period 2

Pluriactivity

Something similar holds for pluriactivity. Only in the third period households who had gone pluriactive reported statistically significant increasing incomes, relative to the reference group. One interpretation of this is of course that during earlier phases of the transformation, those who for various reasons opted partially out of farming had few choices except low remunerative jobs or self-employment in the informal sector, and that the situation seems to have improved since the mid-90s. This is obviously an effect of the ST and a positive one at that. However, this result is clearly at odds with what is reported from studies of income and livelihood studies of the informal sector, so it needs to be treated with caution.[6]

Control variables

Coming to the demographic controls, there is a negative effect of logged age of head of household on income development in the first period, but it disappears in the second and third ones. Partition had a similar effect in the first period and third periods. This means that heirs who had taken over during the period tended to report lower income changes than households that had not been partitioned. It is not straightforward to reconcile this result with the one in Chapter 6 (p. 106), according to which descendants had lower odds of being stable in size-class in the third period, i.e. both their upward and downward mobility was higher than that of the reference group of undivided households. That their income on the average seems to have gone down during the third period obviously does not mean that all of them became poorer – a minority did increase their income. Thus the discrepancy between these and those in Chapter 6 could be deceptive.

Size of family, however is interesting. In the first period there was a highly significant and negative elasticity of income change to family size. Thus larger families were losers in a relative sense. This changed in the second period and the disadvantage of initial large family size disappeared, so that we now get a small but positive association with change in income. This could however be an effect of the longer period (17 years) in the second panel than in the first one (11 years). The longer panel period makes for more generational shifts over the years.

Trends turned again in the third period where the negative regression coefficient from Period 1 is reiterated. Since methods of selecting descendants differ between surveys, these results are again difficult to interpret.

Farm type

The results for farm type are strong and contrasting between periods. Several of them go from positive in the first period to negative in the second, and return to positive in the third period. In terms of the family farm hypothesis, this means that in the first period, incomes changed in line with the hypothesis: family farms, smallholder–agricultural labourers and landless labourers gained relative to the reference group of large landowners. Tables turned in the second period when large landowners tended to gain more in income than other farm and household types.

This seems to be one of the reasons why Binswanger-Mkhize described this period[7] as one of 'stunted development' (Binswanger-Mkhize 2013). We have the advantage of also using HDPI-IHDS and can see that the development apparently returned to the patterns of the 70s from the late 90s onwards (see also Mohan 2008, who calls the 70s an interregnum in the growth history of India, compare also Vakulabharanam and Motiram 2011, and Mehrotra *et al.* 2014).

In both the first and the third period then, the hypothesis about large landowners plays out exactly according to expectation, although since they are the reference group it is not directly visible in the table. What can be seen however is that all other groups increased their incomes more than the large landowners, meaning that they may also have increased theirs but less than other groups. For two periods of three we get an effect according to the hypothesis, with incomes of large landowners increasing less than for other groups. Thus change of incomes for family farmers and smallholders–agricultural labourers were higher than for the large landowners.

Landless agricultural labourers increased their income even more than family farmers and smallholders in the third period (1994/95–2004/05),[8] strengthening the hypothesis that wage inflation, unlike in the preceding period, was driving the development. Lastly, there is a very clear pattern for the non-agricultural households compared again to large landowners. During the second period, like for all other farm and household types, their incomes changed less than for large landowners. But for the former too, the pattern reversed in the last period, when income changes for non-agricultural households were significantly higher than in both the preceding periods. Inequality between the farm sector and the agrarian sectors generally is considered to have increased over the years (Deaton and Drèze 2002).

The contrasting development in the 80s and 90s compared both to the preceding and succeeding periods may be due to different sources of agricultural growth in these periods. This again may depend on factors both internal and external to the farm sector.

Beginning with the internal factors, there may be something to the observation made above, that in the later phase of the Green Revolution, from the 80s onwards, agricultural growth came to increasingly depend on private investment in small-scale irrigation, as opposed to the large-scale public investments in the early phase.[9] Private investments privileged farmers with good economic resources and may also have given them rewards in terms of better income development than family farmers, whose main asset, their labour resources, became less of an advantage. Something similar can be said about the smallholders–agricultural labourers, who were not disadvantaged in terms of income development during the first period, but whose incomes grew proportionally less than those of large landowners in the second one. Moreover, the driving force during the early phases of the Green Revolution, besides public investments in infrastructure was seed technology (Lipton and Longhurst 1989), which was partible and brought benefits even for the landless in terms of increased labour demand.

The effects of what in India is called the neo-liberal reforms of the Manmohan Singh government should also be brought in here. There are few rigorous and empirically grounded studies of their effects on the agrarian sector. A doctoral thesis dealing with Telengana, the State recently chipped off from Andhra Pradesh, and presented by V. Vakulabharanam is an exception (Vakulabharanam 2005: 103 ff.).[10] For agriculture the reforms led to India signing the Dunkel agreement in 1994 and to a number of policy measures summarized by the author. They included measures like: trade liberalization for a long list of products including rice, wheat, cotton, pulses and oil seeds, all common crops in India; liberalization of the seed industry, allowing imports; gradual reduction of fertilizer and power subsidies (still on-going) and reduction of state-supported credit in agriculture (Vakulabharanam 2005: 128). By means of econometric modelling the author manages to demonstrate the immiserizing effect of these policies in Telengana during the decade 1995–2005. To quote his conclusions:

> Large farmers have improved their welfare between 1983 and 1994 but have experienced a decline in their welfare between 1993 and 2000, i.e. during the liberalization period. For medium farmers, while the coefficient for the liberalization period has a negative sign, it is not significant. For the small farmers too, the results look identical to those of the medium farmers. For marginal farmers and landless laborers, the coefficient for the liberalization period is not only negative but also significant at 5 per cent confidence interval. These two groups are clearly worse off after liberalization.
>
> (op. cit. pp. 116–17)[11]

The time periods, as well as the operationalization of farm types are not the same ones that we have used. These differences notwithstanding, immiserizing effects of the liberalization of agriculture from the mid-90s tally at least partly with the results we have achieved. Together with the increasing share of private investment in irrigation etc., this may be one explanation of the contrasting distribution profiles we get from our second panel (1982–99) compared both to the first (1971–82) and third panel (1994/95–2004/05).

Ecotype

We spot no significant difference between the ecotypes in terms of income development, except for the intermediate ecotype in the last period, when incomes of households in that ecotype changed less than in the other two ecotypes. As previously discussed there are problems with the reliability of the ecotype variable, so we will leave the issue of the causes of this result unresolved.

Joint family

In this model the pattern for joint families conforms to the one we detected in the Tamil Nadu study. It is striking that the pattern displayed by farm type recurs for the joint family dummy. In the first period joint family formation had positive effects on income development, in the second period the sign of the regression coefficient turned negative and turned positive again in the third period (in all cases strongly significant). One admittedly *ad hoc* explanation of the contrasting patterns would hold if the advantage of joint families had to do with their control of labour rather than their ability to mobilize capital and if the latter is the main resource explaining the contrasting patterns between the three periods. If that is the case we would expect regression coefficients for the joint family dummy to mirror those for the farm types, more specifically for the contrast between large landowners and family farmers and the large swings in the odds for both mobility in size-class and for income change. The best bet then seems to be that the advantages of joint families is their control of larger pools of labour resources, which in many circumstances can be turned into an advantage, as they seem to have been both in the first period of the Green Revolution and more currently in the development from the mid-90s to the mid-00s.

Education

Like in previous models we get weak or no effects for the education dummy. Since this effect crosscuts the models, there must be something to this. Could it mean that people who are educated are more likely to opt out of agriculture, so that because of their leaving the sample, we don't find effects of education, in either of the models, i.e. neither in mobility between size-classes nor in income development? Reviewing all three models and the effects of education it is indeed striking that the only statistically significant finding is in Model 1 for Period 3 where there is a strong association between education and the tendency to have exited farming (see page 69).

Caste groups

Caste groups are poor proxies for agrarian class and the farm type indicator performs better. As repeatedly pointed out, there is no high correlation between farm types and caste groups. Thus the caste group classification should mostly model the effects of caste independent of farm type. As we had expected, the caste group dummies do not yield much, except the strong tendency for Scheduled Caste to have gained less in income during the first period than others. From a normative point of view, it is thus a positive finding that this association is not repeated in later periods and that caste groups have little association with income change. It is an obvious sign of less discrimination.

Conclusions

It is striking how the focus in this chapter on relative change in income gives another perspective on developments in the Indian agrarian sector than the usual focus on absolute changes. Obviously this approach does not falsify the usual and depressing findings on the resilience of poverty in rural India, but it gives a more nuanced view of what has happened in the sector. This is because with our model we concentrate on changes for specific groups in comparison to others, for example the contrast between large landowners and family labour farms.

Progress in alleviating poverty during the period of study was indeed slow, but behind or below the bleak performance lie patterns of mobility, which diverge from those inferred from cross-sectional rather than panel data. One pattern central to the concern in this book relates to family labour farms versus large landowners dependent on hired (or tenant) labour. First of all, the early Green Revolution period, here dated to 1970–82, was family farm and smallholder friendly, as claimed by Djurfeldt and Jirström (2005). The second phase of same Revolution, when in the Indian case it spread from the pioneer areas in northwestern India, to the rice-growing areas in the eastern and southern parts of the country, the smallholder friendliness was compromised. This can be explained by less "State-drivenness" (or more *laissez-faire)* than during the first period which led to features like: less public investments in irrigation, neglect of extension services, farmers' cooperatives and rural banking and a comparatively larger role for private investments, especially in irrigation. These explain, we believe, the changing distribution profile (Mohanty and Lenka 2016).[12]

Frankly, we did not expect the distribution profile to change in the third period and with the HDPI-IHDS data. Model 3 in this chapter, as well as Models 1 and 2 in the earlier chapters also indicate a reversal of trends, and so we are fairly confident that this finding is not a statistical fluke. As we argue, in the 90s and early 00s, several States seem to have reached an LTP, a "Lewis Turning Point" (cf. above p. 88 ff.) . Reaching the LTP seems to have led to the expected outcome, according to our hypothesis, that is competition between the farm sector and the service and industrial sectors for labour. Large landowners dependent on hired or tenant labour thus faced rising wages and difficulties in finding tenants, again rigging the odds against their resilience or survival in farming. This did not lead to a complete exit from farming, but to partial disposal of land and relative loss of income.

Although many narratives focus on caste, the above development on the whole is not a caste phenomenon, but one more dependent on economic position ("class") than on caste. As we pointed out, caste is poor proxy for class.

Notes

1 On measuring multidimensional poverty, see: http://hdr.undp.org/en/content/multidimensional-poverty-index-mpi.

2 Regularly published by the Government of India, Labour Bureau. See: http://labourbureau.nic.in/press.htm, last accessed January 13, 2016.

3 Dhamija and Bhide made a study of income change based on the same ARIS REDS data as here. They used other methods but arrived at findings largely comparable with ours, Dhamija, N. and S. Bhide (2011). "Dynamics of Chronic Poverty: Variations in factors infuencing entry and exit of chronic poor." *CPRC-IIPA Working Paper No. 38*, Indian Institute of Public Administration, New Delhi, Chronic Poverty Research Centre.

4 For a discussion of this method, its drawbacks and advantages, see Fields, G. S. and E. A. Ok (1996). "The Meaning and Measurement of Income Mobility." *Journal of Economic Theory* **71**: 349–77.

5 The number of non-farm workers in the household could play a role here, but unfortunately the variable is only available for the first period, so it is not included in the model.

6 Compare however Mehrotra *et al.* who argue that "since 2004–05 the structural shifts in employment, significant increases in rural wages, increase in per capita consumption expenditure and therefore a sharp decline in absolute numbers of the poor as demonstrated by the National Sample Surveys (NSS) of 2009–10 and 2011–12 has promoted inclusive growth… (Tendulkar poverty line)" Mehrotra, S., J. Parida, S. Sinha and A. Gandhi (2014). "Explaining Employment Trends in the Indian Economy: 1993–94 to 2011–12." E*conomic and Political Weekly* **XLIX**(32): 49–57. The authors moreover show that in the five-year period 2004/05 to 2009–10, "as many as 23.7 million of India's agricultural workforce abandoned agriculture, or nearly 10 per cent of the work force" (op. cit. p. 50). Finally, the authors found that "about 30 million rural workers (women comprising 60 per cent of that number, who were often aged women) joined the workforce as self-employed in agriculture" (p. 51). On female labour, see Garikipati, S. and S. Pfaffenzeller (2012). "The Gendered Burden of Liberalisation: The impact of India's economic reforms on its female agricultural labour." *Journal of International Development* **24**(7): 841–64.

7 Also supported by the problematic 1999–2006 round of REDS.

8 About double the effect, which given the small standard errors is highly significant (0.1 per cent).

9 Mohanty and Lenka cite Dev and statistics showing the decline of public investment in agriculture over a 15-year period from 1989/90 to 2003/04 from 34 to 20 per cent in 1999/2000 prices Mohanty, B. B. and P. K. Lenka (2016). "Neoliberal Reforms, Agrarian Capitalism and the Peasantry." *Critical Perspectives on Agrarian Transition: India in the global debate*. B. B. Mohanty (ed.). Abingdon and New York, Routledge; Dev, M. S. (2012). "A Note on Trends in Public Investment in India." *IGIDR Proceedings/Projects series*. Mumbai, Indira Gandhi Institute of Development Research.

10 Rahul Mukherji, personal communication February 2016.

11 The author is using the size-class categories of the Agricultural Census as proxies for farm and household types.

12 See also Misra and Rao who also cite statistics on the increasing level of private investment in agriculture. They also show that growth increased in the 90s, thanks to more emphasis on high value crops and increasing exports. The latter declined in the last part of the decade and the early 00s, due to decreasing international prices before the world food price crisis from 2008, Misra, V. and M. G. Rao (2003). "Trade Policy, Agricultural Growth and Rural Poor: Indian experience, 1978–79 to 1999–2000." *Economic and Political Weekly*: 4588–603. To this should be added the report by Birthal *et al.* who show that "the gradual diversification of Indian agriculture towards high-value crops exhibits a pro-smallholder bias, with smallholders playing a proportionally larger role in the cultivation of vegetables versus fruits... The comparatively high labor endowments of the small farmers, as reflected in their greater family sizes, induce them to diversify towards vegetables. Although fruit cultivation is also labor intensive (as compared to cultivation of staples), fruits are relatively capital intensive, making them a less advantageous choice for smallholders who tend to have low capital endowments. Furthermore, both the probability of participation in fruit and vegetable cultivation as well as land allocation to horticulture decreases with the size of landholdings in India. Small or medium holders do not appear to allocate a greater share of land to fruits or

vegetables. However, the share allocated to vegetables is significantly higher if the family size is bigger, while the reverse is true in the case of fruits." Joshi, P. K., A. Gulati, P. S. Birthal and L. Tewari (2004). "Agriculture Diversification in South Asia: Patterns, determinants and policy implications." Ibid. **XLI** (June 30): 2457–67, Birthal, P. S., P. K. Joshi, D. Roy and A. Thorat (2007). "Diversification in Indian Agriculture towards High-Value Crops: The role of smallholders. Washington, D.C., International Food Policy Research Institute.

8 Conclusion

No place for family farms?

Coming down a winding country road our trip has ended; we are ready to summarize and conclude on our research questions. We set out with a question on family farms. Quoting FAO studies and statistics we showed that family farms are almost universal and make up around 95 per cent of all farms worldwide. The concept of family farm as defined by FAO and used in estimating this statistic (see page 3) is too general and heterogeneous to be interesting as an object of research. Instead we are interested in the narrower concept of "family labour farms."

Using Weberian methodology, we defined an ideal type family farm as dependent on family labour in production and primarily managed by members of the family. This definition still includes a huge majority of the 570 million family farms worldwide. It follows that the ideal type of capitalist farm constitutes a minority of the world's farms and as we have shown, a surprisingly small one at that. We define this ideal type as an agricultural production unit in which all factors of production (land, labour, capital and management) are procured on the market, which is another way of saying that factors of production are commodities and have market value. In contrast to the family labour farm, the ideal typical capitalist farm (or firm) is: (1) worked by labourers hired for wages (rather than recruited by non-market means; (2) managed by professional managers (rather than by family members); (3) owned by corporations having invested their capital into the farm. As for family farms, its capital includes land that may be owned or leased.

It is a paradox, more of scholarship than of history that the ideal type capitalist farm is so rare a bird that you need binoculars to spot it. It constitutes a tiny minority of the five per cent of world farms that are not family farms. The main part of the five per cent is large estates, dependent on non-family labour but not fulfilling all the above criteria of ideal type capitalist farms (see p. 5 ff.). The rarity of the capitalist farm contrasts with the prophecies of its supremacy, repeatedly issued since the classical economists and Marx – prophecies that we deem belong to the most frequently failed ones in intellectual history. Alas, the ideological influence of these forecasts has had catastrophic effects in countries where politicians have attempted to forestall development and design purportedly more effective production units than family labour farms by administrative means, causing agrarian stagnation in countries like Russia (since the 1920s), China (before 1974) and Ethiopia after 1974. (See Chapter 1 for details).

In contrast to the many studies of agricultural development basing themselves on the flawed expectation of capitalist farms growing in prevalence, we investigated instead the hypothesis of the growing prevalence of family labour farms in India from 1970.

Against this background we formulated the main hypothesis of this book: has the agrarian structural transformation brought with it an increasing prevalence and will it lead to an eventual predominance of family labour farms? Obviously this question presupposes a process and a concept of structural transformation (ST).

Using the standard definition of the ST, as a process in which the share of agriculture in GDP decreases, at the same time as the share of agricultural labour in the total labour force goes down, we concluded that worldwide[1] since 1965, the share of agricultural labour in the labour force has gone down by about one per cent per year. Defined in this way there is no doubt that the structural transformation is ongoing.

Theoretically the main driver of the decline of large landholdings and the rising commonness of family labour farms is competition for labour. As the growth of industry and services proceeds it causes competition between these sectors and the farm sector, leading to increasing real wages in agriculture. This again leads to advantages for family-organized farming (see "The competitive advantage of family farms," p. 12 ff.). Has this been the case in India?

We concluded that during colonial time "the agrarian ST stood still for about 60 years, to take off only in the in the 1990s" (see pp. 64 ff.). Macro statistics show than since then, the ST has not only proceeded but increased in pace. This substantiates our least controversial hypothesis that India is no exception in this respect. What effects has the ST had on agrarian structures? Are we able to corroborate our second main hypothesis about the increasing prevalence of family labour farms? If so, or if not, what is the role of competition for hired labour between the farm and non-farm sectors?

Answering the above questions requires the development of indicators; primarily of the farm types referred to above, i.e. family labour farms and large landed properties dependent on hired labour, where the latter is a wider category than the ideal type of capitalist farms. Since our databases do not contain detailed data on inputs of family and hired labour on the farms studied, we are forced to rely on more approximate indicators. This operationalization is made in Chapter 5 and results in a farm and household typology centring on large landowners dependent on hired labour, family labour farms, smallholders–agricultural labourers, landless agricultural labourers, petty landlords and non-agrarian households (see "Operationalizing the family labour farm," pp. 69 ff.).

Before coming to the results of this inquiry, we note another paradox in the social science studies of agrarian structures, viz. that they have tended to abstract from a crucial dimension of farmers' livelihoods, which moreover is growing with the ST and affecting the resilience both of family farms and of large landed properties. We are referring to *pluriactivity*, which tends to lead to an increasing prevalence of combination farms, i.e. farms on which cultivators' livelihoods depend on a combination of farm and non-farm sources of income (see pp. 16 ff.).

In our models we use pluriactivity as a cross–cutting dimension to the farm and household typology, both crucial tools for our enquiry.

Methodology and sources of data

Popular both among sociologists and economists, we use statistical tools developed for the study of social mobility. We primarily study and model three processes: (1) mobility out of and into the farm sector: the entry/exit model in Chapter 5; (2) mobility between size-classes of cultivated area in Chapter 6; and (3) relative change in income per capita in Chapter 7. See Appendix 2 for mathematical descriptions of the models.

For all three models we draw on data from the ARIS REDS and HDPI-IHDS databases (see Appendix 1), which gives models for three periods: 1970–82, 1982–1999 and 1994/95–2004/05.

While writing this book a second round of the India Human Development Survey (IHDS-II) was published.[2] We have refrained from applying our models to the period covered there, i.e. 2004/05–2011/12, but we will quote some descriptive statistics from the database with a bearing on the conclusions of this study. Thus we note that the proportion of cultivators in the rural population as estimated by this panel[3] stayed constant over the panel period at 39 per cent of the rural population. The total sample included both urban and rural households; the rural ones declined from 72 per cent in 2004/05 and 68 per cent in 2011/12, an expected drop over the 10-year period. However, the fall was not precipitous, which partly should have to do with the "unseen" urbanization, discussed in Chapter 3. One would expect that many of the villages, classified as "rural" have not yet been upgraded to "Census Towns" although they have many small-town characteristics (cf. Chapter 3). Thus the agrarian ST is proceeding and may be underestimated also in the IHDS-II data, which depend on official classifications of "rural" and "urban."

Transformation of agrarian structure

The other part of our main research question, which is concerned with the transformation of the agrarian structure as a consequence of the ST is not as easy to answer. Drawing on the results of the statistical models and the operationalization used there, we conclude that family labour farms are *not* getting more common. Unlike the hypothesis on the ST in general, the hypothesis on the growing proportion of family labour farms does not survive unscathed. In fact, we answered it in the negative and had to reject both the family labour farm hypothesis itself but also the obverse hypothesis of a growing proportion of large landed properties dependent on hired labour. The latter hypothesis implies a polarization of the agrarian structure with "factories in the fields" and "armies" of agricultural labourers, as a consequence of capitalist development; a hypothesis which fails to get support from our inquiry.

Statistics from the latest round of IHDS are not suited to replicate the models applied to data collected in earlier rounds because the indicators used for drawing the boundaries between family labour farms and large landholdings dependent on hired labour may be good enough for modelling, but not for describing the changes in the relative size of each type of farm over time. Model results are quite clear however. When in the second part of Chapter 5 we studied the drivers of exit and entry to the farm sector, we were forced to conclude negatively on the hypothesis that the competition for labour between the service and industrial sectors and the farm sector would lead to wage inflation and increasing difficulties for large farms to survive. In all three periods covered in the analysis, we saw no tendencies in that direction – on the contrary. This would seem a knock-back for the family labour farm hypothesis, but as we saw from Model 2 it does not imply that large landowners continue to dominate the Indian agrarian sector.

The last statement rests on the results of Model 2 in Chapter 6, in which we attempted to model the mobility of farming households between size-classes of cultivated holdings. The results considerably qualify the conclusions drawn in Chapter 5 and partly salvage the family labour farm hypothesis. It turns out that in all three periods, family labour farmers and the category of smallholder–agricultural labourers faced considerably lower relative risks of being downwardly mobile in size-class than large landowners. Concerning the latter, we conclude that, although they face lower risks of exit, the propensity of large landowners to be downwardly mobile in size-class is higher. We take this to mean that survival in farming for a large landowner is not so much an either/or question as it is for family farmers and smallholders. Large landowners more often dispose of parts of their holdings to finance the education of their children, building a house in town etc. Thus they tend to stay on in the farm sector but with reduced landholdings. The same options are not open to family farmers and smallholder–agricultural labourers, especially not to the latter. As the name implies, smallholders are often in found in the smallest size-classes. To them, in case of a crisis (or for that matter, in case of opportunity), the option of selling parts of the land is often closed. This tallies with the statistics on change in average size of holdings, which show a sharply falling trend over the period covered (compare Table 5.7 on page 83). From 1971 to 2004–05 the average size of area cultivated went down from 4.06 hectares to 0.59. According to IHDS-II it has only marginally changed since then.

Our study of mobility in size-class further brought a tendency towards unimodality, not centring on the family labour farms as our second major hypothesis predicted, but towards smallholder–agricultural labourers. Kept together with the finding from Chapter 5 (see page 89) of an increasing share of smallholders and landless agricultural labourers in the rural population, the ST of the agrarian sector points to a smallholder–agricultural labourer pattern, where large landowners dispose of land, acquired not so much by family labour farms, as by smallholders. We thus discern a pattern in which India may be approaching conditions seen in East and South East Asia (see the previous chapter and Rigg, Salamanca *et al.* 2016). Obviously it is a blow to the family labour farm hypothesis, apparently its time has not yet come, if it ever will. Thus, India after all may not be a place for family labour farms.

Spatial diversity

The structural transformation proceeds at different pace in different places, especially in the vastly heterogeneous country of India. In studying this we drew on the concept of "Lewis Turning Point" (LTP, for an exact definition see endnote on page 91), after one of the founding fathers of development studies, W. Arthur Lewis. Inspired by a study by Reddy *et al.* (2015) dividing the major India states into "advanced," "intermediate" and "backward"[4] in terms of reaching the LTP, our results are cross-validated by theirs and the other way round. Thus we concluded from Model 1 that households in States that are "advanced" in terms of the ST in the late 90s and early 00s shared higher odds of exit from the farm sector, with one notable exception, which is Himachal Pradesh. The low rates of entry/exit for Himachal Pradesh, in an *ad hoc* interpretation can be due to its being a pioneer State, with high rates of transformation already in earlier periods.

Leaving the farms?

Pluriactivity has often been seen as a push-driven process in which wretched farmers or labourers seek income outside agriculture, but get locked in to exploitative low wage, low return and often part-time occupations. Undoubtedly part- or full-time *émigrés* from the farm sector tend to get locked in to exploitative informal sector jobs or activities, but the analysis in Chapter 6 pointed to another process, in which smallholders use off-farm incomes to invest in agriculture and increase their resilience in farming. Here too the parallel between India and East and South East Asia is evident.

The results of the mobility study in Chapter 6 are reinforced by the study of the drivers of change in income in Chapter 7. The model used confirmed both the contrasting distribution profiles in the second period studied (1982–99), i.e. the late Green Revolution and the first years after the "neo-liberal" reforms from 1991 to 1994 during the Manmohan Singh government. In the third period (1994/95–2004/05) the equalizing effects, which prevailed in the early phase of the Green Revolution (1970–82), reappeared. In both the second and the third periods the large landowners lost out relatively speaking, contrasted to some extent with family labour farms, but even more with smallholder–agricultural labourers and most of all with the landless labourers;[5] and according to the model *all farm and household types mentioned improved their incomes relative to the large landowners.*

Competition for labour?

Finally, a comment on the hypothesis that demand-driven competition for agricultural wage labour would drive a process of increasing wages. The hypothesis seems difficult to validate, given the increasing share of landless labour in the agricultural population. One can obviously interpret this increase as evidence of an insufficient demand for such labour from the non-farm sectors. It could also be construed as a possibly unintended consequence of political interventions.

Before coming to the details of this, we recall the results of the comparative study of the ST in 85 countries by Timmer and Akkus already referred to (2008). The authors document a mismatch between the two processes of a decreasing share of agriculture in total GDP and the decrease of the agricultural labour force as part of the total labour force. As a result of the mismatch the latter gets retarded compared to the first one so that the gap tends to increase in the process. The authors attribute the growing mismatch to political interventions, motivated by politicians' wariness of increasing inequalities between agriculture and the rest of the economy and between urban and rural areas. They mention the classical price subsidy policies, characteristic of Europe and the US since the New Deal and current subsidy regimes (see "Comparative studies of structural transformaton," pp. 28 ff.).

Political interventions slowing the structural transformation

In the Indian case, primarily two policies come to mind: the Minimum Support Programme (MSP), which under various names has been in place since the first phase of the Green Revolution (see pp. 34 ff.). There are reasons to believe that the minimum prices, motivated by the need to support small and family farms, increases the resilience of large-scale farms who too enjoy the minimum prices and, since they sell more, in absolute terms get more in terms of subsidies. This seems to be a universal result of price subsidies, so it should not surprise us (see for example Kumar, Darbha *et al.* 2003).

The other policy intervention, which has grown in importance during recent years, and which could have similar effects is the MGNREGA – Mahatma Gandhi National Rural Employment Guarantee Act. Although there are reports of employers complaining that the scheme is leading to increased wages, our analysis opens up another interpretation. The scheme is officially marketed as "a social security scheme that attempts to provide employment and livelihood to rural labourers in the country."[6] To the extent that it is successful, the MGNREGA could contribute to keeping rural labourers in the villages, by subsidizing their consumption and thus the labour costs of the employers. Indirectly it would add to the resilience, not only of owners of large estates, but also other parts of the farm sector, especially where the competition for labour is less, like in the "backward" LTP States. We do not know of many studies that have addressed this aspect of MGNREGA, but that by Harish *et al.* is an exception. In the case of a district in Karnataka they found that "the implementation of MGNREGA led to labour scarcity to the tune of 53 per cent and 30 per cent for agriculture operations like weeding and sowing, respectively. There has been a decline in area for labour-intensive crops like tomato and ragi[7] to the extent of 30 per cent" (Harish, Nagaraj *et al.* 2011: 485). Similar results have been reported for Tamil Nadu (Carswell and Neve 2014) and Haryana (Ahuja, Tyagi *et al.* 2011).

The above quote refers not to the welfare effects of the MGNREGA programme, which undoubtedly are substantial and well documented (compare Drèze, 2013; see also Sameeksha, 2012). We have in mind its side effects of indirectly subsidizing the labour costs of employers and thus dampening the pace of the structural transformation.[8]

The above is one aspect where Indian development seems to deviate from that in East and South East Asia where, outside the plantation sector, the large estates dependent on hired labour have decreased in importance and preponderance compared to India.

Perpetuating caste discrimination?

Above we quoted Sugihara and Japanese economic historians who claim that the whole of East Asia as well as parts of South East Asia went through an "industrious revolution" (see p. 22 f.), in which the balance between family and hired labour was different than one historically obtaining in India. We suggested that India did not go through a similar type of revolution, because unfree labour was institutionalized through its caste segmented labour markets (see p. 10 ff.). It is easy to believe that the availability of low-wage, mainly Scheduled Caste labour is a factor that has so far and outside some specific areas hampered the establishment of family labour farms. Against this background it is obviously interesting that our models point to few correlations between mobility chances and caste groups. In the farm sector, to repeat, caste is a poor proxy for class, which could be the reverse of conditions in the non-agrarian sector (Majumder 2010, Motiram and Singh 2012). Perhaps after all, many years of affirmative action, together with the effects of the agrarian ST, is pointing towards less, although far from absent caste discrimination in the sector?

Nationally representative, long-term panel data for households work like a radio-telescope into a micro-cosmos of changing agrarian realities. It is powerful enough to blow asunder standard narratives on Indian agriculture as stagnant, landlord-dominated and immiserizing for the lowliest of the low, like the Scheduled Castes and Tribes. The agrarian structural transformation has brought much volatility to the farm sector and, be sure: more is to come!

Notes

1 More precisely in the 85 countries included in the study by Timmer and Akkus Timmer, C. P. and S. Akkus (2008). "The Structural Transformation as a Pathway out of Poverty: Analytics, empirics and politics." *Working Paper no. 50*. Washington D.C., Center for Global Development..

2 Desai, S. and R. Vanneman (2016). India Human Development Survey-II (IHDS-II), 2011–12, Inter-university Consortium for Political and Social Research (ICPSR) [distributor].

3 So far in this book we have used the unweighted sample means, which for the earlier rounds of ARIS REDS and HDPI-IHDS tend to agree quite well with the weighted ones. In IHDS-II there appears to be considerable panel bias: apparently the reason for the larger discrepancies between weighted and unweighted and figures. The figures quoted from IHDS-II here and below are weighted population estimates.

4 "Advanced" towards reaching the LTP are the following major States: Kerala, Tamil Nadu, Punjab, Haryana and Himachal Pradesh, with the "intermediate" group containing: Andhra Pradesh, Maharashtra, Gujarat, West Bengal. "Backward" ones

were: the undivided States of Bihar, Madhya Pradesh, Orissa and Uttar Pradesh. The following States were not classified by the authors cited: Karnataka and Rajasthan.

5 Chavan and Bedamatta found the same pattern of development of real wages for agricultural labourers as we have done here Chavan, P. and R. Bedamatta (2006). “Trends in Agricultural Wages in India 1964–65 to 1999–2000.” *Economic and Political Weekly*: 4041–51.

6 See www.mapsofindia.com/my-india/government/mnrega-progress-made-by-modi-government-in-one-year, accessed 19 February 2016.

7 “Ragi” is a variety of millet, grown in rainfed lands and not exactly known as labour intensive.

8 A case study in Haryana, a State “advanced” in terms of its structural transformation, found that the MGNREGA had not reduced migration since the wages paid by the programme could not compete with the wages paid in the destination areas Ahuja, U. R., D. Tyagi, S. Chauhan and K. R. Chaudhary (2011). “Impact of MGNREGA on Rural Employment and Migration: A study in agriculturally-backward and agriculturally-advanced districts of Haryana.” *Agricultural Economics Research Review* **24**: 495–502. On the other hand, the study by Carswell and de Neve in Tamil Nadu concluded that MGNREGA contributed to increasing the wages of landless labour Carswell, G. and G. Neve (2014). “MGNREGA in Tamil Nadu: A story of success and transformation?” *Journal of Agrarian Change* **14**(4): 564–85. Thus the evidence is mixed.

Appendix 1

Data sources

The primary data source in this book is the ARIS-REDS panel study (1969–71, 1982, 1999 and 2006) covering 250 villages in 99 districts in 12 states.[1] The survey in 1970–72 was called the 'Additional Rural Income Survey' (ARIS) with a sample size of 5115. The subsequent rounds were called the 'Rural Economic and Demographic Survey' (REDS). The data set is therefore called the ARIS-REDS.

One of the basic ideas behind the panel surveys was to study the effect of the Green Revolution on rural households in terms of income and assets and their distribution within the population. Therefore, the sample was stratified by type of district:

- **Stratum 1:** The IADP districts refer to the Intensive Agricultural Development Programme started in 1961 to boost agricultural production in 16 districts in the major states in India. The programme meant a strong government effort to provide farmers with know-how, technology, modern inputs, price incentives, marketing support, and credit. This strategy was later used in the implementation of the Green Revolution from 1967 onwards. About 20 per cent of the sample comes from these 16 districts.
- **Stratum 2:** The IAAP districts refer to Intensive Agricultural Area Programme started in 1964 in 114 districts. The same strategy as in the IADP districts was applied and became a major force in the successful broadening of the Green Revolution in the late sixties and onwards. About 40 per cent of the sample comes from these districts
- **Stratum 3:** The rest of the sample is made up from most major states and districts, which was originally thought to represent those regions where agriculture was still based on traditional technologies.

Within each stratum and the districts selected there was a three stage sample design:

1 selection of blocks based on probability proportional to size (PPS) (in stratum 2 and 3 also based on cropping pattern)
2 selection of on average two villages within the blocks based on PPS
3 within each village selected, there was, finally, a selection of around 20 households based on a stratification of the households according to their income:

> about 10–20 per cent belonging to the richest households; about 20–40 per cent belonging to the middle income households; and the rest belonging to the poorer households. Since the two first groups are estimated to be only about 10 per cent of the population, this stratified sample was made in order to ensure statistical representativity for each sub-group.[2]

In order to get estimates representative of the population sampled, weighting of individual households is required. In modelling, however, we use unweighted data. Cases of non-response and inconsistent data are excluded. We have selected the entire cross section samples for 1971 and 1982. For 1999 and 2006 we have selected the entire cross section sample of un-partitioned households and added a number of descendant households, sampled at random, if there was more than one household descendant from a 1982 household. By including the descendants, one can control for the bias arising from the ageing of the panel.

The cross sectional and panel data are shown in Table A1.1.

We have compared the attrition cases with those who responded in the panel in 1982 on a number of characteristics in 1971 such as cultivated area, income, proportion of non-farm income, family type, agricultural labourers and literacy. It turns out that the two populations are very similar but for the tendency that attrition is positively correlated with proportion of non-farm income, indicating that households with lower stakes in the farm sector were less interested in participating or more difficult to get hold of. This may underestimate the effect of non-farm income in the models.

Similarly we have compared the attrition cases in 1999 with those who responded in the panel in 1982. Also here the similarities strike the eye, though

Table A1.1 Details about ARIS REDS samples and panels

Cross–sections	*Sample size (n)*	*(%)*	*Weighting*
1971	4121	–	Weights in the original sample make for statistical representativity
1982	4983	–	Descendants selected inherit the original weight of the household
1999	5933	–	Ditto
2006	119034	–	Ditto
Panels			
1971 to 1982	2859	–	
1982 to 1999	2790	–	
1999 to 2006	1755		
Attrition			
1971 to 1982	1262	31	
1982 to 1999	2193	47	
1999 to 2006	4178	70	

the attrition cases are slightly poorer, rely somewhat more on non-agricultural income, and have slightly less area under cultivation. However, the differences are small and do not warrant any conclusion about significant dissimilarities between the two populations.

Bardhan noted that the sample of ARIS-REDS villages in the first round often had many villages with factories in them.[3] He is right in suspecting that this may imply a bias in the sample and that it may overstate the ST. Together with the severe attrition for the 1999 to 2006 wave, this has to be kept in mind when interpreting the results.

Weighting, attrition and pairing problems in REDS

The weighting system in ARIS-REDS thus makes it easy to derive population estimates and compute confidence intervals for 1971, but attrition makes them increasingly problematic for the other waves. Problems are compounded by the fact that no separate weights are available for the later waves. Thus the surveys have not been balanced to make each cross-sectional sample statistically representative of the entire population (as was the case in 1971). Moreover, only the 1971 weights are available, making it problematic to work out population estimates for the later rounds.

The researcher is consequently put into a situation where (s)he can either use the unweighted data, thus making estimates descriptive of the sample, rather than of the population. Alternatively, one can use the 1971 weights to compute population estimates but these would be biased and marred by attrition for the later rounds. We have chosen just to describe the sample.[4]

Trying to pair data based on the information available at the secure server[5] proved a virtual nightmare. Thanks to dogged efforts by our colleagues, Sultana Nasrin and Björn Holmquist, we were able to sort out some of the pairing problems.[6]

The 2006 household listing IDs in *hlist06* in *hdeck00f* are not unique to the different households. Merging of the files *listing2006* and *hdeck00f* based on *hlist06* results in a close to random matching.

There are indications that the numbers in *hlist06* may be unique to households on the village level. In that case a combination of the variables *villageid* and *hlist06* may tentatively be used for the matching. Such a variable may for example be computed as = *villageid*10000+hlist06*, which can be calculated in both files and then be used for merging. In that case the 1999 interview numbers in *hdeck00f* can be incorporated into the file *listing2006*. But this presumes that the correspondence between the *hlist06* numbers and the 1999 interview numbers for the households in *hdeck00f* is correct. Unfortunately there are many errors in this description. Some of these may be typing errors, but others seem to be gross errors e.g. when assigning the wrong set of 1999 interview numbers to a village.

Excel sheets available at the website mentioned describe how the *hlist06* numbers (given in 2006) and the 1999 interview numbers (given in 1999) have been connected, but these are totally missing for some States and many villages.

The matching technique used for this book draws on the listing of serial numbers of households in 1999, which are also available in *listing2006* (variable *q2*). These are unique to households on the village level. We then calculate: *=villageid 99*10000+q2*. This can be used as a merging variable with any file containing village identifiers in 1999 and household listing numbers in 1999.

For files containing 1999 interview numbers only, household listing numbers for the different villages can be derived from the Excel files (describing the match between these listing numbers and the 1999 interview numbers), which are available for all states except West Bengal, Madhya Pradesh Uttar Pradesh and Assam.

The incomplete matching of the 1999 and 2006 REDS waves and problems of attrition and bias in the data are the reasons for drawing upon another survey, in addition to ARIS-REDS. This is the Human Development Profile of India (HDPI) collected in 1994/95 and made into a panel with the collection of India Human Development Survey in 2004/05. These datasets are exemplary, reasonably clean, with good data descriptions and good weighting systems. They have been used instead of the REDS 1999–2006 panel.

In the summer of 2015, the second wage of the India Human Development Survey (IHDS-II) was published (Desai and Vanneman 2016). We deemed it too late to be incorporated in the models. Since these were originally designed to capture the situation in the late twentieth century, trying to fit them to more recent data would have called for changes in model design. The IHDS-II data have been drawn upon as population estimates in the Conclusion. They are then weighted according to the weighting regime designed by the original researchers (ibid.)

Notes

1 See http://adfdell.pstc.brown.edu/arisreds_data/

2 The description here is based on Additional Rural Incomes Survey Desai, S. and R. Vanneman (2016). *India Human Development Survey-II (IHDS-II), 2011–12*, Inter-university Consortium for Political and Social Research (ICPSR) [distributor].

3 Pranab Bardhan, personal communication.

4 Dhamija and Bhide reached the same conclusion Dhamija, N. and S. Bhide (2011). "Dynamics of Chronic Poverty: Variations in factors infuencing entry and exit of chronic poor." *CPRC-IIPA Working Paper No. 38*, Indian Institute of Public Administration, New Delhi, Chronic Poverty Research Centre..

5 At Brown University: adfdell.pstc.brown.edu/arisreds_data/, a site maintained by Andrew Foster at the University and as per agreement with the data owners: National Council of Applied Economic Research, New Delhi (www.ncaer.org).

6 We acknowledge contributions in mail communications with Andrew Foster, Hans Binswanger-Mkhize, Sudhir K. Singh, Anirudh Tagat and Hari Nagarajan.

Appendix 2

Multilevel modelling with MLWin

The models in this book (Chapters 5–7) were fitted with multilevel techniques and the software package MLWin (Rasbash *et al.* 2010). Thus the dependent variable in all three models was defined as four levels (State, district, village and household), which allows for decomposition of the total variance into parts stemming from variation at all four levels. The link functions were binomial logit in Model 1, multinomial ordered logit in Model 2, and normal in Model 3. The models contain higher-level variables at the village level, such as village ecotype, but not at higher levels such as district[1] or State. Other village-, district- and State effects are captured in the random parts of the models. All models were fitted with Maximum Likelihood (ML) estimation, in some cases using the ML estimates as priors in a second stage, using Markov-Chain Monte Carlo (MCMC) methods. An exception here is Model 2, which proved hard to fit with the routines available in MLWin. Here we resorted to an SPSS routine: GENLINMIXED, which was up to the task (for more details see Chapter 6).

Model 1: entry into and exit from farming

In Chapter 5 we model a household-level binary variable, "cultivator status." Thus the dependent variable for the first period (y_{t1}) is the odds of being a cultivator at (t_1) regressed on, first of all, cultivator status at the beginning of the period (t_0). Basically we model four outcomes:

Table A2.1 Cultivator status at t_0 and t_1, number of cases (n)

	Cultivator status at t_1		
	No	*Yes*	*Total*
Cultivator status at t_0			
No	n_{00}	n_{01}	n_{0+}
Yes	n_{10}	n_{11}	n_{1+}
Total	n_{+0}	n_{+1}	n_{++}

The logged odds of being a cultivator at (t_1) are taken to be a function of a vector of independent variables. Thus for t_1 we work with the following binary logistic regression model:

$$\ln(p_{1t1ijkl}/(1-p_{1t1ijkl}) = \alpha_{0jkl} + \lambda y_{t0ijkl} + \beta_1 x_{1ijkl} + \ldots + \beta_n x_{nijkl}, + e_{ijkl}$$

where:

$p_{1t1ijkl} = E(y_{t1ijkl})$;

$\ln(p_{1t1ijkl}/(1-p_{1t1ijkl}))$ is the natural logarithm of the odds $(p_{1t1ijkl}/(1p_{1t1ijkl}))$ of being a cultivator in t_1

α_{0jkl} = constant

λ = regression factor for:

y_{t0ijkl}, i.e. the value of the dependent variable at t_0

β_{nijkl} = regression factors for:

x_{ijkl} = independent variables, measuring change either (1) between t_0 = 1969–71 and t_1 = 1982, (2) between 1982 and 1999; or (3) 1994/95 and 2004/05.

e_{ijkl} = residual, in this multilevel model partitioned into state, district village and household level.

Subscripts refer to the levels of the model, i.e. i = household, j = village, k = district and l = State.

Independent and control variables are:

1 the autoregressive component, i.e. having been a cultivator in (t_0) (y_{t0})
2 having partitioned the household since (t_0), i.e. a dummy[2]
3 age of head of household at t_1, logged
4 a number of other variables. For details see Chapter 5.

Since the dependent variable (y_{t1}) is a binary variable coded =1 for being a cultivator and = 0 otherwise, without the autoregressive component (y_{t0}) we would be modeling the log odds of being a cultivator at t_1. Introducing the autoregressive variable, we are instead modeling the odds cultivator status not changing (y_{t0} = 1; y_{t1} = 1, or the obverse: y_{t0} = 0; y_{t1} = 0). In other words, for those who were cultivators at t_0 we model the odds of remaining a cultivator also at t_1 and, for those who were not cultivating any land at t_0 we model the odds of their still being non-cultivators at t_1.

Out of the four outcomes in Table A2.1 then, only two outcomes are directly modeled. But since both the dependent and the autoregressive variables are binary, the model implies the other two outcomes.[3] Of these, the first outcome is most interesting, since it models the odds for a cultivator to exit farming. Multiplying all regression coefficients, including the constant by –1, as has been done in the tables, gives the equation for both these outcomes.

Model 2: mobility between size-classes of cultivated area

The question asked and answered in Model 2 concerns factors influencing the probability of being downwardly or upwardly mobile in size-class of cultivated area. Formulated this way, the problem can be addressed with a multinomial logistic regression model. Once again we need three models for the three periods already mentioned.

While logistic regression was originally worked out for binary dependent variables, multinomial logistic regression is a variety adapted to nominal scales. In ordinary binomial logistic regression the dependent variables are the natural logarithm of the odds ((p/(1–p)). In multinomial regression y is similarly *the probability of one outcome* (say downward (p_1)) *relative to a reference category* (i.e. p_2 = the probability of stability in size-class)). The dependent variable y_1 of outcome 1 is the natural logarithm or the logit of the relative risk (p_1/p_2) where p_2 is set = 1. For the reference category there is an implicit equation with all β-values = 0 and the intercept equal to the log of the of the overall odds of downward mobility ($p_2/(1-(p_1+p_3))$)). Since the latter need not be reported, the output in this case gives two equations, one for downward and the other for upward mobility.

$$y_{ijklm} = g\,(cons_{jklm}, \pi + 03c0_{ijklm})$$

$$1\mathrm{n}(\pi_{1jklm} / \pi_{2jklm}) = \alpha_{1jklm} + (X\beta_{1jklm}) + h_{jklm}$$

$$1\mathrm{n}(\pi_{3jklm} / \pi_{2jklm}) = \alpha_{3jklm} + (X\beta_{2jklm}) + h_{jklm}$$

$$h_{jklm} = X\beta_{3jklm}$$

$$\mathrm{cov}\,(y_{sjklm}\, y_{rjklm}) = -\pi_{sjklm} * \pi_{sjklm} : s \neq r;\ \pi_{sjklm}(1-\pi_{rjklm}) : s = r;$$

Where subscripts denote the levels of the model: j = household, k = village, l = district and m = state. Subscript i refers to a fifth level created by the software and denoting three variables at sub-household level containing three dummies, where one is coded = 1 and the others = 0, depending upon the value of the dependent variable.

y_{ijklm} = the dependent variable, taking 3 values: 1 = downwardly mobile; 2 = stable and 3 = upwardly mobile in size-class of cultivated area.

g = the link function, in this case multinomial logit[4]

$cons_{jklm}$ = a vector of 1's
π_{1jklm} = the relative risk of a given value (1) of y compared to the reference category (stable, $y = 2$)

The model contains two equations modelling the natural logarithm, or logit of $\pi_{1jklm} / \pi_{2jklm}$ and $\pi_{3jklm} / \pi_{2jklm}$ as a function of:

α =an intercept for each outcome, α_{1jklm} and α_{3jklm} respectively

β = regression factors for each independent variable (X) at two levels of the model, household (j) and village (k).

We use no data at district and State level, but control for variance at this level in the random part of the models. As before we will list the independent variables as we formulate the hypotheses to be tested.

Model 3: Change in income

As a final step in the analysis we run an income change function as follows:

$$\ln\Delta y_{t1} = \ln(y_{t1}) - (y_{t\_1}) = \alpha + x'\beta$$

Where:

$E\ (y_t)$ = the expected value (E) of log income change (Δy_t) defined as:

$\ln(y_t) - \ln(y_{t\_1})$ = the difference between logged income in (t_1) and logged income in (t_{-1}), i.e. the equivalent to dividing income in (t_1) with income in (t_{-1})

α = constant

β is a vector of regression coefficients for independent variables

x is a vector of independent variables.

The independent variables are much the same as in the other models and defined text. As before we use no data at district and State level, but control for variance at this level in the random part of the models.

Notes

1 A partial exception would be the variable "Large landowner, belonging to the 20 per cent largest landowners in the District," which builds on a ranking at district level to code individual households.
2 A dummy is regression terminology for a binary variable, usually coded 0 and 1.
3 That is, ceasing to be a cultivator ($y_{t0} = 1$; $y_{t1} = 0$), or the obverse, becoming one ($y_{t0} = 0$; $y_{t1} = 1$).
4 The dependent variable is in effect ordinal, but with our way of modelling, with the same independent variables in the equations for both outcomes, we are in effect only drawing on the nominality of the dependent variable.

Appendix 3

Detailed model results and analyses of residuals

Table A3.1 Model 1: drivers of exit/entry to the farm sector, binomial logistic regression, detailed results

Parameter	*Panel 1, 1971–82*			*Panel 2, 1982–99*			*Panel 3, 1994/95–2004/05*			*Comparison of panels 1 and 2*			*Comparison of panels 2 and 3*		
	B	*SE*	*Sig.*	*B*	*SE*	*Sig.*	*B*	*SE*	*Sig.*	*B diff*	*SE*	*Sig.*	*B diff*	*SE*	*Sig.*
Constant	–1.41	0.81		–2.56	0.91	**	1.81	0.43	***	–1.15	1.22		4.37	1.01	§§§
Autoregressive component: Cultivator status at start of period	–1.78	0.29	***	–0.37	0.43		–2.07	0.14	***	1.41	0.52	§§	–1.70	0.45	§§§
Ecotype															
Intermediate ecotype	0.40	0.20		0.01	0.20		0.09	0.09		–0.38	0.29		0.08	0.22	
Wet ecotype	0.15	0.23		0.19	0.23		0.20	0.11		0.04	0.32		0.01	0.25	
Partitioned	–1.26	0.20	***	0.03	0.10		0.00	0.07		1.29	0.22	§§§	–0.03	0.12	
Age of HH, logged	0.19	0.20		0.34	0.19		–0.30	0.10	**	0.15	0.27		–0.64	0.21	§§
Caste groups															
Brahmin and other Upper Caste	0.08	0.19		–0.21	0.18		–0.41	0.11	***	–0.28	0.26		–0.20	0.21	
Scheduled Caste	0.38	0.21		0.47	0.21	*	0.25	0.10	*	0.08	0.30		–0.21	0.23	
Scheduled Tribe	0.09	0.28		–0.17	0.29		–0.25	0.13		–0.26	0.40		–0.08	0.31	
Other Backward Caste	–0.06	0.19		0.15	0.18		–0.20	0.10		0.20	0.26		–0.34	0.20	
Farm type, large farmer, among 20% largest landowners in District															
Family farmer, narrow definition	0.87	0.24	***	0.45	0.26		0.40	0.07	***	–0.42	0.35		–0.05	0.27	
Smallholders – agricultural labourer	2.19	0.36	***	1.25	0.31	***	0.66	0.08	***	–0.94	0.48	§	–0.59	0.32	
Landless agricultural labourer	1.36	0.23	***	2.26	0.52	***	0.12	0.15		0.90	0.57		–2.13	0.54	§§§
Non–agricultural household	0.93	0.25	***	1.71	0.51	***	0.00	0.00		0.78	0.57				
Petty landlord	0.00	0.00	1.16	0.32	***					1.16	0.32	§§§			
Gone pluriactive since start of period	0.04	0.20		–0.48	0.36		–0.01	0.16		–0.52	0.41				
Joint family, at the end of period	–0.80	0.12	***	–0.72	0.10	***	–0.91	0.08	***	0.08	0.16		–0.19	0.13	
Head of household studied beyond primary level, dummy	–0.22	0.24		0.21	0.11		–0.21	0.05	***	0.43	0.27		–0.42	0.13	§§§
Proportion of non–farm income, village level mean	0.97	0.23	***	1.10	0.18	***	1.40	0.07	***	0.13	0.29		0.30	0.20	
No. of cases	2844			2731			10255								
Missing (%)	43			45			1								
–2*Loglikehood, null model	3203.41			3477.22			13165.10								
–2*Loglikehood, full model	1456.96			2687.60			9106.94								

Parameter	*Panel 1, 1971–82*			*Panel 2, 1982–99*			*Panel 3, 1994/95–2004/05*			*Comparison of panels 1 and 2*			*Comparison of panels 2 and 3*		
	B	*SE*	*Sig.*	*B*	*SE*	*Sig.*	*B*	*SE*	*Sig.*	*B diff*	*SE*	*Sig.*	*B diff*	*SE*	*Sig.*
Chi^2, p–value of	0.00		***	0.00		***	0.00		***						
Random effects:	Estimate	SE		Estimate	SE		Estimate	SE							
State	0.25	0.14		0.04	0.06		0.42	0.16	**						
District	0.31	0.12	**	0.28	0.12	*	0.14	0.04	***						
Village	0.22	9.21		0.42	0.11	***	0.24	0.04	***						
Household	1.00	0.00		1.00	0.00		1.00								

Source: ARIS and HDPI-IHDS data

Note: For a detailed version see Table A3.3. "Constant" denotes the estimated ($\hat{\alpha}$). Similarly "B" denotes the estimated regression coefficients ($\hat{\beta}$). Arrows denote positive and negative associations so that an upward pointing arrow indicates a positive correlation with exit/entry, while *, ** and ***, and §, §§ and §§§ denote 5, 1 and 0.1 per cent level of significance. Results are after removal of 8 outliers in period1 , 18 in period 2

Table A3.2 Model 2: drivers of mobility in size–class of operated area. Multilevel multinomial logistic regression, detailed results

Fixed part		*Panel 1, 1971–82*		*Panel 2, 1982–99*		*Panel 3, 1994/95–2004/05*		*Comparison of panels*			
Parameter	*Direction*	*B*	*Sig.*	*B*	*Sig.*	*B*	*Sig.*	*Coeff ch*	*Sig.*	*Coeff ch*	*Sig.*
Constant	Downward	–1.58		2.47	*	–0.26		4.05	§§	–2.74	§
	Upward	–1.64		–3.70	*	–2.05	**	–2.06		1.65	
Ecotype						0.93					
Intermediate ecotype	Downward	–0.03		–0.07		0.56	***	–0.04		0.63	§§
	Upward	0.03		–0.12		0.65	***	–0.15		0.77	§§§
Wet ecotype	Downward	0.01		–0.20		0.11		–0.20		0.31	
	Upward	0.08		0.21		0.12		0.13		–0.10	
Partitioned	Downward	0.49	***	0.42	**	0.14		–0.07		–0.28	
	Upward	–0.43	**	–0.24		0.07		0.19		0.31	
Age of HH, logged	Downward	0.53	*	–0.46		–0.60	***	–0.98	§§	–0.15	
	Upward	0.23		0.50		0.07		0.27		–0.42	
Caste groups, ref cat: Brahmin and other Upper Caste											
Scheduled Caste	Downward	–0.12		–0.21		–0.19		–0.10		0.02	
Scheduled Tribe	Downward	–0.09		–0.21		0.17		–0.13		0.38	
Other Backward Caste	Downward	0.01		–0.18		–1.23	***	–0.19		–1.05	§§§
Other caste	Downward	–0.07		–0.22		–1.56	***	–0.15		–1.34	§§§
Scheduled Caste	Upward	–0.53	*	–0.17		0.58	***	0.36		0.76	§
Scheduled Tribe	Upward	–0.09		–0.03		0.38		0.07		0.41	
Backward caste	Upward	–0.33		–0.04		0.53	***	0.29		0.57	§
Other caste	Upward	–0.18		–0.07		0.48	*	0.11		0.55	
Farm type, large farmer, among 20% largest landowners in District											
Family farmer, narrow definition	Downward	–1.05	***	–0.86	***	–1.23	***	0.20		0.75	§§
Smallholders – agricultural labourer	Downward	–2.72	***	–2.54	***	–1.56	***	0.18		2.42	§§§
Landless agricultural labourer	Downward										
Petty landlord	Downward										
Non–agricultural household	Downward										

Fixed part		*Panel 1, 1971–82*		*Panel 2, 1982–99*		*Panel 3, 1994/95–2004/05*		*Comparison of panels*			
Parameter	*Direction*	*B*	*Sig.*	*B*	*Sig.*	*B*	*Sig.*	*Coeff ch*	*Sig.*	*Coeff ch*	*Sig.*
Family farmer, narrow definition	Upward	0.11		0.82		–0.10		0.71		–0.92	§
Smallholders – agricultural labourer	Upward	–0.26		0.58		–0.12		0.84		–0.70	
Landless agricultural labourer	Upward										
Petty landlord	Upward										
Non–agricultural household	Upward										
Gone pluriactive since start of period	Upward	–0.27		0.02		0.12		0.29		0.09	
	Downward	0.10		–0.60		0.14		–0.70		0.74	
Joint family, at the end of period	Upward	–0.39	***	0.34	**	0.07		0.73	§§§	–0.27	
	Downward	0.25		0.12		–0.60	***	–0.13		–0.72	§§
Head of household studied beyond primary level, dummy	Upward	0.01		0.15		0.07		0.15		–0.08	
	Downward	–0.08		0.57	***	0.06		0.06		–0.51	§§
Proportion of non–farm income, village level mean	Upward	–0.46		–1.13	*	–0.19		–0.67		0.94	
	Downward	–0.46		–0.20		0.17		0.26		0.36	
No. of cases		1772		1437		8869					
Missing (%)		38		48		3					
Deviance of null model		3873.92		3031.76		6936.92					
Deviance of full model		3480.23		2718.58		3971.03					
Chi^2		8.56	***	6.96	***	65.91	***				
Random part											
Variance shares	**Estimate**	**Sig.**	**Estimate**	**Sig.**	**Estimate**	**Sig.**					
State, Downward/Downward	Downward/ Downward	0.02				0.55					
State, Upward/Downward		–0.08				–0.82					
State, Upward/Upward		0.19				1.30					
District, Downward/Downward	Downward/ Downward	0.22	*	0.13	*	0.30					

(Continued)

Table A3.2 Continued

Fixed part		*Panel 1, 1971–82*		*Panel 2, 1982–99*		*Panel 3, 1994/95–2004/05*		*Comparison of panels*			
Parameter	*Direction*	*B*	*Sig.*	*B*	*Sig.*	*B*	*Sig.*	*Coeff ch*	*Sig.*	*Coeff ch*	*Sig.*
District, Upward/Downward		–0.09		–0.28	***						
District, Upward/Upward		0.33	*	0.26	*	0.73					
Village, Downward/Downward	Downward/ Downward	0.27		0.24							
Village, Upward/Downward		–0.18				–0.06					
Village, Upward/Upward		0.27	*								

Source: ARIS and HDPI-IHDS data

Note: Constant" denotes the estimated ($\hat{\alpha}$). Similarly "B" denotes the estimated regression coefficients ($\hat{\beta}$), while *, ** and *** denote 5, 1 and 0.1 per cent level of significance. This model is the best approximation possible with the MLWin programme. The iteration did not converge why the results are not fully reliable. Compare the results of the GENLINMIXED model reported in Chapter 6

Note 1: For Period 2, the co–variance structure has been simplified to two district level variances

Note 2: In the last period, there were too few cases for using 'Gone Pluriactive' as an indicator. Instead we used the non–agricultural share of household income

Table A3.3 Model 3: drivers of change in income, log–log ordinary least square regression, detailed results

Model 3 Income change	*Panel 1, 1971–82*			*Panel 2, 1982–99*			*Panel 3, 1994/95–2004/05–99*			*Comparison of panels 1 and 2*			*Comparison of panels 2 and 3*		
Parameter	*B*	*SE*	*Sig.*	*B*	*SE*	*Sig.*	*B*	*SE*	*Sig.*	*B diff*	*SE*	*Sig.*	*B diff*	*SE*	*Sig.*
Constant	1.13	0.23	***	–0.33	0.37		–0.22	0.18		–1.46	0.44	§§§	–1.24	0.47	§§
Ecotype															
Intermediate ecotype	–0.05	0.07		0.09	0.08		–0.12	0.04	**	0.14	0.11		0.26	0.11	§
Wet ecotype	–0.11	0.09		–0.05	0.10		–0.07	0.05		0.06	0.13		0.13	0.14	
Partitioned	–0.10	0.04	**	0.01	0.05		–0.20	0.02	***	0.11	0.06		0.31	0.06	§§§
Age of HH, logged	–0.20	0.05	***	–0.01	0.09		–0.02	0.04		0.20	0.10		0.22	0.11	§
Household size at the start of period, logged	–0.34	0.03	***	0.05	0.01	***	–0.24	0.02	***	0.39	0.03	§§§	0.63	0.04	§§§
Caste groups															
Scheduled Caste	–0.20	0.05	***	–0.07	0.08		–0.07	0.03	*	0.13	0.09		0.20	0.10	§
Scheduled Tribe	–0.08	0.08		–0.05	0.11		–0.07	0.05		0.04	0.13		0.11	0.14	
Other Backward Caste	–0.10	0.04	*	–0.15	0.06	*	–0.04	0.03		–0.05	0.07		–0.01	0.08	
Other Castes	–0.09	0.05		0.02	0.08		–0.03	0.05		0.11	0.10		0.14	0.11	
Farm type, large farmer, among 20% largest landowners in District															
Family farmer, narrow definition	0.31	0.04	***	–0.23	0.09	*	0.44	0.03	***	–0.53	0.10	§§§	–0.97	0.11	§§§
Smallholders – agricultural labourer	0.30	0.10	**	–0.33	0.13	**	0.36	0.03	***	–0.63	0.16	§§§	–0.99	0.17	§§§
Landless agricultural labourer	0.27	0.06	***	–0.53	0.13	***	0.89	0.04	***	–0.79	0.14	§§§	–1.68	0.14	§§§
Non–agricultural household	0.46	0.07	***	–0.47	0.13	***	0.81	0.05	***	–0.93	0.14	§§§			
Petty landlord	0.51	0.07	***	–0.45	0.12	***				–0.96	0.13	§§§	–1.77	0.14	§§§
Gone pluriactive since start of period	0.05	0.05		–0.11	0.13		0.33	0.04	***	–0.15	0.14		–0.49	0.14	§§§
Joint family, at the end of period	0.38	0.03	***	–0.52	0.05	***	0.55	0.03	***	–0.90	0.06	§§§	–1.45	0.06	§§§
Head of household studied beyond primary level, dummy	–0.02	0.06		0.01	0.05		0.04	0.02		0.03	0.08		0.00	0.08	

(Continued)

Table A3.3 Continued

Model 3 Income change	*Panel 1, 1971–82*			*Panel 2, 1982–99*			*Panel 3, 1994/95–2004/05–99*			*Comparison of panels 1 and 2*			*Comparison of panels 2 and 3*		
Parameter	*B*	*SE*	*Sig.*	*B*	*SE*	*Sig.*	*B*	*SE*	*Sig.*	*B diff*	*SE*	*Sig.*	*B diff*	*SE*	*Sig.*
Proportion of non–farm income, village level mean	0.23	0.16		–0.01	0.23		0.28	0.08	***	–0.24	0.28		–0.52	0.29	
No. of cases	2835			2754			10562								
Missing (%)	43			45			12								
Deviance of null model	7024.43			4702.44			29015.86								
Deviance of full model	6343.57			4348.18			27049.00								
Chi²	29.60		***	15.40	***		85.52		***						
Random effects by level	Estimate	SE		Estimate	SE		Estimate	SE		Estimate	SE				
State	0.06	0.03	*	0.11	0.05	*	0.04	0.02	*	0.20					
District	0.08	0.02	***	0.00	0.01		0.06	0.01	***	0.30					
Village	0.08	0.02	***	0.08	0.02	***	0.08	0.01	***	0.40					
Household	0.50	0.01	***	0.68	0.02	***	0.86	0.01	***	0.50					

Source: ARIS and HDPI-IHDS data

Note: Constant" denotes the estimated ($\hat{\alpha}$). Similarly "B" denotes the estimated regression coefficients ($\hat{\beta}$). *, ** and ***, and §, §§ and §§§ denote 5, 1 and .1 per cent level of significance. Results are after removal of 8 outliers in period, 18 in period 2

Analysis of residuals, Models 1 to 3, all periods

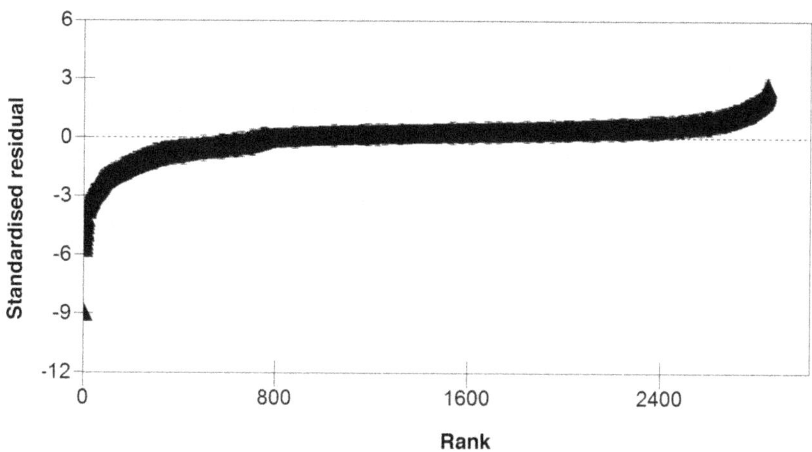

Figure A3.1a Model 1, Period 1: Household-level residuals

Note: One extreme value (extreme left in the graph) has been removed from the model. The other outliers on the left-hand side of the graph have been kept

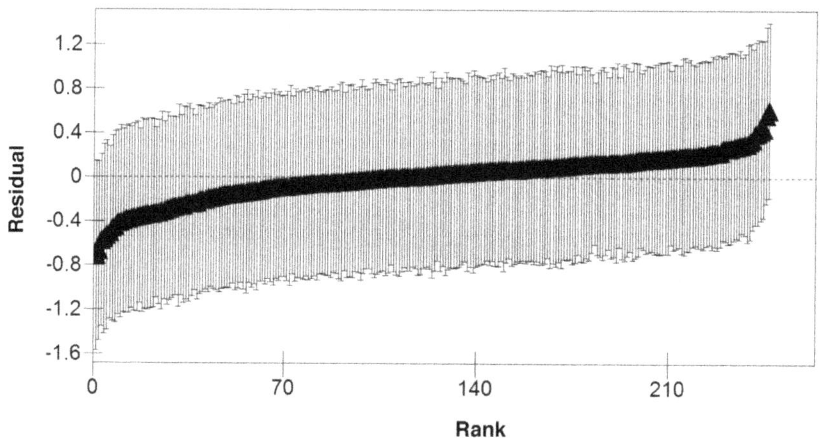

Figure A3.1b Model 1, Period 1: Village-level

Note: The black triangles above show the residual values of villages and the "legs" show a 95 per cent confidence interval. As can be seen the intervals in all cases include the value of zero, which is the mean residual. Thus no village deviates significantly from the mean

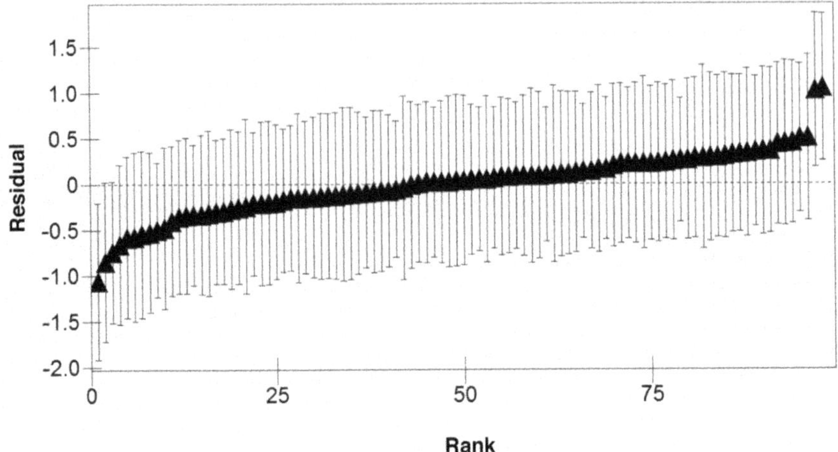

Figure A3.1c Model 1, Period 1: District-level

Note: District-level residuals contain one outlier to the left and two to the right. They are: Mallapuram in Kerala, Santhal Parganas in Bihar, i.e. a tribal district and Palghat in Kerala. These have been kept in the model. For State-wise residuals see Figure 5.6 State-wise residuals for Model 1, Periods 1, 2 and 3, p. 90

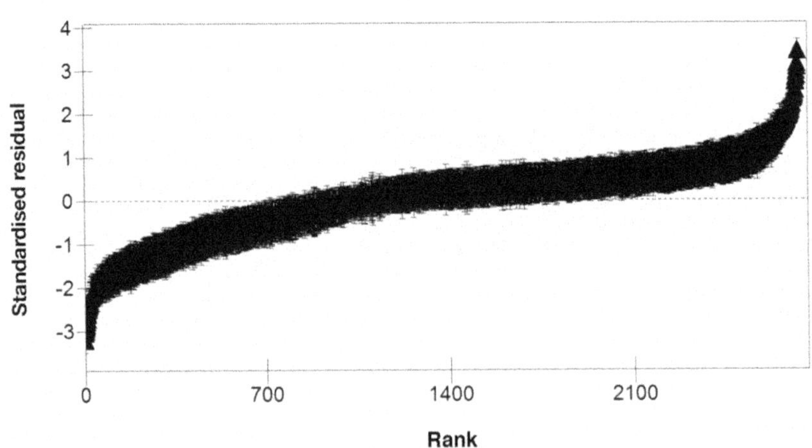

Figure A3.2a Model 1, Period 2: Household-level residuals

Note: There are no marked outliers; the distribution is approximately normal

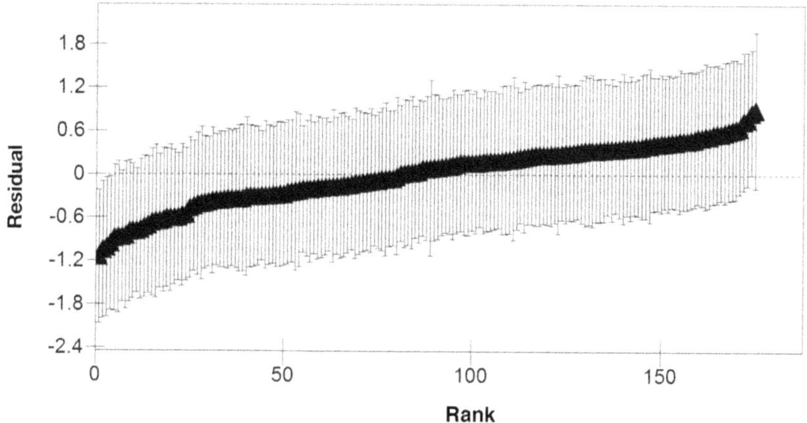

Figure A3.2b Model 1, Period 2: Village-level

Note: There are four outlying villages among the lower ranking one: one each in Orissa and Himachal Pradesh and two in Rajasthan

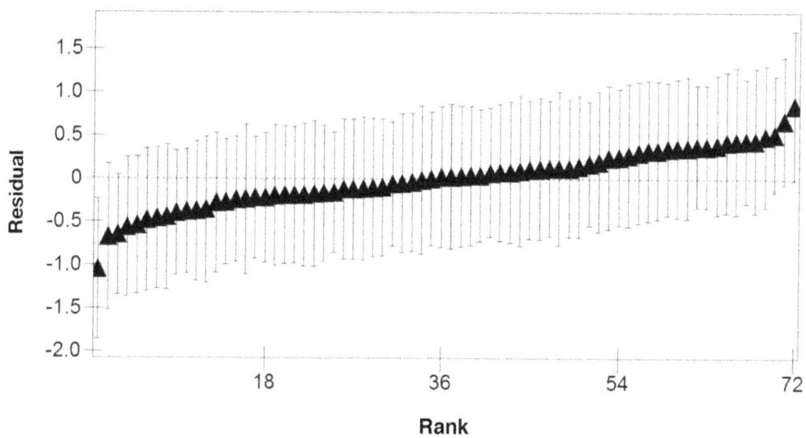

Figure A3.2c Model 1, Period 2: District-level

Note: One outlier at rank 1: Rajkhot in Gujarat. For State-wise residuals see Graph 5.6. State-wise residuals for Model 1, Periods 1, 2 and 3, p. 90

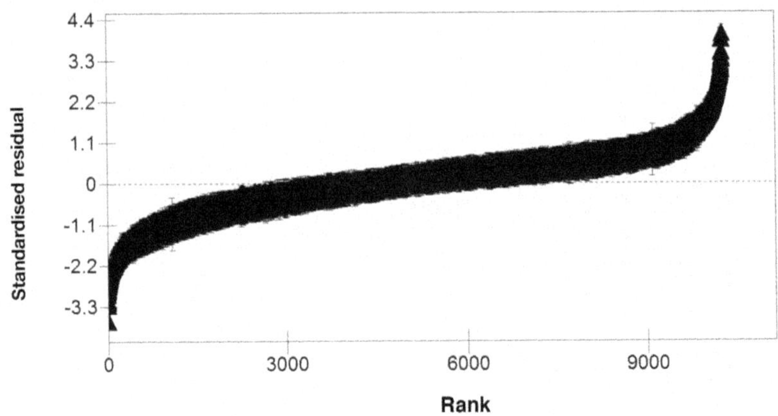

Figure A3.3a Model 1, Period 3: Household-level residuals

Note: There are no extreme cases and outliers have been kept in the model

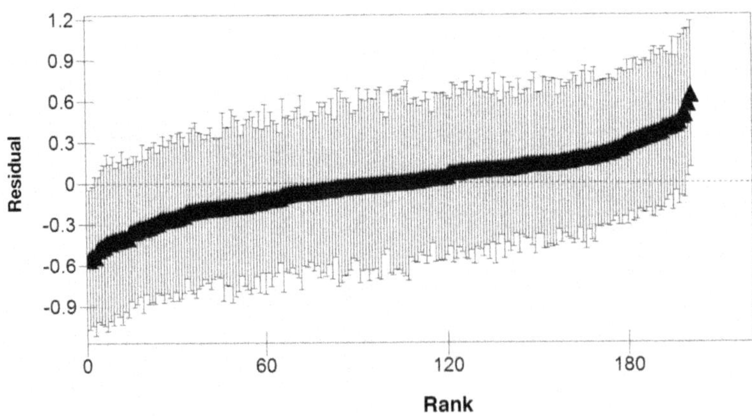

Figure A3.3b Model 1, Period 3: Village-level

Note: There are cases which are significantly different from zero (at 5 per cent level of confidence) but their z-values are not extreme, so they have been kept in the model

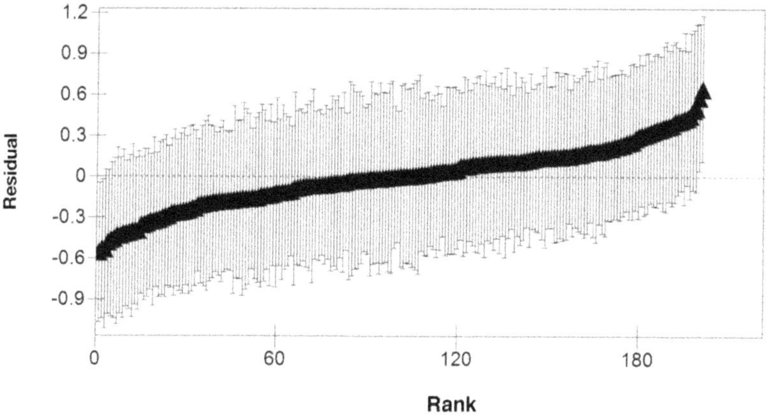

Figure A3.3c Model 1, Period 3: District-level

Note: Of the four outlying districts at each end of the distribution two are in Bihar and one each in Punjab and Andhra Pradesh. For State-wise residuals see Figure 5.6 State-wise residuals for Model 1, Periods 1, 2 and 3, p. 90

The image below shows the situation before using Hansen–Hurwitz estimators: Cases are clustering away from outcome C1 (upwardly mobile) and towards C2 (stable) and C3 (downwards). There are some outliers to the right of main cluster.

Figure A3.4a–d Model 2, Periods 1–3: Individual level residuals, before and after weighting

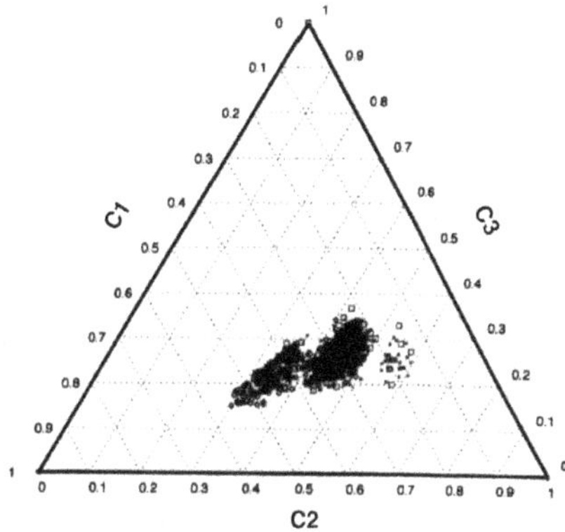

Figure A3.4a Period 1 (unweighted)

After weighting, the cases tend to cluster in the middle of the triangle, indicating an approximately normal distribution of residuals, while the outliers are clustering as before to the right of the main cluster.

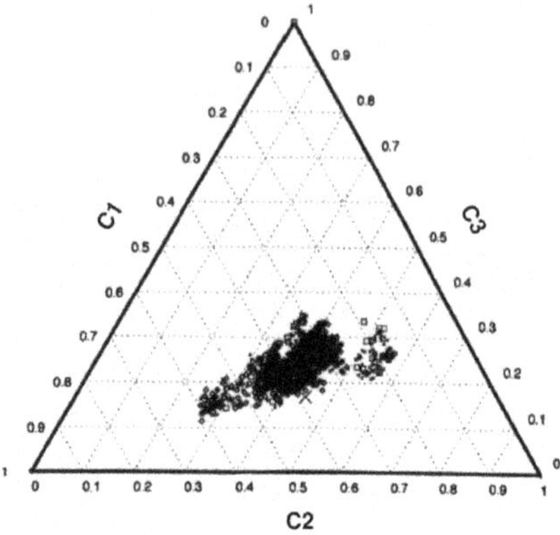

Figure A3.4b Period 1 (weighted)

Scattergrams for Period 2 are not reproduced here and look much the same for Period 2, but different in Period 3 when the number of cases is much higher.

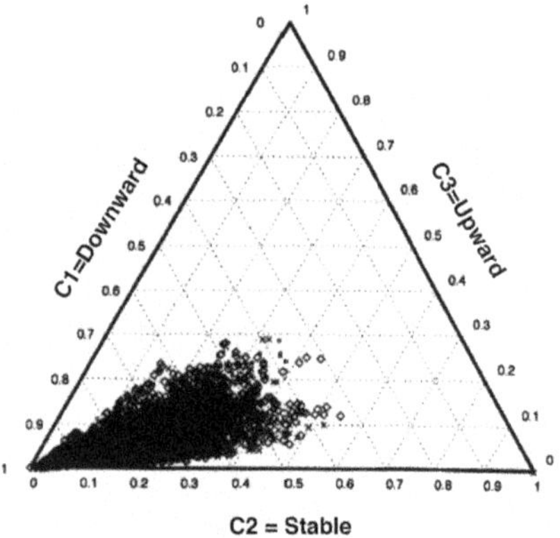

Figure A3.4c Period 3 (unweighted)

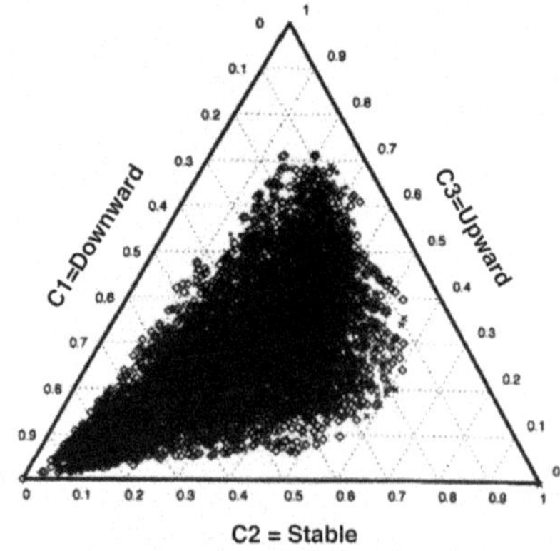

Figure A3.4d Period 3 (weighted)

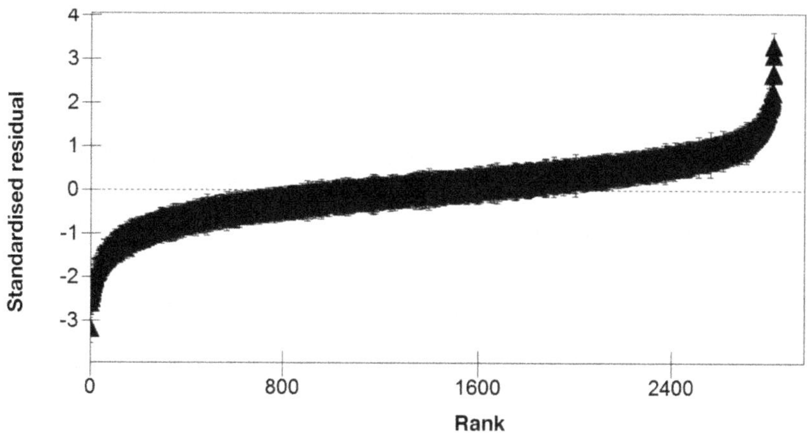

Figure A3.5a Model 3, Period 1: Household-level

Note: No extreme cases. Outliers have been kept in the model

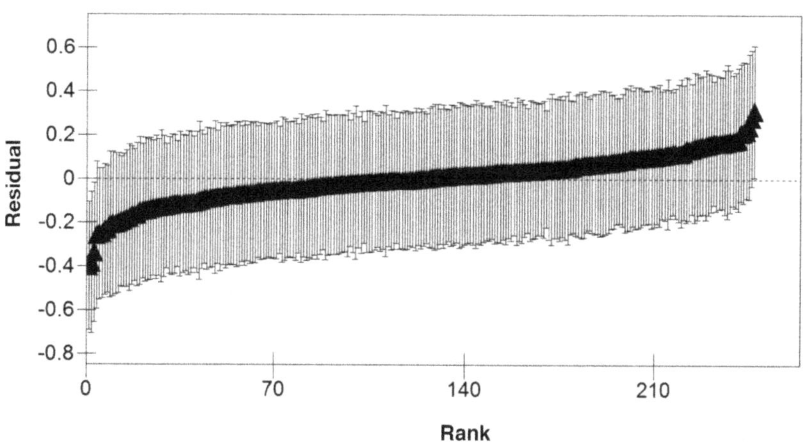

Figure A3.5b Model 3, Period 1: Village-wise

Note: The confidence intervals are wide but only a few means are significantly different from zero

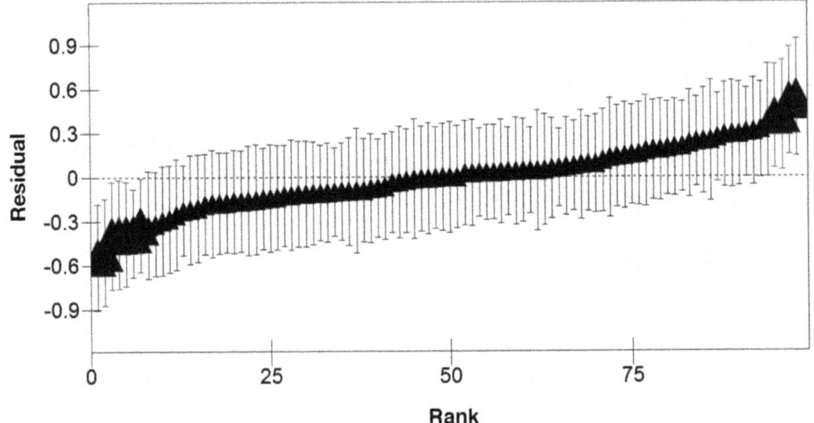

Figure A3.5c Model 3, Period 1: District-wise

Note: Around 10 districts significantly deviate from zero. These districts include Purnea Bihar, Chatarpur Madhya Pradesh, Chandrapur Maharashtra, Kutch Gujarat, Purulia West Bengal, Thanjavur Tamil Nadu, Khargone (West Nimar) Madhya Pradesh; and at the lowest ranks: Mandi Himachal Pradesh, Barda Gujarat, Bhojpur Bihar, Pune Maharashtra

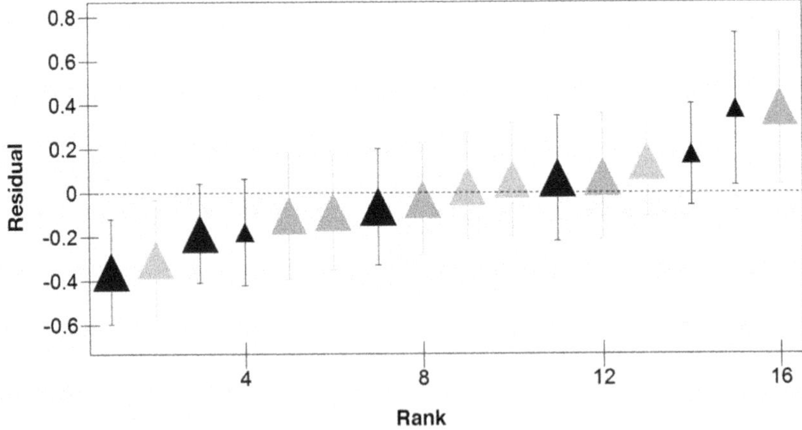

Figure A3.5d Model 3, Period 1: State-wise

Note: From low to high: Madhya Pradesh, West Bengal, Uttar Pradesh, Karnataka, Kerala, Bihar, Tamil Nadu, Gujarat, Andhra Pradesh, Orissa, Punjab, Maharashtra, Rajasthan, Jammu and Kashmir, Himachal Pradesh

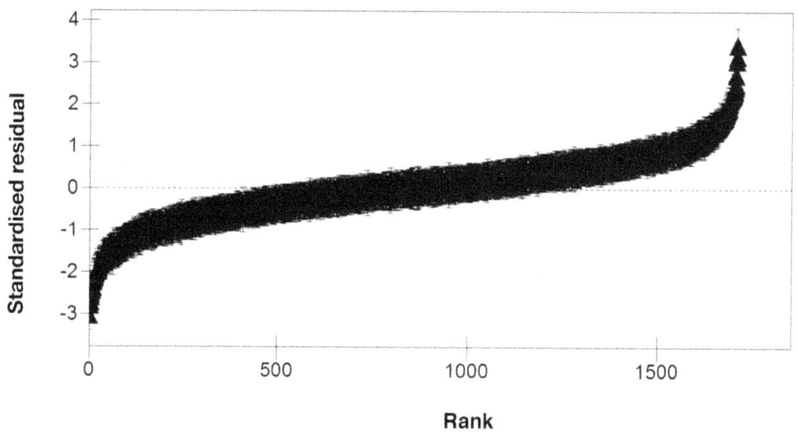

Figure A3.6a Model 3, Period 2: Household-level

Note: There are no outliers

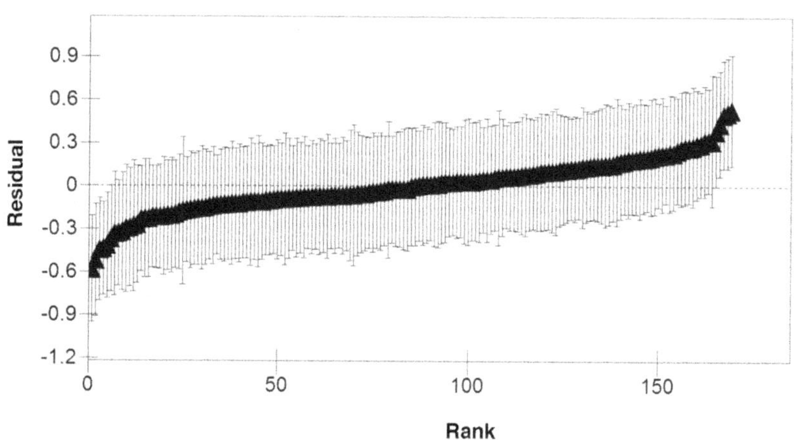

Figure A3.6b Model 3, Period 2: Village-level

Note: There are no extreme cases but 10 outliers which have been kept in the model

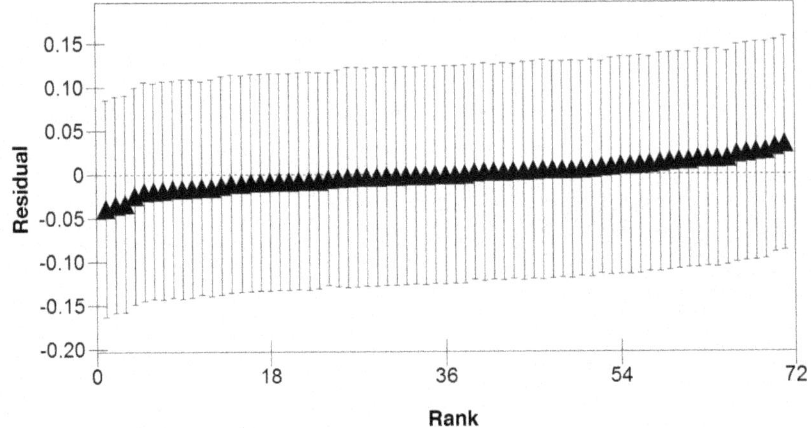

Figure A3.6c Model 3, Period 2: District-level

Note: No outliers but very broad confidence intervals. There may be something wrong with the district definitions

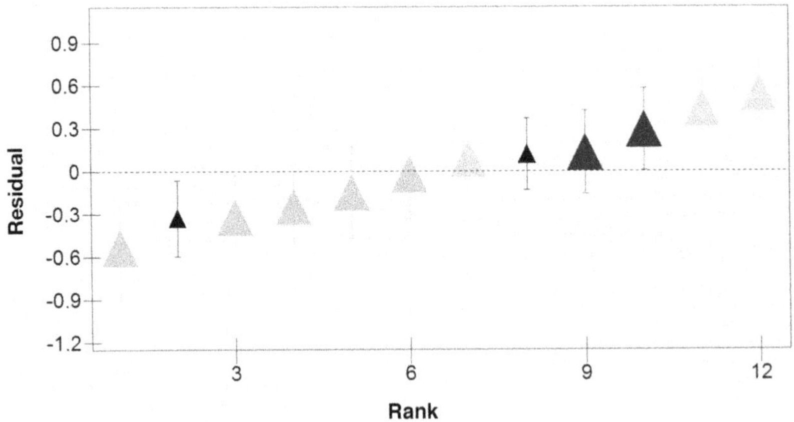

Figure A3.6d Model 3, Period 2: State-level

Note: From low to high rank: Himachal Pradesh, Karnataka, Kerala, Tamil Nadu, Punjab, Haryana, Gujarat, Rajasthan, Orissa, Bihar, Maharashtra, Andhra Pradesh

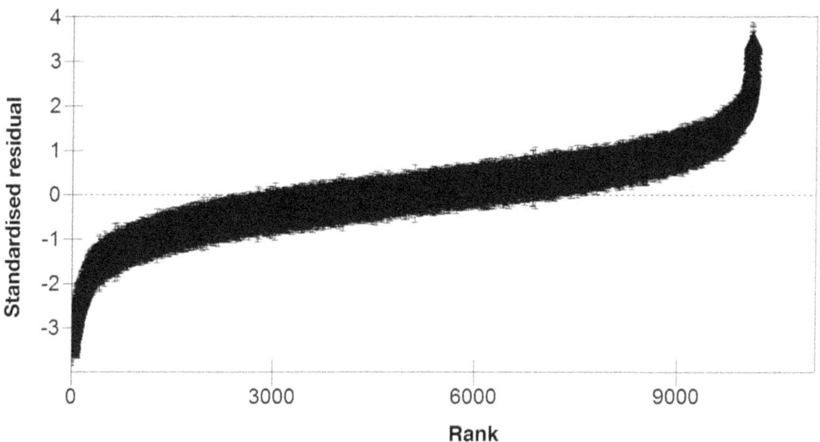

Figure A3.7a Model 3, Period 3: Household-level

Note: Looks normal, no extreme cases

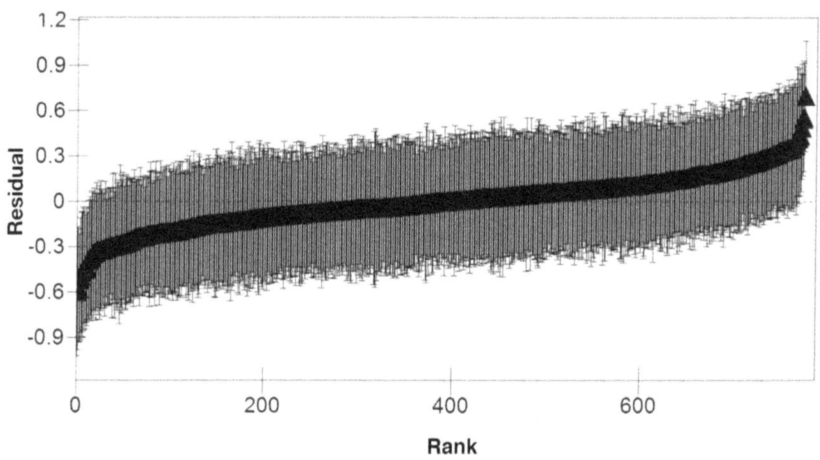

Figure A3.7b Model 3, Period 3: Village-level

Note: Broad confidence intervals and quite a number of outliers which have been kept in the model

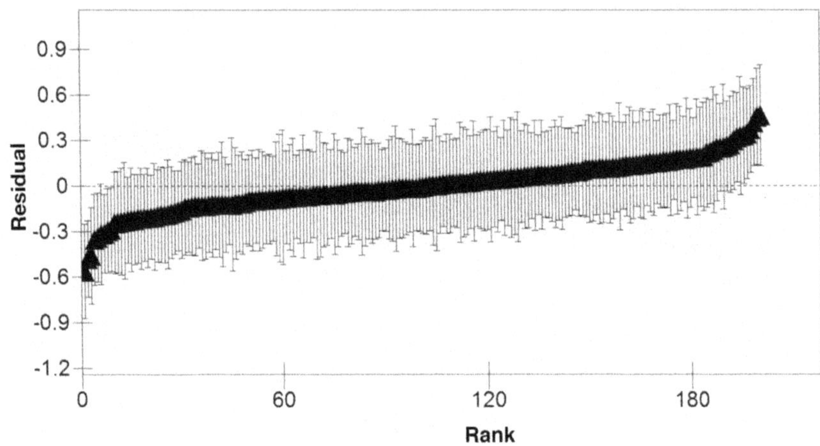

Figure A3.7c Model 3, Period 3: District-level

Note: Looks normal, no extreme cases

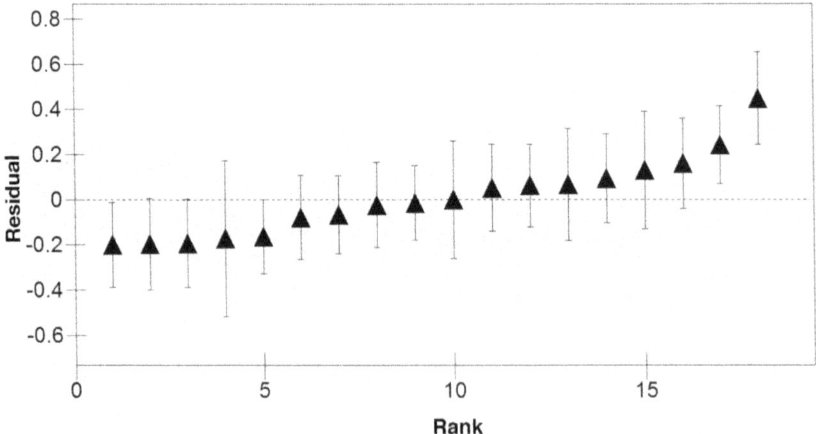

Figure A3.7d Model 3, Period 3: State-level

Note: Two outlying States: Himachal Pradesh and Rajasthan. Otherwise from 1: Andhra Pradesh, Tamil Nadu, Bihar, Assam, Madhya Pradesh, Gujarat, Orissa, Maharashtra, Jharkand, Chhattisgarh, Haryana, Kerala, West Bengal, Uttaranchal, Punjab

Appendix 4

Descriptive statistics

Table A4.1 Descriptive statistics of variables used in the analysis, cross–sectional means by survey round

	ARIS REDS 1971			*ARIS REDS 1982*			*HDPI 1994/95*			*IHDS I 2004/05*			*IHDS–II 2011/12*		
	m	*SE*	*missing (%)*	*m*	*SE*	*missing (%)*	*m*	*SE*	*missing (%)*	*m*	*SE*	*missing (%)*	*m*	*SE*	*missing (%)*
Cultivator status	0.72	0.007	7	0.70	0.006	0	0.66	0.003	0	0.36	0.002	0	0.45	0.002	0
Ecotype															
Dry ecotype	0.41	NA	0.07	0.33	NA	0	0.34	NA	1				0.28	NA	35
Intermediate ecotype	0.28	NA	7	0.33	NA	0	0.30	NA	1				0.24	NA	35
Wet ecotype	0.31	NA	7	0.34	NA	0	0.35	NA	1				0.47	NA	35
Partitioned	0.23	0.008	35	0.56	0.009	44				0.06	0.001	0			
Age of HH, logged	3.84	0.004	0	3.88	0.004	0				3.81	0.001	0	3.87	0.001	0
Caste groups															
Brahmin and other Upper Caste				0.37	NA	0				0.23	NA	0	0.19	NA	0
Scheduled Caste				0.13	NA	0				0.20	NA	0	0.18	NA	0
Scheduled Tribe				0.06	NA	0				0.08	NA	0	0.07	NA	0
Other Backward Caste				0.31	NA	0				0.34	NA	0	0.28	NA	0
Other Caste				0.14	NA	0				0.15	NA	0	0.28	NA	0
Farm type															
Large landowner, among 20% largest landowners in District	0.14	NA	0	0.02	NA	0	0.20	NA	0	0.13	NA	0	0.15	NA	16
Family farmer, narrow definition	0.55	NA	0	0.57	NA	0	0.31	NA	0	0.14	NA	0	0.15	NA	16
Smallholders – agricultural labourer	0.02	NA	0	0.06	NA	0	0.16	NA	0	0.12	NA	0	0.14	NA	16
Landless agricultural labourer	0.13	NA	0	0.10	NA	0	0.16	NA	0	0.13	NA	0	0.12	NA	16
Non–agricultural household	0.09	NA	0	0.18	NA	0	0.18	NA	0	0.39	NA	0	0.45	NA	16
Petty landlord	0.06	NA	0	0.06	NA	0		–		0.10	NA	0	0	NA	16

	ARIS REDS 1971			*ARIS REDS 1982*			*HDPI 1994/95*			*IHDS I 2004/05*			*IHDS–II 2011/12*		
	m	*SE*	*missing (%)*	*m*	*SE*	*missing (%)*	*m*	*SE*	*missing (%)*	*m*	*SE*	*missing (%)*	*m*	*SE*	*missing (%)*
Gone pluriactive since start of period or Share of non–agricultural income	0.09	0.005	0	0.01	0.002	0	–			0.18	0.002	0	0.74	0.002	0
Joint family	0.40	0.009	0	0.37	0.009	44	0.10	0.002	0	0.20	0.002	0	0.14	0.002	
Head of household studied beyond primary level, dummy	0.07	0.000	0	0.27	0.006	5	0.37	0.003	0	0.26	0.002	0	0.18	0.002	35
Proportion of non–farm income, village level mean	0.22	0.002	0	0.22	0.003	0	0.58	0.000	0	0.64	0.001	0	0.67	0.001	0

Notes:

1) All statistics are sample estimates. Weighting has not been applied
2) On farm types: the division between large landowners is arbitrary and these statistics cannot be used to draw inferences on the relative prevalence of each category
3) On ecotype 2004–05: data are inconsistent and withheld
4) 'Gone pluriactive' refers to 1971 and 1982, 'share of non-farm income' refers to 1994/95, 2004/05 and 2011–12

Table A4.2 Descriptive statistics of variables used in the analysis, means by panel

	ARIS REDS 1971–82				*ARIS REDS 1982–99*				*HDPI–IHDS 1994/95–2004/05*			
	n	*mean or prop*	*SE*	*Missing (%)*	*n*	*Mean or prop*	*SE*	*Missing (%)*	*n*	*Mean or prop*	*SE*	*Missing (%)*
Cultivator status at start of period	2857	0.73	0.008	35.32	2857	0.72	0.008	43	10255	0.69	0.005	0
Ecotype, at the start of period												
Dry ecotype	1231	0.43	NA	35	1014	0.36	NA	44	3315	0.32	NA	0
Intermediate ecotype	794	0.28		35	1045	0.38	NA	44	3203	0.31	NA	0
Wet ecotype	832	0.29		35	726	0.26	NA	44	3737	0.36	NA	0
Partitioned, at the end of period	2857	0.23	0.008	35	2766	0.56	0.009	44	10255	0.85	0.033	0
Age of HH at the end of period, logged	2853	3.82	0.005		2783	3.88	0.005	44	10255	3.88	0.003	0
Caste groups												
Brahmin and other Upper Caste	See 1982–99				958	0.34	NA	44	2198	0.21	NA	0
Scheduled Caste	See 1982–99				357	0.13	NA	44	2552	0.25	NA	0
Scheduled Tribe	See 1982–99				160	0.06	NA	44	1014	0.10	NA	0
Other Backward Caste	See 1982–99				923	0.33	NA	44	3436	0.34	NA	0
Other Caste					387	0.14	NA	44	1055	0.10	NA	0
Farm type, at the beginning of period												
Large landowner, among 20 largest landowners in District	403	0.14	NA	35	142	0.05	NA	44	2285	0.23	NA	0
Family farmer, narrow definition	1620	0.56	NA	35	1702	0.61	NA	44	3024	0.30	NA	0
Smallholders – agricultural labourer	62	0.02	NA	35	171	0.06	NA	44	1717	0.16	NA	0
Landless agricultural labourer	365	0.13	NA	35	235	0.08	NA	44	1604	0.15	NA	0
Non–agricultural household	218	0.08	NA	35	374	0.13	NA	44	1624	0.16	NA	0
Petty landlord	197	0.07	NA	35	161	0.06	NA	44	NA		NA	0

	ARIS REDS 1971–82				*ARIS REDS 1982–99*				*HDPI–IHDS 1994/95–2004/05*			
	n	*mean or prop*	*SE*	*Missing (%)*	*n*	*Mean or prop*	*SE*	*Missing (%)*	*n*	*Mean or prop*	*SE*	*Missing (%)*
Gone pluriactive since start of period or Share of non–agricultural income	2857	0.09	0.054	35	2785	0.03	0.003	44	10255	0.13	0.003	0
Joint family, at the end of period	See 1982–99				2785	0.37	0.009	44	10255	0.14	0.003	0
Head of household studied beyond primary level, dummy	2850	0.06	0.005	35	2750	0.28	0.009	45	10255	0.35	0.005	0
Proportion of non–farm income at the beginning of period, village level mean	2857	0.20	0.003	35	2784	0.28	0.003	44	10255	0.44	0.005	0

Notes:

1) All statistics are sample estimates. Weighting has not been applied

2) On farm types: the division between large landowners is arbitrary and these statistics cannot be used to draw inferences on the relative prevalence of each category

3) On ecotype 2004–05: data are inconsistent and withheld

4) ‘Gone pluriactive’ refers to 1971 and 1982, ‘share of non-farm income’ refers to 1994/95, 2004/05 and 2011–12

Table A4.3 Farm and houseold type by caste groups and survey round, per cent within rows

Year:	*Farm and household type (%)*	*Brahmin and upper castes (%)*	*Scheduled caste (%)*	*Scheduled tribe (%)*	*Other Backward Caste (%)*	*Other (%)*	*Total (%)*
1971	Large landowner, among 20% largest in District	47.90	6.70	2.70	30.30	12.40	100
	Family farmer, narrow definition, exluding 20% largest landowners in District	38.10	10.20	6.00	34.00	11.80	100
	Smallholder – agricultural labourer	22.60	33.90	6.50	27.40	9.70	100
	Landless agricultural labourer	15.70	30.30	12.70	25.70	15.70	100
	Non-agricultural household	35.90	13.00	2.20	30.00	18.80	100
	Petty landlord, agrarian household not cultivating any land, earning no agricultural wages	49.20	6.40	3.20	19.30	21.90	100
	Total	36.80	12.80	6.00	31.00	13.60	100
1982	Large landowner, among 20% largest in District	56.50	5.60	3.20	28.20	6.50	100
	Family farmer, narrow definition, exluding 20% largest landowners in District	39.70	9.30	5.00	33.30	12.70	100
	Smallholder – agricultural labourer	12.40	19.80	10.20	48.00	9.60	100
	Landless agricultural labourer	17.00	28.90	10.80	35.00	8.30	100
	Non-agricultural household	40.40	14.40	4.30	21.50	19.40	100
	Petty landlord, agrarian household not cultivating any land, earning no agricultural wages	40.70	12.20	7.10	20.80	19.20	100
	Total	36.70	12.80	5.90	31.00	13.60	100
1999	Large landowner, among 20% largest in District	45.00	3.60	2.80	36.80	11.80	100
	Family farmer, narrow definition, exluding 20% largest landowners in District	38.90	8.30	6.00	33.70	13.20	100
	Smallholder – agricultural labourer	20.30	21.30	9.80	39.60	9.10	100
	Landless agricultural labourer	19.10	28.30	5.90	34.80	11.90	100
	Non-agricultural household	33.40	14.60	3.20	33.70	15.10	100
	Petty landlord, agrarian household not cultivating any land, earning no agricultural wages	41.20	8.50	5.70	33.20	11.40	100
	Total	33.50	13.60	5.40	34.70	12.80	100

Year:	*Farm and household type (%)*	*Brahmin and upper castes (%)*	*Scheduled caste (%)*	*Scheduled tribe (%)*	*Other Backward Caste (%)*	*Other (%)*	*Total (%)*
HDPI							
1994/95	Large landowner, among 20% largest in District	32.30	6.20	6.50	41.60	13.40	100
	Family farmer, narrow definition, exluding 20% largest landowners in District	26.40	13.10	8.60	36.90	15.00	100
	Smallholder - agricultural labourer	12.20	23.40	18.20	40.80	5.40	100
	Landless agricultural labourer	7.30	38.20	11.80	32.10	10.70	100
	Non-agricultural household	27.00	18.90	4.90	29.80	19.40	100
	Total	22.30	20.70	8.40	33.40	15.10	100
IHDS-1							
2004/05	Large landowner, among 20% largest in District	31.60	6.40	6.60	39.80	15.60	100
	Family farmer, narrow definition, exluding 20% largest landowners in District	26.60	14.70	8.50	37.20	13.00	100
	Smallholder – agricultural labourer	12.60	22.00	19.10	40.90	5.50	100
	Landless agricultural labourer	7.30	38.20	11.80	32.00	10.60	100
	Non-agricultural household	29.10	17.70	4.20	29.50	19.60	100
	Petty landlord, agrarian household not cultivating any land, earning no agricultural wages	19.40	23.20	7.80	34.60	15.00	100
	Total	23.00	20.10	8.30	33.90	14.80	100

Source: ARIS REDS and HDPI IHDS surveys

References

Ahuja, U. R., D. Tyagi, S. Chauhan and K. R. Chaudhary (2011). "Impact of MGNREGA on Rural Employment and Migration: A study in agriculturally-backward and agriculturally-advanced districts of Haryana." *Agricultural Economics Research Review* **24**: 495–502.

Alkire, S. and J. Foster (2011). "Counting and Multidimensional Poverty Measurement." *Journal of Public Economics* **95**(7): 476–487.

Anonymous (undated). *Additional Rural Incomes Survey* Sample Design, Concepts and Definitions, and Data Available on Tape. National Council of Applied Economic Research. New Delhi.

Athreya, V. B., G. Djurfeldt and S. Lindberg (1990). *Barriers Broken: Production relations and agrarian change in Tamil Nadu*. New Delhi, Sage.

Bailey, W. R. (1973). *The One-Man Farm*. Washington, D.C., Economic Research Service, United States Department of Agriculture.

Bardhan, P. (1970). "Green Revolution and Agricultural Labourers." *Economic and Political Weekly* **5**: 29–31, 1239–1240.

Batra, L. (2009). "A Review of Urbanization and Urban Policy in Post-Independent India." *Working Paper Series*. New Delhi, Centre for the Study of Law and Governance, Jawaharlal Nehru University

Bhalla, G. S. and G. Singh (2001). *Indian Agriculture: Four decades of development*. New Delhi, Sage.

Bhalla, S., A. K. Karan and T. Shobha (2006). "Rural Casual Labourers, Wages and Poverty: 1983 to 1999–2000." *Chronic Poverty and Development Policy in India*. A. K. Mehta and A. Shepherd (eds). New Delhi, Sage: 86–147.

Bhan, G. (2009). "This Is No Longer The City I Knew: Evictions, the urban poor and the right to the city in millennial Delhi." *Environment & Urbanization* **21**(1): 127–142.

Bhan, G. and K. Menon-Sen (2007). *Swept off the Map: Surviving eviction and resettlement in Delhi*. New Delhi, Yoda Press.

Bhaskar, R. (1975). *A Realist Theory of Science*. Brighton, Harvester Press.

Bhaskar, R. (1989). *Reclaiming Reality: A critical introduction to contempary philosophy*. London, Verso.

Binswanger, H. P., K. Deininger and G. Feder (1995). "Power, Distortions, Revolt and Reform in Agricultural Land Relations." *Handbook of Development Economics*. Jere R. Behrman and T. N. Srinivasan (eds). Amsterdam, Elsevier. **3B**: 2659–2772.

Binswanger-Mkhize, H. P. (2013). "The Stunted Structural Transformation of the Indian Economy." *Economic & Political Weekly* **XLVIII**(26–27).

Birthal, P. S., P. K. Joshi, D. Roy and A. Thorat (2007). "Diversification in Indian Agriculture towards High-Value Crops: The role of smallholders." Washington, D.C., International Food Policy Research Institute.

Bjerén, G. (1981). "Female and male in a Swedish Forest Region: Old roles under new conditions." *Antropologiska Studier* (30–31): 56–85.

Bloom, D. E., D. Canning and J. Sevilla (2003). *The Demographic Dividend: A new perspective on the economic consequences of population change.* Santa Monica, CA: Rand.

Bosc, P.-M., J. Marzin, J.-F. Bélières, J.-M. Sourisseau, P. Bonnal, Bruno Losch, P. Pédelahore and L. Parrot (2015). Defining, Characterizing and Measuring Family Farming Models. *Family Farming and the Worlds to Come.* J.-M. Sourisseau (ed.). Dordrecht, Springer.

Boserup, E. (1965). *The Conditions of Agricultural Growth: The economics of agrarian change under population pressure* . London, Allen & Unwin.

Breman, J. (1985). *Of Peasants Migrants and Paupers: Rural labour circulation and capitalist production in West India.* Delhi, Oxford University Press.

Breman, J. (1996). *Footloose Labour: Working in India's informal economy.* New Delhi, Cambridge University Press.

Brenner, R. (1976). "Agrarian Class Structure and Economic Development in Preindustrial Europe." *Past and Present* **70**(Feb 1976): 30–75.

Brookfield, H. (2008). "Family Farms are Still Around: Time to invert the old agrarian question." Geography Compass **2**(1): 108–126.

Brown, L. (1997). "Higher Crop Yields? Don't bet the farm on them." *WorldWatch* (4, July August).

Brox, O. (1969). *Hva Skjer i Nord-Norge?* Pax Forlag.

Caird, J. (1961, 1878). *The Landed Interest and the Supply of Food.* London, Frank Cass.

Caldwell, J. C., P. H. Reddy and P. Caldwell (1984). "The Determinants of Family Structure in Rural South India." *Journal of Marriage and the Family* **46**(1): 215–229.

Carswell, G. and G. Neve (2014). "MGNREGA in Tamil Nadu: A story of success and transformation?" *Journal of Agrarian Change* **14**(4): 564–585.

Chakrabortty, A. (2008). "Secret Report: Biofuel caused food crisis. Internal World Bank study delivers blow to plant energy drive." London. *The Guardian.*

Chambers, J. D. and G. E. Mingay (1966). *The Agricultural Revolution 1750–1880.* London, B. T. Batsford Ltd.

Chand, R., Prasanna, P. Lakshmi and A. Singh (2011). "Farm Size and Productivity: Understanding the strengths of smallholders and improving their livelihoods." *Economic and Political Weekly* **46**: 5–11.

Chavan, P. and R. Bedamatta (2006). "Trends in Agricultural Wages in India 1964–65 to 1999–2000." *Economic and Political Weekly* **41**(38): 4041–4051.

Chayanov, A. V. (1977). "The Journey of my Brother Aleksei to the Land of Peasant Utopia." The Russian Peasant 1920 and 1984. Edited by R. E. F. Smith. London, Frank Cass: 63–108.

Chayanov, A. V. (1986). *On the Theory of Peasant Economy.* Madison, WI: The University of Wisconsin Press.

Chayanov, A. V. (1986, 1966). *A. V. Chayanov and the Theory of Peasant Economy.* Madison, WI: The University of Wisconsin Press.

Chenery, H. and M. Syrquin (1975). *Patterns of Development 1950–1970.* New York, Oxford University Press.

Christman, M. C. (2002). "Hansen–Hurwitz Estimator." *Encyclopedia of Environmetrics.* John Wiley & Sons.

Coase, R. H. (1937). "The Nature of the Firm." *Economica* **4**(16): 386–405.

Cotula, L., S. Vermeulen, R. Leonard and J. Keeley (2009). "Land Grab or Develoment Opportunity? Agricultural investment and international land deals in Africa." IIED, FAO, IFAD.

Das, D. (2014). "Changing Distribution of Land and Assets in Indian Agriculture." *Review of Radical Political Economics* **47**(3): 412–423

Das, S. K. and H. Tripathi (2014). "India's Green Revolution: Fact and fallacy." *International Journal of Bio-resource and Stress Management* **5**(1): 153–158.

Datt, G. and M. Ravallion (1998a). "Farm Productivity and Rural Poverty in India." *The Journal of Development Studies* **34**(4): 62–85.

Datt, G. and M. Ravallion (1998b). "Why Have Some Indian States Done Better than Others at Reducing Rural Poverty?" Economica **65**(257): 17–38.

Datt, G. and M. Ravallion (2010). "Shining for the Poor Too?" *Economic and Political Weekly* **XLV**(7): 55–60.

Deaton, A. and J. Drèze (2002). "Poverty and Inequality in India: A re-examination." *Economic and Political Weekly* **37**(36): 3729–3748.

Deininger, K. and D. Byerlee (2012). "The Rise of Large Farms in Land Abundant Countries: Do they have a future?" *World Development* **40**(4): 701–714.

Deininger, K., S. Jin and H. K. Natarajan (2007). "Land Reforms, Poverty Reduction, and Economic Growth: Evidence from India." *Policy Research Working Paper 4448*. Washington D.C., World Bank.

Denis, E., P. Mukhopadhyay and M. Zerah (2012). "Subaltern Urbanization in India." *Economic & Political Weekly* **XLVII**(30): 52–62.

Desai, S. and R. Vanneman (2016). *India Human Development Survey-II (IHDS-II), 2011–12*, Inter-university Consortium for Political and Social Research (ICPSR) [distributor].

Deshingkar, P. and S. Akter (2009). "Migration and Human Development in India." *Human Development Reports*, United Nations Development Programme.

Dev, M. S. (2012). "A Note on Trends in Public Investment in India." *IGIDR Proceedings/Projects series*. Mumbai, Indira Gandhi Institute of Development Research.

Dhamija, N. and S. Bhide (2011). "Dynamics of Chronic Poverty: Variations in factors infuencing entry and exit of chronic poor." *CPRC-IIPA Working Paper No. 38*, Indian Institute of Public Administration, New Delhi, Chronic Poverty Research Centre.

Dhanagare, D. N. (1984). "Agrarian Reforms and Rural Development in India: Some observations." *Research in Social Movements, Conflict and Change* **7**(1): 178–193.

Dhanagare, D. N. (2016). "Declining Credibility of the Neo-liberal State and Agrarian Crisis in India: Some observations." *Critical Perspectives on Agrarian Transition: India in the global debate*. B. B. Mohanty (ed.). Abingdon and New York, Routledge.

Dixon, J., A. Tanyeri-Abur and H. Wattenbach (2004) "Framework for Analysing Impacts of Globalization on Smallholders." *FAO Corporate Document Repository*.

Djurfeldt, G. (1981). "What Happened to the Agrarian Bourgoisie and the Rural Proletariat Under Monopoly Capitalism?" *Acta Sociologica* **24**(3): 167–191.

Djurfeldt, G. (1993). "Classes as Clients of the State. Landlords and laborers in Andalusia." Comparative Studies in Society and History **35**(1): 159–182.

Djurfeldt, G. (1994). *Gods och Gårdar: Jordbruket i ett sociologiskt perspektiv*. Lund, Arkiv.

Djurfeldt, G. (1996). "Defining and Operationalising Family Farming from a Sociological Perspective." *Sociologia Ruralis* **36**(3): 340–351.

Djurfeldt, G. (2000). Mariyamma and the Logic of Realist Explanation in Sociology. *Methodology in Social Research. Dilemmas and Perspectives: Essays in honour of Ramkrishna Mukherjee*. P. N. Mukherji (ed.). New Delhi/Thousand Oaks/London, Sage Publications: 199–212.

Djurfeldt, G. (2010). "Foreign Land Investments in Developing Countries." *Foreign Land Investments in Developing Countries: Contribution or threat to sustainable development?* Stockholm, Ministry of Agriculture: Swedish FAO Committee.

Djurfeldt, G., V. B. Athreya, N. Jayakumar, S. Lindberg, R. Vidyasagar and A. Rajagopal (2008a). "Agrarian Change and Social Mobility in Tamil Nadu." *Economic and Political Weekly* **43**(45): 50–61.

Djurfeldt, G., V. B. Athreya, N. Jayakumar, S. Lindberg, R. Vidyasagar and A. Rajagopal (2008b) "Modelling Social Mobility in Rural Tamil Nadu." DOI: Lund University Publications: http://luur.lub.lu.se/luur?func=downloadFile&fileOId=1267070

Djurfeldt, G. and M. Jirström (2005). The Puzzle of the Policy Shift: The early green revolution in India, Indonesia and the Philippines. *The African Food Crisis: Lessons from the Asian Green Revolution*. G. Djurfeldt, H. Holmén, M. Jirström and R. Larsson (eds). London, CABI.

Djurfeldt, G. and C. Waldenström (1996). "Towards a Theoretically Grounded Typology of Farms: A Swedish case." *Acta Sociologica* **39**: 187–210.

Dovring, F. (1965, 1955). *Land and Labor in Europe in the Twentieth Century: A comparative survey of recent agrarian history* 3rd revised edition of *Land and Labor in Europe, 1900–1950*). The Hague, Martinus Nijhoff.

Dyer, G. (1998). "Farm Size and Productivity: A new look at the old debate revisited." *Economic and Political Weekly* A113–A116.

Eastwood, R., M. Lipton and A. Newell (2010). "Farm size." *Handbook of Agricultural Economics*. P. L. Pingali and R. E. Evenson (eds). North Holland, Elsevier.

Eaton, G. (2012). "Revealed: How we pay our richest landowners millions in subsidies." The Staggers: The New Statesman's rolling politics blog. Online at: www.newstatesman.com/blogs/politics/2012/09/revealed-how-we-pay-our-richest-landowners-millions-subsidies

Eicher, C. K. and J. M. Staatz, (eds). (1990). *Agricultural Development in the Third World*. Baltimore, MD: The Johns Hopkins University Press.

Errington, A. (1996). "A Comment on Djurfeldt's Definition of Family Farming." *Sociologia Ruralis* **36**(3): 352–355.

Eswaran, M. and A. Kotwal (1986). "Access to Capital and Agrarian Production Organisation." *Economic Journal* **96**(382): 482–498.

FAO (2014). "The State of Food and Agriculture: Innovation in family farming." Food and Agriculture Organization of the United Nations.

Fields, G. S. and E. A. Ok (1996). "The Meaning and Measurement of Income Mobility." *Journal of Economic Theory* **71**: 349–377.

Foster, A. D. and M. R. Rosenzweig (1996). "Technical Change and Human-Capital Returns and Investments: Evidence from the Green Revolution." *The American Economic Review* **86**(4): 931–953.

Foster, Andrew D. and Mark R. Rosenzweig (2004). "Agricultural Productivity Growth, Rural Economic Diversity, and Economic Reforms: India, 1970–2000." *Economic Development and Cultural Change* **52**(3): 509–542.

Frankel, F. R. (1978). India's Political Economy, 1947–1977: The gradual revolution. Princeton, NJ: Princeton University Press.

Friis, C. and A. Reenberg (2010). Land Grab in Africa: Emerging land system drivers in a teleconnected world. *GLP Report No. 1*. Copenhagen, Global Land Project International Project Office.

Fuller, A. and B. Ray (1992). "Pluriactivity Among Farm Families: Some West European, US and Canadian comparisons." *Contemporary Rural Systems in Transition*. I. R.

Bowler, C. R. B. and M. D. Nellis (eds). London, CAB International. Volume 2: Economy and Society: 201–212.
Garikipati, S. and S. Pfaffenzeller (2012). "The Gendered Burden of Liberalisation: The impact of India's economic reforms on its female agricultural labour." *Journal of International Development* **24**(7): 841–864.
Garner, E. and A. P. de la O Campos (2014). "Identifying the 'Family Farm': An informal discussion of the concepts and definitions." *ESA Working Paper 14–10*. Rome, Agricultural Development Economics Division, Food and Agriculture Organization of the United Nations.
Gasson, R. (1987). Family Farming in Britain. *Family Farming in Europe and America*. B. Galeski and E. Wilkening. Boulder, CO: Westview Press: 5–37.
Gatti, F. (2007). *Bilal: viaggiare, lavorare, morire da clandestini*. Milano, BUR.
Gerschenkron, A. (1962). *Economic Backwardness in Historical Perspective: A Book of Essays*. Cambridge, MA: The Belknap Press of Harvard University Press.
Gibbon, P. (1992). "A failed agenda? African agriculture under structural adjustment with special reference to Kenya and Ghana." *The Journal of Peasant Studies* **20**(1): 50–96.
Giddens, A. (1984). *The Constitution of Society: Outline of the theory of structuration*. Cambridge, Polity Press.
Government of India (1985). *The 7th Five Year Plan*. New Delhi, Planning Commission.
Government of India (2012). *Agriculture Census 2010–11 Phase 1. All India report on number and area of operational holdings (Provisional)*. New Delhi, Ministry of Agriculture.
Government of India (2014). "Draft Concept Note on Smart City Scheme." New Delhi, Ministry of Urban Development.
Government of India Planning Commission (1958). *Appraisal and Prospects of the Second Five Year Plan*. New Delhi, The Commission.
Grindle, M. S. (1996). *Challenging the State: Crisis and innovation in Latin America and Africa*. Cambridge, Cambridge University Press.
Harish, B., N. Nagaraj, M. Chandrakanth, P. S. Murthy, P. Chengappa and G. Basavaraj (2011). "Impacts and Implications of MGNREGA on Labour Supply And Income Generation for Agriculture in Central Dry Zone of Karnataka." *Agricultural Economics Research Review* **24**(3): 485–494.
Harris, J. R. and M. P. Todaro (1970). "Migration, Unemployment and Development: A *Two Sector Analysis*." *The American Economic Review* **51**(4): 566–593.
Harrison, A. (1975). *Farmers and Farm Businesses in England*, Miscellaneous Study Number 62. Reading: Reading University, Department of Agricultural Economics and Management.
Hazell, P. B. and C. Ramasamy (1991). *The Green Revolution Reconsidered: The impact of high-yielding varieties in South India*. Baltimore, MD: The Johns Hopkins University Press.
Himanshu (2008). "What Are These New Poverty Estimates and What Do They Imply?" *Economic and Political Weekly* **43**(43).
Hjejle, B. (1967). *Slavery and Agricultural Bondage in South India in the Nineteenth Century*. Copenhagen, Scandinavian Institute of Asian Studies.
Hobsbawm, E. J. (1969). *Industry and Empire: An economic history of Britain since 1750*. London, Weidenfeld & Nicolson.
Holmes, D. and J. Qataert (1986). "An Approach to Modern Labor: Worker peasantries in historic Saxony and Friuli region over three centuries." *Comparative Studies in Society and History* **28**(2): 191–216.

International Rice Research Institute (IRRI) (2004). *World Rice Statistics: Area planted (or harvested) to modern varieties, selected Asian countries, 1965–1999.* Luzon, IRRI.

Jirström, M. (2005). "The State and Green Revolutions in East Asia." *The African Food Crisis: Lessons from the Asian Green revolution.* G. Djurfeldt, H. Holmén, M. Jirström and R. Larsson (eds). Wallingford, CABI: 25–42.

Jirström, M., A. Andersson and G. Djurfeldt (2011). "Smallholders Caught in Poverty: Flickering signs of agricultural dynamism." *African Smallholders: Food crops, markets and policy.* E. Aryeetey, G. Djurfeldt and A. Isinika (eds). London, CABI.

Jodhka, S. (2013). "Beyond the Binaries of 'India' and 'Bharat': Reimagining the rural-urban in contemporary times." *Workshop on Urbanization and Migration in Transnational India Organized by South Asian Studies Network (SASNET) and Institute for Social and Economic Change (ISEC)* March 5–7, 2013 Bangalore.

Jodkha, S. S. (2015). *Caste in Contemporary India.* New Delhi, Routledge.

Joshi, P. K., A. Gulati, P. S. Birthal and L. Tewari (2004). "Agriculture Diversification in South Asia: Patterns, determinants and policy implications." *Economic and Political Weekly* **XLI**(June 30): 2457–2467.

Kapur, A. M. and A. Shah (2003). "Chronic Poverty in India: Incidence, causes and policies." *World Development* **31**(3): 491–511.

Kar, S. and S. Sakthivel (2007). "Reforms and Regional Inequality in India." *Economic and Political Weekly* 42(47): 69–77.

Karanth, G. K. (1996). "Caste in Contemporary Rural India." *Caste: Its twentieth century avatar.* M. N. Srinivas (ed.). New Delhi, Penguin.

Kasimis, C. and A. G. Papadopoulos (1997). "Family Farming and Capitalist Development in Greek Agriculture: A critical review of the literature." *Sociologia Ruralis* **37**(2): 209–227.

Kolenda, P. M. (1968). "Region, Caste, and Family Structure: A comparative study of the Indian 'joint' family." *Structure and Change in Indian Society* (47): 339.

Kumar, A. G., G. Darbha and K. Parikh (2003). "Growth and Welfare Consequences of Rise in MSP." *Economic and Political Weekly* **9**(38): 891–895.

Kumar, D. (1965). *Land and Caste in South India: Agricultural labour in the Madras Presidency during the nineteenth century.* Cambridge, Cambride University Press.

Kumar, D. and M. Desai (eds). (1983). *Cambridge Economic History of India.* Cambridge, Cambridge University Press.

Kundu, A. (2011a). "Method in Madness: Urban data from 2011 census." *Economic and Political Weekly* **XLVI**(40): 13–16.

Kundu, A. (2011b). Trends and Processes of Urbanisation in India. Human Settlements Group London, IIED, Populations and Development Branch.

Lenin, V. I. (1960, 1899). *The Development of Capitalism in Russia.* Moskva, Foreign Languages Publishing House.

Lewis, W. A. (1954). "Economic Development with Unlimited Supplies of Labor." *Manchester School of Economic and Social Studies* **22**: 139–191.

Lin, J. Y. (1992). "Rural Reforms and Agricultural Growth in China." *The American Economic Review* **82**(1): 34–51.

Lindberg, S., V. B. Athreya, G. Djurfeldt, A. Rajagopal and R. Vidyasagar (2014). "Progress Over the Long Haul: Dynamics of agrarian change in the Kaveri delta." *Persistence of Poverty in India.* N. Gooptu and J. Parry (eds). New Delhi, Social Science Press: 344–369.

Lindberg, S., V. B. Athreya, R. Vidyasagar, G. Djurfeldt and A. Rajagopal (2011). "A Silent 'Revolution'? Women's empowerment in rural Tamil Nadu." *Economic and Political Weekly* **46**(13): 111–120.

Lipton, M. (2005). "The Family Farm in a Globalizing World: The role of crop science in alleviating poverty." Washington, D.C., IFPRI.

Lipton, M. and T. John (1991). *Does Aid Work in India? A study of the impact of official development assistance.* London, Routledge.

Lipton, M. and R. Longhurst (1989). *New Seeds and Poor People.* Baltimore, MD: The Johns Hopkins University Press.

Loehlin, J. C. (2004). *Latent Variable Models: An introduction to factor, path, and structural equation analysis.* Mahwah, NJ: Lawrence Erlbaum Associates.

Lowder, S. K., J. Skoet and S. Singh (2014). "What do we really know about the number and distribution of farms and family farms in the world?" Background paper for *The State of Food and Agriculture*: 8.

Mackinnon, N., J. M. Bryden, C. Bell, M. Fuller and M. Spearman (1991). "Pluriactivity, Structural Change and Farm Household Vulnerability in Western Europe." *Sociologia Ruralis* **XXXI**(1): 59–70.

McMichael, P. (1995). *Food and Agrarian Orders in the World Economy.* Westport, CT: Praeger Publishers.

Mahadevia, D. (2003). *Globalisation, Urban Reforms and Metropolitan Response: India*, Manak Publications.

Mahendra Dev, S. and C. Ravi (2007). "Poverty and Inequality: All-India and States, 1983–2005." *Economic and Political Weekly* **42**(6): 509–521.

Majumder, R. (2010). "Intergenerational Mobility in Educational and Occupational Attainment: A comparative study of social classes in India." *Margin: The Journal of Applied Economic Research* **4**(4): 463–494.

Marx, K. (1977). *Capital: A critique of political economy.* London, Lawrence & Wishart.

Mayer, H. and P. Knox (2010). "Small-town Sustainability: Prospects in the second modernity." *European Planning Studies* **18**(10): 1545–1565.

Mehrotra, S., J. Parida, S. Sinha and A. Gandhi (2014). "Explaining Employment Trends in the Indian Economy: 1993–94 to 2011–12." *Economic and Political Weekly* **XLIX**(32): 49–57.

Mehta, A. K. and A. Shah (2001). *Chronic Poverty in India: Overview study*, Chronic Poverty Research Centre.

Mellor, J. (1984). "Agriculture on the Road to Industrialization." *Agricultural Development in the Third World.* C. K. Eicher and J. M. Staatz (eds). Baltimore, MD: The Johns Hopkins University Press: 70–88.

Merton, R. K. (1968). *Social Theory and Social Structure.* New York, Free Press.

Misra, V. and M. G. Rao (2003). "Trade Policy, Agricultural Growth and Rural Poor: Indian experience, 1978–79 to 1999–2000." *Economic and Political Weekly* **38**(43): 4588–4603.

Mitchell, D. (2008). *A Note on Rising Food Prices.* Prepared by Donald Mitchell. The World Bank Development Prospects Group. Washington D.C., The World Bank.

Mohan, R. (2008). "Growth Record of the Indian Economy, 1950–2008: A story of sustained savings and investment." *Economic and Political Weekly* **XLIII**(19): 61–71.

Mohanty, B. B. and P. K. Lenka (2016). Neoliberal Reforms, Agrarian Capitalism and the Peasantry. *Critical Perspectives on Agrarian Transition: India in the global debate.* B. B. Mohanty (ed.). Abingdon and New York, Routledge.

Motiram, S. and A. Singh (2012). "How Close Does the Apple Fall to the Tree? Some evidence on intergenerational occupational mobility from India." *Economic and Political Weekly* **47**(40).

Mukherjee, R. (1963). "Urbanization and Social Transformation in India." *International Journal of Comparative Sociology* **4**(2): 178–210.

Nagarajan, H. K., K. Pradhan and A. Sharma (no year). "The Curse of Location: Investigating links between income mobility, migration and location premium." New Delhi, NCAER.

Newby, H., C. Bell, C. Rose and P. Saunders (1978). *Property, Paternalism and Power*. London, Hutchinson.

Patnaik, U. (1990). "Some Economic and Political Consequences of the Green Revolution in India," in H. Bernstein *et al.* (eds), "The Food Question," *Monthly Review*: 80–90.

Perkins, J. H. (1997). *Geopolitics and the Green Revolution: Wheat, genes and the cold war*. New York, Oxford University Press.

Perry, P. J. (1972). *British Agriculture, 1875–1914*. London, Methuen.

Pfeffer, M. (1983). "Social origins of Three Systems of Farm Production in the United States." *Rural Sociology* **48**: 540–562.

Polanyi, K. (2001, 1944). *The Great Transformation: The political and economic origins of our time*. Boston, MA: Beacon Press.

Portes, A. (2010). *Economic Sociology: A systematic inquiry*. Princeton, NJ: Princeton University Press.

Pradhan, K. (2012). "Unacknowledged Urbanization: The new census towns of India." New Delhi, Centre for Policy Research.

Prowse, M. (2011). "A Century of Growth? A History of Tobacco Production and Marketing in Malawi-1890–2005." Universiteit Antwerpen, Institute of Development Policy and Management (IOB).

Prowse, M. (2013). "A History of Tobacco Production and Marketing in Malawi, 1890–2010." *Journal of Eastern African Studies* **7**(4): 691–712.

Prowse, M. and A. Chimhowu (2007). "Making Agriculture Work for the Poor." *Natural Resource Perspectives*. London, Overseas Development Institute.

Puja, D. and H. K. Nagarajan (no year). "Spatial Inequality among Indian Villages: Do initial conditions matter?" New Delhi, NCAER.

Rama, M., T. Béteille, Y. Li, P. K. Mitra and J. L. Newman (2015). *Addressing Inequality in South Asia*. Washington, D.C., World Bank. .

Rao, Y. M., K. R. Chand, V. Kiresur and M. Bantilan (2011). "Documentation of Second-Generation Village Level Studies (VLS) in India (2001/02–2004/05)." Patancheru, 502304 Andhra Pradesh, India, ICRISAT, International Crop Research Institute for the Semi-Arid Tropics.

Rastogi, A., (ed.) (2006). *India Infrastructure Report: Urban infrastructure*. Oxford University Press, New Delhi.

Ravallion, M. (2008). "A Global Perspective on Poverty in India." *Economic and Political Weekly* **43**(43).

Reardon, T., C. B. Barrett, J. A. Berdegué and J. F. M. Swinnen (2009). "Agrifood Industry Transformation and Small Farmers in Developing Countries." *World Development* **37**(11): 1717–1727.

Reardon, T., C. P. Timmer, C. Barrett and J. Berdegué (2003). "The Rise of Supermarkets in Africa, Asia and Latin America." *American Journal of Agricultural Economics* **85**(5): 1140–1146.

Reddy, A. A. (2015). "Growth, Structural Change and Wage Rates in Rural India." *Economic & Political Weekly* **50**(2).

Reddy, D. N., A. A. Reddy, N. Nagaraj and C. Bantilan (2014). "Emerging Trends in Rural Employment Structure and Rural Labor Markets in India." *Research Program Markets, Institutions and Policies*, Working Paper Series no 56. Patancheru, Telegana, India ICRISAT.

Rigg, J., A. Salamanca and E. C. Thompson (2016). "The Puzzle of East and Southeast Asia's Persistent Smallholder." *Journal of Rural Studies* **43**: 118–133.

Riskin, C. (1995). "Feeding China: The experience since 1949," *The Political Economy of Hunger: Selected essays*. J. Drèze, A. Sen and A. Hussain (eds). Oxford, Clarendon Press: 401–444.

Rodrik, D. (2011). *The Globalization Paradox: Why global markets, states, and democracy can't coexist.* Oxford, Oxford University Press.

Roumasset, J. (1995). "The Nature of the Agricultural Firm." *Journal of Economic Behavior and Organization* **26**: 161–177.

Roy, D. (2012). "Caste and Power: An ethnography in West Bengal, India." *Modern Asian Studies* **46**: 947–974.

Rudra, A. (1978). "Organisation of Agriculture for Rural Development: The Indian case." *Cambridge Journal of Economics* **2**: 381–406.

Rudra, A. (1996). *Prasanta Chandra Mahalanobis: A biography*. New Delhi, Oxford University Press India.

Sainath, P. (1996). *Everybody Loves a Good Drought: Stories from India's poorest districts.* Penguin Books India.

Samanta, G. (2014). "The Politics of Classification and the Complexity of Governance in Census Towns." *Economic and Political Weekly, Review of Agriculture* **49**(22): 55–62.

Schmitt, G. (1991). "Why is the Agriculture of Advanced Western Economies Still Organized by Family Farms. Will this continue to be so in the future?" *European Review of Agricultural Economics* **18**: 443–458.

Scott, J. C. (1998). *Seeing Like a State: How certain schemes to improve the human condition have failed*. New Haven, CT: Yale University Press.

Scrase, T. J., M. Rutten, R. Ganguly-Scrase and T. Brown (2015). "Beyond the Metropolis—Regional Globalisation and Town Development in India: An introduction." *South Asia: Journal of South Asian Studies* **28**(2): 216–229.

Sen, A. (1981). *Poverty and Famines: An essay on entitlement and deprivation*. Oxford, Clarendon Press.

Sen, A. K. (2001). *Development as Freedom*. Oxford, Oxford University Press.

Sen, A. K. (2009). *The Idea of Justice*. London, Penguin.

Shah, T., O. P. Singh and A. Mukherji (2006). "Some Aspects of South Asia's Groundwater Irrigation Economy: Analyses from a survey in India, Pakistan, Nepal Terai and Bangladesh." *Hydrogeology Journal* **14**(3): 286–309.

Sharma, A. (2005). "Agrarian Relations and Socio-Economic Change in Bihar." *Economic and Political Weekly* March 5: 960–972.

Sharma, H. R. (1994). "Distribution of Landholdings in Rural India, 1953–54 to 1981–82: Implications for land reforms." *Economic and Political Weekly* **29**(13): A12–A25.

Shaw, A. (1999). "Emerging Patterns of Urban Growth in India." *Economic and Political Weekly, Review of Agriculture* (April 17–23): 968–979.

Shiva, V. (1991). *The Violence of the Green Revolution: Third world agriculture, ecology and politics*. London; Atlantic Highlands, NJ, Zed Books.

Sircar, S. (2012). *Where 'Everyone' has Migrated: Exploring social transformation under the impact of labour migration*. Masters thesis.

Sircar, S. (2016, forthcoming). "Census Towns in India and what it Means to be Urban: Competing epistemologies and potential new approaches," Department of Human Geography, Lund Univesity.

Skocpol, T. and K. Finegold (1982). "State Capacity and Economic Intervention in the early New Deal." *Political Science Quarterly* **97**(2): 255–278.

Skrondal, A. and S. Rabe-Hesketh (2004). *Generalized Latent Variable Modeling: Multilevel, longitudinal and structural equation models*. Boca Ration, FL: Chapman & Hall/CRC.

Smith, A. (1904 (1776)). *An Inquiry into the Nature and Causes of the Wealth of Nations*. Edited by E. Cannan. London: Methuen & Co., Ltd, Library of Economics and Liberty (online).

Stevenson, A. (2014). "Cash Crops With Dividends: Financiers transforming strawberries into securities." *The New York Times*.

Sugihara, K. (2003). "The East Asian Path of Economic Development: A long-term perspective." *The Resurgence of East Asia: 500, 150 and 50 year perspective*. G. Arrighi, T. Hamashita and M. Selden (eds). London and New York, Routledge: 78–123.

Thomas, R. J. (1985). *Citizenship, Gender and Work: Social organization of industrial agriculture*. Berkeley, CA: University of California Press.

Thorat, S. and K. S. Newman (2010). "Introduction: Economic Discrimination, Concept, Consequences and Remedies." *Blocked by Caste: Economic discrimination in modern India*. S. Thorat and K. S. Newman (eds). New Delhi, Oxford University Press.

Timmer, C. P. (1998). The Agricultural Transformation. *International Agricultural Development*. K. E. Eicher and J. M. Staatz (eds). Baltimore, MD: The Johns Hopkins University Press.

Timmer, C. P. and S. Akkus (2008). "The Structural Transformation as a Pathway out of Poverty: Analytics, empirics and politics." Working Paper no. 50. Washington D.C., Center for Global Development.

Timmer, P. (2009). *A World without Agriculture: The structural transformation process in historical perspective*. Washington D.C., The American Enterprise Institute Press.

Tomich, T. P., P. Kilby and B. F. Johnston (1995). *Transforming Agrarian Economies: Opportunities seized, opportunities missed*. Ithaca, NY: Cornell University Press.

Tracy, M. (1989). *Government and Agriculture in Western Europe 1880–1988*, 3rd edition. London: Harvester Wheatsheaf.

UNDP (2015). "Human Development Report: Work for human development." New York, United Nations Development Programme.

Vakulabharanam, V. (2005). *Immiserizing Growth: Globalization and agrarian change in Telengana, South India between 1985 and 2000*. Ph.D, The University of Massachusetts Amherst.

Vakulabharanam, V. and S. Motiram (2011). "Political Economy of Agrarian Distress in India since the 1990s." *Understanding India's New Political Economy: A great transformation?* S. Ruparelia, S. Reddy, J. Harriss and S. Corbridge (eds). London and New York, Routledge: 101–126.

Venables, A. J. (2005). "Spatial Disparities in Developing Countries: Cities, regions, and international trade." *Journal of Economic Geography* **5**(1): 3–21.

Weber, M. Ed. (1997, 1949). *The Methodology of the Social Sciences*. Translated and edited by Edward A. Shils and Henry A. Finch. New York, Free Press.

Wilkening, E. and J. Gilbert (1987). "Family Farming in the United States," in Galeski, B. and Wilkening, E. (eds) *Family Farming in Europe and America*. Boulder, CO: Westview Press: 271–301

Williamson, J. (1989). What Washington Means by Policy Reform. *Latin American Readjustment: How Much has Happened*. J. Williamson (ed.). Washington, Institute for International Economics.

Williamson, O. E. (1979). "Transaction-cost Economics: The governance of contractual relations." *Journal of Law and Economics* **22**(2): 233–261.

Wingender, A. (2014). "Structural Transformation in the 20th Century: A new database on agricultural employment around the World." *Discussion Paper*. Copenhagen, Department of Economics, University of Copenhagen. **14**.

World Bank (2007). "World Development Report 2008: Agriculture for development." Washington D.C., World Bank.

World Bank (2009). *Awakening Africa's Sleeping Giant: Prospects for commercial agriculture in the Guinea Savannah Zone and beyond.* Washington, D.C., World Bank.

World Bank Group (2015). "World Development Report 2015: Mind, society, and behavior." Washington, D.C., World Bank.

Index

www.ingramcontent.com/pod-product-compliance
Ingram Content Group UK Ltd.
Pitfield, Milton Keynes, MK11 3LW, UK
UKHW020951180425
457613UK00019B/619

* 9 7 8 0 3 6 7 8 7 1 9 9 4 *